A HISTORY (
BIRKENHEAD
MUNICIPAL
BUS UNDERTAKING

by
T. B. Maund, FCILT

The Omnibus Society

Published by
THE OMNIBUS SOCIETY
Provincial Historical Research Group
7 Nursery Close
Emsworth
Hampshire
PO10 7SP

Printed by
Modern Graphic Arts Ltd
52-54 Milton Road
Westcliff-on-Sea
SS0 7JX

Cartography and assistance in production:
Mike Harris, Peter Bale and Peter Figg

ISBN 978 0 901307 66 8

Contents

Introduction

Before the Industrial Revolution, the Wirral peninsula was a thinly populated area given over to farming and fishing. The main centre was Neston which, with its neighbour Parkgate, enjoyed some prosperity in the late 17th and early 18th century as a port for Ireland. However, as the River Dee silted up, navigation moved closer to the estuary and eventually to the Mersey. Second in size and importance was Tranmere. In 1801 the population of the whole of the Hundred of Wirral was only 9,500 but, in the next forty years it had more than trebled to 32,000. The population continued to increase for the next hundred years, settlement being mainly in the north-eastern corner where the old parishes grew together to form the towns of Birkenhead and Wallasey. Many of their inhabitants lived there and worked in Liverpool, population growth on the Wirral shore being a direct result of the adoption of steam on the ferries between 1816 and 1825, but transport services in Wirral had been influenced by Liverpool's rise as a port long before that.

Until the mid-19th century, most towns were sufficiently compact for the inhabitants to walk wherever their affairs took them. Most people had no reason to move very far from their birth-place and many born on the Cheshire side of the Mersey never crossed to the other bank in the course of a lifetime. Stage coaches catered for the middle classes who needed to travel between towns.

The Liverpool and Manchester Railway was the first orthodox inter-city line and it was only ten years later, by which time a basic network of lines covered much of England, that the railway arrived in Birkenhead with the ceremonial opening of the Chester and Birkenhead Railway on 22nd September 1840. As the railways spread, the coaches were withdrawn and a great many people and horses became redundant. The urban omnibus was a product of this transport revolution as the shrewd entrepreneurs realised that there would be an enormous increase in travel and that feeder services would be needed to the railheads. Resources made redundant by the coming of the railway could be redeployed in this way. The first omnibuses in Birkenhead were dedicated railway feeders.

Following the adoption of steam power on the ferries, improvements in embarkation facilities on both sides of the river resulted in much higher standards of safety and reliability. Timid passengers, and especially ladies, were encouraged to cross and a sail on the river became an acceptable part of the work journey. Many well-to-do people forsook the cramped, unhealthy environment of Liverpool and built houses on cheap land on the Cheshire side of the river. Fine family houses were built in Oxton and horse-drawn omnibuses were provided to take these Victorian daily passengers to and from the ferry. Some came in every day from Hoylake and the early omnibuses catered specifically for this category of passenger.

As the towns spread, the need for internal transport increased and the omnibuses ran throughout the day, but they remained middle-class conveyances throughout the Victorian years as the customary minimum fares of 2d, 3d and sometimes 6d were quite beyond the pocket of the working man.

Birkenhead was the first town in Britain to have a purpose-built street tramway but detailed consideration of this mode is outside the scope of this book. The reader is referred to *The Tramways of Birkenhead and Wallasey* which also deals with the horse bus services of the Victorian era. Suffice to say that by 1877 Birkenhead had three separate tramway companies with lines to Oxton, New Ferry and along the Line of Docks, another line to Prenton being added later.

Although railway companies pioneered some motor bus services in Birkenhead in the Edwardian era, these did not endure and it was municipal enterprise which brought the motor bus to the streets of the large Wirral towns, World War I delaying its debut from 1914 to 1919. From being an auxiliary to the electric tramcar, the motor bus succeeded in usurping its railbound predecessor completely within 18 years. During that time, technological developments in motor bus design were such that the machines that replaced the last trams in 1937 bore little resemblance to the crude vehicles of 1919. Private enterprise was soon represented by one large company which, after tough battles against the entrenched interests of the municipalities, at last achieved a *modus vivendi* through intervention from what might earlier have been considered an unlikely catalyst - the railway companies. Simultaneously, new regulatory laws brought an end to parochial restraints and both public and private operators were able to expand their businesses in an orderly fashion which, in general, provided the public with a highly satisfactory level of service.

The 1939-45 war placed a great strain on the operators but they acquitted themselves magnificently. The post-war years brought bus patronage to its zenith, economic constraints, short-sighted government policies and social change contributing to a gradual decline in the industry's fortunes. The resultant merger of the three Merseyside municipal transport undertakings in 1969 and the closer integration of company services brought palliatives which a government of a different complexion considered to be too demanding on public funds. Thus followed, in 1986, the deregulation of the industry which radically changed the face of the bus service network.

Many of the places mentioned in this book have disappeared or changed beyond recognition in urban redevelopment schemes. Thus the Haymarket and Market Place South, once important termini, have been overwhelmed by tunnel approach roads and Grange shopping precinct straddles what was once the main road to Oxton and Woodchurch. The Fire Station, at the corner of Borough Road and Whetstone Lane, once an important stage point, has been relocated to Exmouth Street. Woodside railway station closed in 1967 and both Woodside and Seacombe ferries have declined almost to the status of landing places on a pleasure cruise.

Money

The British coinage was changed on 15th February 1971 from pounds, shillings and pence (£.s.d) to pounds and new pence. All references to fares are in the old currency as it is impossible to translate the value of money into the present currency. The 3d of the horse bus fare has to be compared with the contemporary manual worker's wage of perhaps 16 shillings (80p) per week. As a guide, a bus driver's wage in 1939 was about £3.15.0d (£3.75) per week.

1 – The Edwardian Years

At the turn of the century, having obtained Parliamentary powers to own and operate electric tramways, Birkenhead, like many other towns, agreed terms with the horse tramway companies and worked out a scheme for its own network. Because electric cars were so much heavier than horse cars, all existing tracks on routes being retained had to be replaced by heavier section rail and traffic was disrupted throughout the town as this was done. The first electric cars ran in public service between New Ferry and Brandon Street on 4th February 1901. There was no ceremony as the nation was in mourning following the death of Queen Victoria a few days earlier. The route was extended down to Woodside ferry terminal on 6th June following completion of a six-track terminal layout. The first parts of the main town system opened on 14th August with proper ceremony and by the end of the year, seven routes radiated from Woodside as follows:-

> New Ferry via New Chester Road
> Higher Tranmere (Bebington Road) via Argyle Street South and Church Road
> Prenton (Storeton Road) via Borough Road and Prenton Road West
> Shrewsbury Road via Borough Road and Balls Road
> Palm Grove (Egerton Road) via Claughton Road
> Laird Street via Conway Street
> Line of Docks via Cleveland Street and Beaufort Road

The Shrewsbury Road and Laird Street routes were linked to form the Oxton and Claughton Circle in March 1902 and thereafter there were no more extensions. The impact of electrification on public transport was underestimated in most towns. Cheap fares and frequent services brought transport within the reach of many working class people and, within months of opening, single lines had to be doubled. The planned fleet of 44 cars was soon increased to 59. The main depot was built in Laird Street and the horse car shed and stables at New Ferry were rebuilt to house the cars used on that route.

A few horse buses struggled on but the superior service given by the tramways defeated those in the town by 1903 when the Birkenhead Carriage Co. went into liquidation. An hourly service between New Ferry and Bromborough Cross, with some trips to Bromborough Pool Village, was run by the Oxton Carriage Co. and continued until about 1914, probably being a war casualty. The timetable for 1908 show it running from 1.15pm (2.15 on Sundays) until 9.15pm. By 1913, however, Crosville buses were running an infrequent service over the route. A service between Charing Cross and Seacombe started in 1903 and is described in Chapter 2.

Railway Buses

The Wirral Peninsula was served by no fewer than five railway companies, the London & North Western, Great Western, Great Central, Wirral and Mersey. Of these, three examined the motor bus as an auxiliary to their lines in the early years of the twentieth century.

6

The Mersey Railway had been opened as a steam railway in 1886 and many people would not use it because of the fumes which filled the stations and tunnels. In 1903 the effectively bankrupt railway company was electrified by the British Westinghouse company on special terms after which it attracted a substantial part of the cross-river ferry traffic from both Woodside and Rock Ferry. The ferries carried just over one million fewer passengers in 1903-04 than in the previous year, a loss of 8.7% of the traffic and crossings by Woodside continued to decline for the next few years. The railway management believed that their patronage would increase even further if their stations were better served by the Birkenhead tramways. Being in common ownership, it is not surprising that the ferries were favoured by the tramways. At this time there was only a single line along Borough Road between Central Station and Whetstone Lane and there was a complicated arrangement whereby trams used this part of Borough Road in different directions at various times of the day, cars in the opposite direction using the line along Claughton Road and a 'temporary line' across Charing Cross. The cars which ran by the latter route did not pass Central Station.

The railway company placed an order with the Motor Car Emporium Ltd. of Shepherds Bush for four chain-driven Saurer 24/28hp double-deck buses with open top bodies by Bayleys. They were typical of the times with seats for 18 on forward-facing benches upstairs and 16 on two longitudinal seats inside. They were registered CM 501-4 and garaged on railway land off Argyle Street South, adjacent to Birkenhead Central Station.

The company's intentions were announced by the Chairman at the half-yearly meeting in September 1905. The Town Clerk of Birkenhead wrote to the railway company asking about powers to operate motor buses, the company's view being that no special powers were needed. However the Town Clerk insisted that such operation would be *ultra vires*. The Mersey Railway applied formally for the grant of ply-for-hire licences under the Town Police Clauses Act, 1889 and at first these were turned down on the flimsy pretext that the buses were unsuitable as there was less than 18in. of seat per passenger even though the Corporation trams allowed only 16in. In an indignant letter to the Town Clerk the railway's traffic manager, R. Bowman Smith, deplored the invocation of an anachronistic by-law framed at a time when omnibus seats were arranged back-to-back on the upper deck and asked for the Corporation to reconsider their decision. He went on to state:-

> 'The inauguration of the proposed omnibus service has been forced on [the directors] by the necessities of a large number of their passengers, and it is regarded by them as a very valuable addition to the travelling facilities of the borough. It is therefore a great disappointment to them that it will be opposed by the Corporation on a ground which has no substance, and which, as they conceive, is devoid even of technical validity'.

On 15th November, the Town Clerk informed the Mersey company that the Watch Committee had recommended the Town Council to grant the licences 'without prejudice to the rights and powers of the Corporation in regard to any steps which they may think fit to take in the matter hereafter'. After confirmation by the Council on 6th December, licences were issued. A number of test runs had been already made as, at the same meeting, the Council received a 'memorial' from ratepayers and residents of Alfred Road, Reedville and other roads complaining about the noise and nuisance caused by the buses.

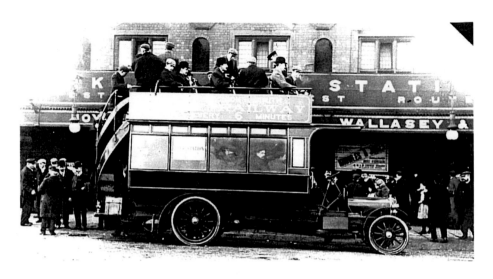

Mersey Railway Saurer bus outside Birkenhead Park station providing a service to an international rugby match on 9th December 1905 as a demonstration project. *T B Maund collection*

On Saturday 9th December, there was an international rugby football match against New Zealand at Birkenhead Park and the buses ran a frequent service between the station and the ground at a fare of 1d. It was later claimed that 1,500 people had been carried and no doubt the stunt had considerable novelty value as most people would never have ridden on a motor bus before. On the following Monday, three of the buses started a regular service between Central Station and Slatey Road via Grange Road, Grange Road West, Westbourne Road and Reedville. Books of 50 $^1/_2$d coupons were sold at railway stations for 2/-. The through fare was $1^1/_2$d (three coupons) with $^1/_2$d and 1d intermediate fares. The buses ran every six minutes throughout the day, the same frequency as the trains.

Acting on an opinion from Mr Stafford Cripps, K.C., on 18th December the Corporation sought an injunction on the grounds that the Mersey Railway had no statutory powers to run omnibuses. This was true, though other railway companies, in particular the Great Western, had started bus services without the legal niceties being considered important. However, two years earlier, the London County Council had been challenged and prevented from running buses as feeders to its tramways on somewhat similar grounds. At this meeting, Dr. H. Laird Pearson, Chairman of the Tramways Committee, calculated that the buses would abstract one eighth of the traffic of both the tramways and the ferries, an estimated loss of £9,425 per annum, equivalent to a rate of $4^1/_2$d in the £.

Meanwhile the Mersey Railway took delivery of two more similar buses with slightly more powerful 28/32hp engines, (which were duly licensed to ply for hire), and ordered a further four to bring the fleet up to 10. On Boxing Day the buses were used on an hourly service between Central Station and the Glegg Arms, Gayton via Woodchurch and Barnston at a fare of 1/- single

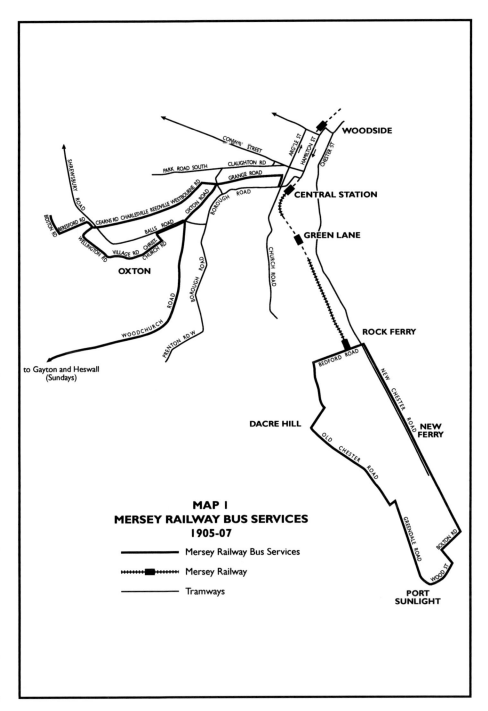

CONWAY STREET

WOODSIDE

ARGYLE ST
HAMILTON ST
CHESTER ST

SHREWSBURY ROAD

PARK ROAD SOUTH   CLAUGHTON RD

GRANGE ROAD

CEARNS RD CHARLESVILLE REEDVILLE WESTBOURNE RD

BOROUGH   ROAD

CENTRAL STATION

BIDSTON RD

BERESFORD RD

OXTON ROAD

BALLS   ROAD

WELLINGTON RD   VILLAGE RD   CHRIST   CHURCH RD

BOROUGH   ROAD

CHURCH ROAD

GREEN LANE

OXTON

BOROUGH ROAD

WOODCHURCH

PRENTON RD W

to Gayton and Heswall
(Sundays)

ROCK FERRY

BEDFORD ROAD

NEW CHESTER ROAD

DACRE HILL

OLD CHESTER ROAD

NEW
FERRY

MAP I
MERSEY RAILWAY BUS SERVICES
1905-07

GREENDALE ROAD
BOLTON RD
WOOD ST

PORT
SUNLIGHT

———————	Mersey Railway Bus Services
┅┅┅■┅┅┅	Mersey Railway
———————	Tramways

9

and 1/6d return. The journey took 50 minutes and continued every Sunday from 7th January 1906 being extended by popular request to the centre of Heswall from Sunday the 14th. The Heswall people would have liked a daily service but the buses were needed in Birkenhead during the week. It must have been a bitterly cold pastime to ride on the exposed upper deck on a mid-winter Sunday but it was a novel experience and no doubt the passengers' inner needs were well catered for by mine host of the Glegg Arms.

On 29th January 1906, the weekday bus service was extended from Slatey Road to the junction of Kingsmead Road South and Bidston Road, via Charlesville, Cearns Road, Shrewsbury Road and Beresford Road. From 26th February, the route was reorganised as a circular so as to serve even more of the Oxton district. Buses ran as before to Cearns Road then via Chetwynd Road, Wellington Road, Village Road, Christchurch Road, Balls Road, Oxton Road and Grange Road to Central Station the loop being traversed every 12 minutes in both directions.

The legal proceedings that followed were quite a *cause célèbre* and were widely reported in the technical press at the time. By early March the buses were carrying 6,000 to 8,000 passengers a week of which a third were not travelling to or from a railway station. After a Chancery Court hearing lasting most of two days, Mr Justice Warrington summed up in the following terms:-

'.....I must confess with some reluctance that I must come to the conclusion that the business of omnibus proprietors which has been carried on by the Mersey Railway Company, is not incidental to or consequential upon the authority given them'.

The injunction was granted on 8th March but held over pending a possible appeal. This was not forthcoming and the buses ceased running after 17th March 1906. The railway later lodged an appeal but in the meantime had deposited a Bill in Parliament to secure powers to run motor buses and to carry passengers, luggage, parcels and mails. This came before a House of Lords Committee only a fortnight after the grant of the injunction and, despite strong Corporation opposition, was sent to the Commons where it came up for second reading on 15th May. A powerful municipal lobby had been organised but some Members quickly got to the heart of the matter sensing that it 'was an attempt by the Corporation of Birkenhead to thwart the wishes, not of the railway company only but of the population and Corporation of Liverpool and of all the districts around Birkenhead. It was an attempt on behalf of a monopolistic body to defend its own isolated position and not in any way an attempt to serve the general public'. The Corporation saw things in a similar light except that, from their point of view, the monopolistic body was the Mersey Railway. On a motion introduced by Mr Vivian, MP for Birkenhead, the House voted 199:108 to instruct the Committee to delete the key clause thus effectively blocking the Bill. The headline in *Commercial Motor* was 'Reactionary Tactics of Municipal Traders and Irishmen', noting that the 91 majority in favour of the motion included many Irish MPs with no interest in the matter.

There were no developments until 14th December 1906 when the Court of Appeal found in favour of the company on condition that undertakings were given to run the buses to and from railway stations and for railway passengers only but, as the Corporation decided to take the matter to the House of Lords, the buses were not immediately reinstated.

Handbills announcing the start of Mersey Railway bus services in December 1905 and May 1907 respectively.

In due course applications were made to the Lower Bebington and Higher Bebington Urban District Councils for licences to run a circular service between Rock Ferry Station and Port Sunlight via New Chester Road and Old Chester Road and vice versa. On 7th May 1907 the Lower Bebington UDC granted licences after some opposition, subject to one month's notice from the Council to discontinue and, on 16th May, the Mersey Railway buses appeared on a new route between Lever Bros. Works at Port Sunlight and Rock Ferry Station via Wood Street, Riverside, Bolton Road and New Chester Road, running every 12 minutes between 7.12am and

7.0pm at a through fare of 1d with a $^1/_2$d fare from The Dell to the station. Books of 50 halfpenny coupons were sold by conductors for 2/-. The issue of licences in Higher Bebington was delayed on the motion of a Lord's Day Observance zealot who objected to Sunday buses. Eventually licences were issued on 27th May for weekdays only and, two days later, the western side of the circular route commenced running via Greendale Road, Old Chester Road and Bedford Road. On Sundays only the New Chester Road route was operated.

Saurer bus CM 509 lettered for the Mersey Railway's Rock Ferry-Port Sunlight service in 1907.   *T B Maund collection*

The buses competed directly with the trams between New Ferry Toll Bar and Bedford Road and employees of the Tramways Department made detailed observations on the service for two weeks, riding as fare-paying passengers and recording all passengers boarding and alighting. Later it was calculated that passengers were being carried at the rate of 530,000 per annum. More than once the Town Clerk informed the company that they were running a pick-up service contrary to the undertaking given to the Appeal Court. The company denied this but invited specific complaints. Details which have survived make it clear that the Corporation's allegations were fair. For example, on 23rd May between 3.7 and 7.30pm, 223 passengers alighted at Rock Ferry station of which only 64 entered the station; 199 passengers boarded buses of whom only 32 came from the station. For the two weeks 3rd-16th June 1907 (inclusive) the breakdown of traffic was as follows:-

Rock Ferry to Port Sunlight

Boarded at the station	3739	75.4%
Boarded at Bedford Road/New Chester Road junction	833	16.8%
Boarded at Rock Lane	386	7.8%
	4958	

Port Sunlight to Rock Ferry

Alighting at Rock Lane	335	6.7%
Alighting at Bedford Road/New Chester Road junction	1433	28.8%
Alighting at the station	3202	64.5%
	4970	

Further legal action by the Corporation was rendered unnecessary as, on 8th July 1907, the Lords found in favour of the Corporation and the Mersey Railway buses were finally withdrawn. Three of the first four plus CM 506, 507 and 509 went to Hull Corporation while CM 505, 508 and 510 were sold to the Station Cab Co. of Belfast. The tenth was dismantled, the engine being used by a local syndicate for experimental purposes.

Reports of the proceedings brought out many interesting facts, not least of which was that of the Corporation fighting a company in which it held stock with a face value of £35,000. The buses were said to have caused considerable damage to the minor roads in Oxton which were surfaced with waterbound macadam. The borough surveyor estimated additional maintenance costs at £1,500 per year saying that the wheels of motor buses had a peculiar sucking action and broke up the macadam very rapidly. The Mersey Railway countered by pointing out that their annual rate bill was £24,502.

The demise of the Mersey Railway buses was followed by rumours of the intention of the LMS & GW Railways to run 'railway motor carriages' to Port Sunlight; this prompted Birkenhead Corporation to formulate plans to extend their tramways but these were frustrated by Lower Bebington UDC whose area included Port Sunlight. Even the rump of the scheme, an extension from Higher Tranmere to Dacre Hill, was thrown out at a Town's Meeting. The sole positive result of these events was the doubling of the tramway track in Borough Road, Birkenhead in August 1906 so that the Corporation trams passed Central Station in both directions but the Corporation's tactics against the Mersey Railway established a pattern which was applied to everyone who sought to usurp the municipal transport monopoly during the next 25 years.

Wirral Railway Powers

The Wirral Railway, whose tracks met those of the Mersey at Birkenhead Park, was also interested in running buses and secured the necessary powers in 1906. However, their victory was a hollow one as the municipal lobby succeeded in having a clause inserted prohibiting the running of buses 'in any city, borough or urban district provided with a system of tramways or omnibuses without the consent of the local authority...'. The company's principal opponent was the Wallasey Urban District Council whose Bill for additional powers to construct a tramway from Seacombe through Poulton to Wallasey Village (which would have taken traffic from the railway) and to run omnibuses, was thrown out by the Lords in the same session of Parliament.

MERSEY RAILWAY

MOTOR BUS SERVICES between ROCK FERRY & PORT SUNLIGHT

ROCK FERRY
MERSEY RAILWAY STATION
←To BIRKENHEAD & LIVERPOOL. TRAINS EVERY 6 MINUTES.

NEW CHESTER ROAD

BEDFORD ROAD

ROCK LANE

KNOWSLEY ROAD

THE DELL

THORBURN ROAD

NEW FERRY ROAD

STANLEY ROAD

BEBINGTON ROAD

BOUNDARY ROAD

LODGE LANE

BROMBORO POOL

BOLTON ROAD

→To BROMBORO, RABY MERE, EASTHAM, HOOTON.

BRIDGE INN

OFFICE & WORKS of Messrs LEVER BROS.

PORT SUNLIGHT
ELAINE LANE

→TO SPITAL, THORNTON HOUGH, TRAFALGAR, & MID WIRRAL.

LOWER BEBINGTON VILLAGE.

WINDY BANK

BEBINGTON STATION

WIRRAL PARK SHOW GROUND

BEBINGTON CEMETERY

←to HIGHER BEBINGTON & STORETON.

TOWN LANE

WOODHEY LANE

KINGS LANE

DACRE HILL

EGERTON PARK

BUSES FOR ROCK FERRY PASS HERE AT 6-18-30-42 & 54 MINS. PAST THE HOUR.

BUSES FOR ROCK FERRY PASS HERE AT 10-22-34-46 & 58 MINS. PAST THE HOUR.

BUSES FOR ROCK FERRY PASS HERE AT 0-12-24-36-48 MINS. PAST THE HOUR.

BUSES leave ROCK FERRY STATION every SIX MINUTES, going round the LOOP in each direction every TWELVE MINUTES.

On SUNDAYS, Buses leave Station every 12 minutes from 1-48 to 7 p.m.; via New Chester Road, returning by same Route every 12 minutes from 2-6 to 7-18 p.m.

TIME TABLE	Via NEW CHESTER RD.	Via DACRE HILL
STATION - - -	7-12 am to 7-0 pm	7-18 am to 7-6 pm
PORT SUNLIGHT	7-36 am to 7-24 pm	7-30 am to 7-18 pm

Fare-ONE PENNY, In or Out, between ROCK FERRY STATION and PORT SUNLIGHT.

Half-Penny FROM THE DELL TO ROCK FERRY STATION.

Books of Half-Penny Coupons 50 for 2/-

R. BOWMAN SMITH, Traffic Manager

Liverpool, May, 1907.

The original of this was a bright yellow poster which was displayed at various places on the Mersey Railway in 1907.

T B Mound collection

The Wirral had no intention of running buses in Birkenhead or Wallasey as then constituted and merely wanted to provide transport between its stations and the various golf courses in the area without the expense of building special halts as it had done in 1888 at Warren on the New Brighton line. The municipalities, who were receiving useful contributions to their General Rate Funds from profitable transport undertakings, were determined that the railway companies should not upset this particular apple-cart.

The Wirral management had, in the meantime, examined the implications of running feeder buses and at the Directors' Meeting on 25th February 1907 the view was expressed that the proposed motor bus service would result in considerable loss to the company and the scheme was quietly shelved.

Great Western Railway Buses

There was to be just one further railway bus service in Birkenhead in the Edwardian era. It had no direct value to Birkenhead people and, in this instance, the Corporation was very happy to co-operate. The Great Western Railway had never succeeded in reaching Liverpool and Birkenhead was its railhead. Both passengers and goods were shipped across the river and no effort was spared to ease the passage. The GWR's route to Birmingham and London (Paddington) was longer but scenically more attractive than the competitive direct route from Liverpool (Lime Street) and the company wooed the American tourist traffic, having the additional advantage of a direct route to Stratford-on-Avon and Oxford. On 20th September 1909 the company inaugurated a motor bus service between Liverpool and Woodside station using the goods ferry, arrangements having been made with the Corporation to give the bus 'pole position' on the boat so that it could disembark first, unobstructed by horse-drawn carts. The *Birkenhead and Cheshire Advertiser* reported the event as follows:-

'A motor bus service between Liverpool and Woodside has been established....as Woodside Station cannot go to Liverpool, Liverpool is being brought to Woodside. With a fleet of three spacious and comfortably upholstered buses, a regular service, running to an official time-table has been organised. Calls are made at the Washington, Imperial, St.George's and Compton hotels and at the GWR Company's office in James Street, where intending passengers with their luggage are picked up. The bus then proceeds to the Landing Stage and runs direct on to the luggage ferry-boat there waiting, and is conveyed forthwith across the river. Having arrived at Woodside, the bus, which is allotted the position exactly opposite the let-down door or flap, at once leaves the boat, and proceeds without a moment's delay to Woodside Station. By having a spare car the Company are in a position to call at intending travellers' private houses without requiring them to go to the offices...... This, in the case of a family or numerous party, is an arrangement which cannot fail to be highly prized.'

The Great Western had the largest bus fleet of any British railway company and three buses were allocated to this service, a garage being erected on Ferries Committee land behind the station. Two of the buses were 20 hp Milnes-Daimlers, CO 125 (No.49) and AX 123 (No.60). The third is not known for sure but may have been AF 86 (No.45). Late September was a strange time of year to start such a venture which foundered after three months for lack of patronage and was not revived.

Under New Management

In Edwardian times the offices of Tramways Manager and Borough Electrical Engineer had been combined but when the incumbent, Mr W. Wyld, an electrical engineer, resigned in April 1913, the Council decided that the two offices should be separated. Cyril Clarke, chief clerk of the tramways department was appointed Acting Tramways Manager at a salary of £275 per year. It is not clear if the 'acting' prefix reflected some doubt as to the wisdom of the policy decision or of the ability of the appointee but Clarke soon proved himself to be an able and energetic manager, traffic rapidly increasing due to his enterprise, and his appointment was confirmed. Clarke was quick to recognise the potential of the motor bus. The Crosville Motor Co. Ltd. had been running from Chester to New Ferry since 25th January 1913 and he urged the Council to refuse licences for them to run through to Woodside. He persuaded the Council that the Corporation needed statutory powers to run motor buses to feed the tramways with passengers from outlying districts and block further attempts by private enterprise to establish bus routes.

The Birkenhead Corporation Bill deposited in November 1913 provoked no fewer than seven petitions, one of which was by Crosville though most were presented by road authorities and railway companies who were seeking safeguards for their own interests. However, by the time the Bill reached the Commons, agreement had been reached with all accept the Wirral Railway who feared competition to Bidston and Moreton. Wallasey was concerned that Birkenhead might be in a position to block its own expansionist ambitions in the future. Lower Bebington and Bromborough Council objected outright but, if granted, reserved the right to veto bye-laws and inspect the buses. There were to be no overhead wires and it reserved the right to run its own buses and trams!

The Birkenhead Corporation Act 1914 received the Royal Assent on 31st July 1914, only five days before the outbreak of war. It permitted the operation of Corporation buses anywhere within the borough and on six routes outside its boundaries, subject to the consent of the various local authorities. These extended to Moreton Cross via Bidston; Upton village; Storeton Road, Prenton (then just outside the borough); Port Sunlight via Old Chester Road and Greendale Road and via New Chester Road and Bolton Road; from New Ferry to Bromborough Cross. Birkenhead agreed not to oppose Wallasey if they sought similar powers in Moreton and Bidston. Even in 1914, Wallasey had its eyes on Leasowe and Moreton as the only areas into which it could expand.

On the eve of World War I, the Corporation brought a London General B-type 34-seat double-deck bus to Birkenhead and members of the Council went on an outing to Moreton. No doubt if war had not broken out, Birkenhead would have had a municipal bus service by the end of 1914. As it was, technical progress under the stimulus of war made the motor bus of 1919 a much more reliable machine than that of 1914.

Finance

It is of interest to set out the way in which money was raised to fund a municipal undertaking of this kind as the financial structure of a municipal trading concern was quite different from that of a joint stock company. Initially, the Act of Parliament sanctioning the enterprise authorised the raising of sufficient capital by means of loans. Thereafter, the cost of new equipment or buildings was met either from revenue or by applying to the government for a loan, financed by the Public Works Loan Board. The department controlling these loans was the Ministry of Health which had a watching brief for all municipal matters.

The repayment period for loans was such as to cover the life of the asset. For trams it was 20 years, trolleybuses 10 years and motor buses seven years. Some transport undertakings renewed their fleets as soon as the loan was discharged (Wallasey was one); others got a little more life out of their assets on which, in commercial terms, there was no depreciation payable for the last few years. The advantage of the system was that capital could be raised cheaply; the disadvantage was that both capital and interest had to be repaid simultaneously. However, municipal trading was seen as a means of serving the inhabitants, not to make a profit and, if substantial surpluses were achieved, it was expected that the fares would be reduced.

In practice it was sometimes convenient to finance capital expenditure from surplus revenue thereby eliminating or reducing the interest charges. This method was also necessary if the Ministry of Health withheld loan sanction either because it did not consider the expenditure justified or it thought that it could not be afforded.

It was normal for sums of money to be set aside in interest bearing Sinking Funds, equivalent to provisions in commercial terms, to meet known future liabilities. In addition, Reserve Funds were created to meet contingencies. In prosperous years, surplus funds would be transferred to the General Rate Fund; this was, of course, the equivalent of declaring a dividend to the shareholders. Although the Transport general manager was in charge of the undertaking, the finances were strictly controlled by the Borough Treasurer to whom the general manager was obliged to defer on financial matters. The accompanying Tables 1 and 2, which set out various aspects of Capital Expenditure, Reserves and contributions to the General Rate Fund cover only the years 1938-69 when the bus undertaking was free from influences of the former tramway undertaking.

17

TABLE I

CAPITAL ACCOUNT & LOAN CHARGES

Year Ended	Capital Account Total Outlay at end of year £	Net Loan Debt at end of year £	% of Loan Debt to total outlay	Loan Charges £
1938	443,884	132,091	30	30,426
1939	445,749	133,733	30	35,831
1940	466,037	155,166	33	41,451
1941	417,260	120,443	29	37,862
1942	411,862	84,195	20	37,840
1943	412,589	54,159	13	31,943
1944	449,862	42,064	9	20,651
1945	468,671	45,626	10	18,534
1946	504,194	54,367	11	9,310
1947	540,862	60,057	11	9,457
1948	536,668	77,062	14	11,891
1949	598,260	132,188	22	16,562
1950	722,784	306,055	42	25,585
1951	785,786	375,762	48	49,421
1952	810,219	350,104	43	65,274
1953	831,423	340,232	41	68,208
1954	842,642	289,377	34	72,664
1955	894,121	299,498	33	71,156
1956	928,448	286,260	31	76,855
1957	990,208	280,864	28	79,869
1958	1,031,632	278,031	27	78,260
1959	1,113,422	269,074	24	55,016
1960	1,148,153	270,109	24	51,017
1961	1,194,425	297,309	25	57,379
1962	1,239,469	306,706	25	67,420
1963	1,317,088	321,588	24	69,335
1964	1,362,023	373,476	27	75,167
1965	1,360,820	342,842	25	83,963
1966	1,392,588	346,770	25	83,092
1967	1,473,813	331,742	23	86,319
1968	1,498,852	369,200	25	81,839
1969	1,555,573	305,347	20	88,332

TABLE 2

APPROPRIATION ACCOUNT & RESERVE FUND
Reproduced from the Municipal Transport Analysis of Accounts

Year Ended 31st March	Net Profit (Loss)	b/f from Previous Year	Appropriations Surplus (Deficit)	Capital	Reserves	Rate Fund	Carried Forward	Reserve Fund Balance
	£	£	£	£	£	£	£	£
1938	43,725	-	43,725	810	841	34,074	-	52,084
1939	47,608	-	47,608	461	9,080	38,067	-	56,210
1940	51,456	-	51,456	14,076	3,895	27,000	6,485	61,106
1941	29,895	6,485	36,380	95	-	26,600	9,685	56,516
1942	18,321	9,685	28,006	-	-	18,000	10,006	55,700
1943	23,974	10,006	33,980	727	10,006	10,825	12,372	57,398
1944	36,630	12,372	49,002	3,015	20,000	14,900	11,087	58,472
1945	37,144	11,087	48,232	810	20,000	15,120	12,301	70,560
1946	40,144	12,301	52,445	448	5,000	35,000	11,997	63,762
1947	41,389	11,997	53,386	1,315	(16,560)	68,600	31	27,461
1948	42,101	31	42,131	6,789	-	35,000	343	16,781
1949	9,451	343	20,696	2,185	(10,902)	15,000	3,510	2,426
1950	8,256	3,510	11,766	1,459	-	-	10,307	2,264
1951	(28,994)	10,307	(18,687)	607	-	-	(19,294)	1,043
1952	(26,333)	(19,294)	(45,327)	1,454	-	-	(47,081)	501
1953	18,277	(47,081)	(28,804)	384	-	-	(29,188)	-
1954	71,350	(29,188)	42,162	2,159	36,659+	-	3,344	13,015
1955	49,256	3,344	52,600	7,703	25,000	-	19,897	38,015
1956	21,773	19,897	41,670	17,508	13,000	-	11,162	51,973
1957	26,125	11,162	37,287	7,335	20,000	-	9,952	58,562
1958	(14,037)	9,952	(4,085)	6,371	-	-	(10,456)	58,154
1959	60,619	(10,456)	50,163	3,946	46,216	-	-	63,570
1960	67,144	-	67,144	5,798	61,346	-	-	108,609
1961	27,999	-	27,999	1,877	-	-	26,122	106,478
1962	(29,005)	26,122	(2,883)	5,416	-	-	(8,299)	76,335
1963	4,319	(8,299)	(3,980)	3,728	-	-	(7,708)	36,596
1964	54,612	(7,708)	46,904	1,402	45,502	-	-	78,391
1965	9,756	-	9,756	2,889	-	-	6,867	66,128
1966	32,858	6,867	39,725	1,117	-	-	38,608	72,099
1967	68,411	38,608	107,019	5,303	-	-	101,716	75,163
1968	(41,064)	101,716	60,652	8,408	2,100	-	52,250	79,075
1969	(92,399)	52,250	(40,149)	2,585	59,414	-	7,266	23,581

+ Includes an Extraordinary contribution to Sinking Fund

2 – 1919 to 1930

Within two months of the Armistice in November 1918, Birkenhead Corporation had invited tenders for the supply of ten motor buses; they accepted that of Leyland Motors Ltd. for 10 single-deck "O" type with 40-48hp engines and 32-seat bodies costing £1,317 each. Alterations were made to New Ferry depot to house six buses and room was found at Laird Street for four. During the next two years, inspection pits and petrol tanks were installed at both depots and accommodation at New Ferry was increased to 11. An essential piece of equipment in the days of solids - a tyre press - was also acquired. There were other administrative matters to be tackled. Skilled drivers were readily available as many men had been trained in the forces. Licensing, scheduling and maintenance facilities all had to be planned and success was achieved against a background of increasing costs and labour unrest.

All the tramway routes ran to Woodside Ferry but the inaugural bus routes had three basic objectives - to link up the tram routes across town and serve important thoroughfares remote from the tramways; to feed passengers to and from the loss-making Rock Ferry and to establish a community of interest between Birkenhead and the outlying villages such as Upton and Moreton, thus turning the eyes of their inhabitants towards Birkenhead and bringing benefits to shopkeepers and ratepayers. The original routes were extremely well thought out and there was great entrepreneurial vigour displayed by the management. Clarke was enthusiastic and enjoyed the confidence of the Committee; doubtless he derived much satisfaction from building up a completely new municipal enterprise. The wise choice of routes was reflected in the almost complete absence of service withdrawals and alterations which figure so largely in the early histories of many motor bus undertakings.

Birkenhead Corporation's first buses were single-deck Leyland O types fitted with 32-seat Leyland bodywork. They were numbered 1-10 (CM 1701-10) and four were delivered in time for the opening of the first route, between Park Station and Rock Ferry on 12th July 1919. By June 1920 all ten had arrived and the route was extended to Moreton Cross. No. 3 is seen at Charing Cross en route to Park Station, probably on the first day of operation. Note the paper destination label. *Leyland Motors*

The original intention had been to run between Rock Ferry Pier and Duke Street Bridge with some early morning workmen's trips between Laird Street and Cammell Laird's but permission was needed to use the Dock Board's private roads and the early morning service would have extracted traffic from the tramways. So the first route was from Park Station to Rock Ferry Pier via Park Road East, Charing Cross, Derby Road, Bebington Road and Bedford Avenue. It started on 12th July 1919 as soon as the first four buses had arrived. A half-hourly service, requiring three buses, ran between 8.0am and 9.30pm and on Saturday afternoons the fourth bus was put on the road so that there was a bus every 23 minutes.

At the end of August 1919, the service was extended from Park Station to Moreton Cross, necessitating a temporary reduction in frequency as the fifth bus was not delivered until December 1919; two more came in January and the order was completed in June 1920. On 30th September 1919, the fourth day of a railway strike, the regular morning and afternoon services were reduced and five trips were run between Hoylake and Laird Street tram terminus in the morning and evening at the request of Hoylake UDC who had posters printed and displayed throughout the district. It is not known for how many days this was done. An emergency service was also run to Upton. Shortage of buses delayed the start of the regular service to Upton.

No trams or buses ran on Sunday mornings and two experimental Sunday bus services were tried in the summer of 1921. A Woodside-Moreton Cross service started in May and from July one trip was run from Laird Street Depot to Woodside via Shrewsbury Road, Balls Road and Oxton Road to connect with the 10.10am boat. The fares were almost double those charged on the trams.

Four Straker-Squire single-deck buses were obtained in 1922, three from Plymouth Corporation (Nos. 13-15, CO 3398-3400) and one (No.16, CM 4006) from a local charabanc operator, W. B. Horn. The latter was not immediately repainted before entering service and retained its previous owner's blue and cream livery for some time; it was thus Birkenhead's first blue bus. Two further Strakers were bought from Plymouth and dismantled for spares, a wise move as the manufacturer went into liquidation in 1925 and spares became rare. One of the Strakers is seen at Rock Ferry Pier.   *T.G.Turner collection*

21

Cross Docks Routes

A horse-bus service, known locally as the 'Penny Jogger' had been run by Thomas Peters over the Four Bridges between Charing Cross and Seacombe Ferry since 1903. The business was sold to the Birkenhead Motor Works in 1919 and the new owners introduced motor buses. Motors had been used for a short time in 1911 in competition with the horse buses but by whom is unknown; they were reported as Ford Model T with specially built 12-seat bodies. The Motor Works occupied the premises at 2-4 Devonshire Road which had been associated with omnibuses since 1853 and are believed to have owned five vehicles including a De Dion and a Dennis, second-hand from Crosville where it had carried the name 'The Alma'. The cross docks service continued to run across the Four Bridges every 15 minutes at busy times and day and half-day tours were also operated.

Birkenhead Corporation now pursued two further objectives - the exercise of the statutory powers to run from New Ferry to Bromborough granted by the 1914 Act (but subject to the approval of the local authority) and the establishment of a service to Wallasey.

Birkenhead and Wallasey had talked about transport between the two boroughs on many occasions since the early days of the century but the dock bridges and railway tracks had been considered insuperable obstacles to the linking of the two tramway systems. Similar problems were overcome elsewhere but the Dock Board, who did not want to be bothered with such matters, was never helpful. So people who did not want to use Peters' archaic conveyances walked over the bridges or quite often took the ferry from Seacombe to Liverpool and then another boat to Woodside. It is surprising that neither borough had had the foresight to include powers to operate into the area of the other in their enabling Acts so any service across the docks would be strictly *ultra vires*. Talks between the two councils in February 1920 were inconclusive. Wallasey was still awaiting delivery of buses and seems to have regarded Birkenhead's offer to provide the whole service with suspicion. However, having obtained the Dock Board's approval to use their private roads, agreement was reached early in 1921 and a 40-minute service started on 19th March 1921 between Charing Cross and Seacombe Ferry via Park Station, Duke Street Bridge and Dock Road. Initially the buses used Exmouth Street, at that time a street of small shops, but the route was later exchanged with the Rock Ferry-Moreton service to use Park Road East. No attempt was made to cater for workmen as the first bus ran at 9.0am (2.30pm on Sundays) and continued until 10.40pm.

The two Corporations agreed on equal shares and, as only one bus was needed, they worked the early and late shifts on alternate weeks. The privately owned service ceased. It is of interest to note that, at least as far as Wallasey was concerned, the Dock Board never gave permission for buses to use the route across Duke Street bridge, their letter dated 18th March 1921, indemnifying the Board against any claims for any loss or damage, specifically mentioning the Four Bridges route which was not used for a scheduled service until 1955.

An hourly summer service from Charing Cross to Harrison Drive was started in June. This followed the same route as the Seacombe bus to Duke Street Bridge then turned left along the Dock Road and Poulton Bridge Road to Poulton then via Breck Road, still little more than a country lane. This ran in the 1922 and 1923 summer seasons. Its withdrawal at the end of the first

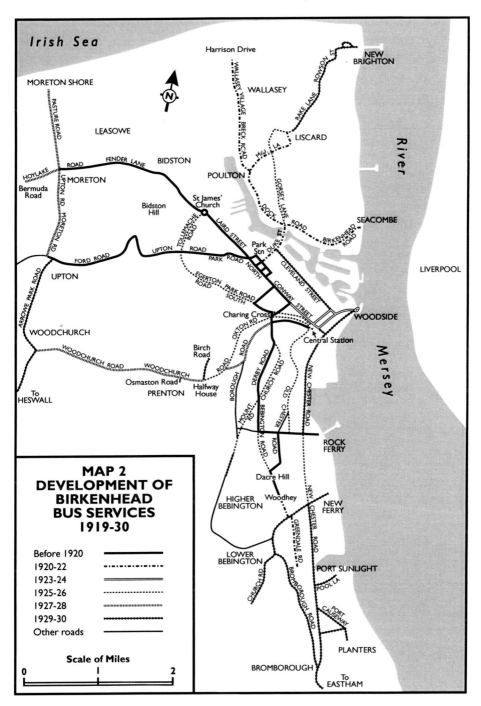

Irish Sea

MORETON SHORE

Harrison Drive

NEW BRIGHTON

WALLASEY

LISCARD

LEASOWE

BIDSTON

PASTURE ROAD

HOYLAKE

ROAD

FENDER LANE

MORETON

Bermuda Road

UPTON RD

MORETON RD

Bidston Hill

St James' Church

POULTON

SEACOMBE

WALLASEY VILLAGE

BRECK ROAD

MILL LA

GORSEY LANE

DOCK

ROAD

BIRKENHEAD ROAD

RAKE LANE

ROWSON ST

River

LIVERPOOL

FORD ROAD

UPTON

ARROWE PARK ROAD

WOODCHURCH

UPTON ROAD

TOLLEMACHE ROAD

LAIRD STREET

Park Stn

PARK ROAD NORTH

EGERTON PARK ROAD

PARK ROAD SOUTH

DUKE ST

CLEVELAND STREET

CONWAY STREET

Charing Cross

WOODSIDE

Central Station

OXTON RD

DERBY ROAD

CHURCH ROAD

OLD CHESTER ROAD

NEW CHESTER ROAD

Birch Road

BOROUGH ROAD

WOODCHURCH ROAD

WOODCHURCH

Osmaston Road

PRENTON

Halfway House

To HESWALL

MOUNT RD

BEBINGTON ROAD

ROCK FERRY

Dacre Hill

HIGHER BEBINGTON

Woodhey

NEW FERRY

LOWER BEBINGTON

GREENDALE RD

NEW CHESTER ROAD

PORT SUNLIGHT

POOL LA

Mersey

CHURCH RD SOUTH

BROMBOROUGH ROAD

PORT CAUSEWAY

PLANTERS

BROMBOROUGH

To EASTHAM

MAP 2
DEVELOPMENT OF BIRKENHEAD BUS SERVICES 1919-30

Before 1920	———
1920-22	—·—·—·
1923-24	═══
1925-26	·········
1927-28	....
1929-30	◆◆◆◆◆
Other roads	———

Scale of Miles

0   1   2

season stimulated a demand for a bus service between Birkenhead and Poulton all the year round so the Charing Cross and Liscard service started in October 1921 running hourly from 10.30am to 9.30pm. It followed the same route as the Harrison Drive bus to Poulton as Gorsey Lane was not built until April 1924. The working arrangements were now altered so that each Corporation ran the whole of the Seacombe or Liscard route on alternate weeks. The Liscard route was more popular than Harrison Drive and the latter service was taken off before the end of the 1923 season. Cheap railway fares were also a factor as there was a frequent train service from Park to Wallasey station. The legal position as far as Birkenhead was concerned was put right by inserting a clause in the Birkenhead Corporation Act, 1923 giving the general right to make agreements about bus services. Wallasey's position was not regularised until 1928.

Problems with Local Councils

An application to Wirral Rural District Council for permission to run into their area to Moreton, Upton and Woodchurch met with limited success, though the Corporation had to agree to pay 3d per mile towards road maintenance. Licences were forthcoming for services to Moreton Cross and Upton Village but authority to use the Moreton-Upton road, which was also being sought by Crosville, was granted subject to payment of £3,500, the cost of widening Moreton Road, Upton which the two applicants eventually agreed to share equally in January 1921. Woodchurch was refused as the Council was satisfied with the service run by J. Pye of Heswall.

On 14th July 1920, Birkenhead Corporation started an approximately hourly service between Charing Cross and Upton via Park Station, extending it to Central Station a month later. Crosville then started a service from West Kirby through Frankby and Upton to the borough boundary at Bidston Hill Waterworks. Clarke was angry at having competition when his Upton service had been running for only three months and he suggested that the company service should terminate at Upton from where the Corporation buses would provide a connecting service. Crosville refused and started to run the buses down the hill to the tram route at Claughton Village which they could do unlicensed so long as the same passenger was not both picked up and set down within the borough. The bus then returned empty to the Waterworks as fare paying passengers could not be picked up in Birkenhead. These were the first exchanges in a battle between the Corporation and Crosville which was not resolved until 1930.

In October 1920, the Corporation started another new route between Rock Ferry Pier and Woodhey (Town Lane) via Bedford Road and Old Chester Road. This was as far as they could get without crossing the borough boundary but, having received the approval of both Higher and Lower Bebington Councils, the route was extended via Bebington Station and Greendale Road to Port Sunlight in March 1921. Promotional and educational tours of Lever Bros. works were very popular in the years between the wars and the new service hoped to attract some of this traffic to the Rock Ferry boats.

Heartened by the success of their Port Sunlight application, the Corporation applied to run from New Ferry to Bromborough but this was refused by the Lower Bebington and Bromborough Urban District Council, an authority which was very jealous of its independence. After delaying its reply for over three months, it refused consent on the grounds that it had completed arrangements with the Crosville company for a "very much improved service in the districts....and it would create unfair competition with the existing service and would lead to confusion and unnecessary deterioration, wear and tear of the roads to have two separate services over the same route in the Districts". It is clear that this diminutive authority gloried in twisting the tail of its larger neighbour and went so far as to refuse authority for the Corporation buses to carry passengers when travelling to or from New Ferry depot.

In August 1922, Birkenhead appealed to the Ministry of Transport but an Arbitrator, after listening to evidence from both sides, reported in June 1923 in favour of retaining the *status quo*. Birkenhead had to wait a few more years to get its buses to Bromborough.

Agreement with Crosville

In the post-war years, the Crosville Motor Co. Ltd. of Chester expanded its network of services in Wirral from bases at New Ferry and West Kirby. An appeal by the company to the Ministry of Transport against refusal of licences to enable buses to pick up passengers at Claughton Village was successful and the service was increased. Three stands were allocated in Park Road West.

In the 1923 Session, Birkenhead Corporation promoted a Parliamentary Bill which included a clause seeking authority to run buses anywhere outside the borough with the approval of the Minister of Transport. Crosville petitioned Parliament and the clause was defeated. In January, the company started a new service of four trips a day between West Kirby and Claughton Village via Meols, Garden Hey Road, Saughall Massie and Upton, as a means of linking Hoylake directly with Birkenhead. The Corporation, perhaps sensing that all-out opposition would be petty, wrote to the company pointing out that the service was unlicensed and Crosville actually suspended the service for a time, presumably as a conciliatory move while other matters were afoot. In March the Corporation was informed by the company that they intended running buses between Heswall and Claughton Village via Thurstaston, Irby and Upton or via Lower Caldy Cross Roads, Frankby and Greasby. There was to be a minimum fare of 5d between Birkenhead and Upton to placate the Corporation. Later correspondence makes it clear that this service was run for a few weekends in 1923. These services were officially approved by the Watch Committee on 4th July 1923 provided that not more than three buses were to stand simultaneously in Park Road West, with a 10 yards gap between them, and Crosville withdrew an appeal they had submitted because of continual delay in dealing with their applications.

In May and June 1923, Crosville applied to Birkenhead for numerous new licences to enable them to extend their Chester services from New Ferry Toll Bar to Woodside together with new routes being planned from Parkgate and North Wales; the West Kirby-Claughton Village services were to continue to Park Station and Woodside and also to Central Station via Park Road West and Charing Cross and an additional service added via Moreton. The company offered to charge higher fares than the Corporation. Between New Ferry and Woodside the company proposed to charge double the tram fare and hand over half the proceeds to the Corporation if the journey was wholly within the borough.

The Corporation regarded these applications with considerable alarm and procrastinated to the extent that Crosville interpreted their inaction as a refusal and appealed to the Ministry of Transport. They had, however, considerable support in local commercial circles and the Birkenhead Traders' Association urged the Council to grant licences for buses to run direct to important shopping centres rather than to the railway and ferry exits.

Having asked the Ministry to defer hearing the appeal, the Corporation appointed a special sub-committee of the Watch Committee which showed great confidence in the chief officers by delegating negotiations to the Chief Constable and the Tramways Manager. The company's case was strengthened by the disclosure at a Municipal Tramways Association Conference in Portsmouth that the Ministry's policy was to allow private buses to penetrate to town centres with protective conditions for local tramway and bus services.

To protect their interests, the Corporation started a daily service between Woodside and Moreton Cross on 16th September 1923 and, about the same time, it seems that some journeys between Central Station and Upton were diverted via Park Roads South and West. No formal evidence of this has been found but the January 1924 time table shows no timing point at Park Station on these trips and five minutes running time instead of the usual eight minutes via Park Station. They were presumably discontinued soon afterwards when the Crosville agreement was settled.

Six all-Leyland 36SG7 32-seat buses (Nos. 18-23, CM 4936-41) were placed in service during 1923. They were similar to Nos. 1-10 but the cab sides were enclosed. No. 20 is seen behind a Leyland PLSC3 at Arrowe Park at the time of the World Boy Scout Jamboree in 1929, by which time it had been fitted with pneumatic tyres.   P.E. Wright

The Corporation took a census at New Ferry and found that Crosville was already carrying more than 500,000 passengers per annum on this group of services, a considerable number of whom started or finished their journeys by Corporation tram. Loss of only half the number would, it was estimated, cost £3,125 per year in lost revenue. This kind of development had been going on throughout the country and in some towns the local authority had already come to terms with company operators.

The company rejected a Corporation suggestion that passengers should change from a Crosville to a Corporation bus and vice versa at Moreton Cross with through tickets between West Kirby,

Hoylake etc. and Birkenhead issued by both operators. There was also disagreement about the picking up limit beyond New Ferry; the Corporation wanted Bromborough Pool Lane whereas Crosville insisted that it must have Bolton Road which would have given the company access to the Port Sunlight works traffic. In this case the company proposed to charge 4d to Woodside and was prepared to pay 3d over to the Corporation. As Cyril Clarke pointed out in a report, this was likely to be a temporary expedient as such an imposition would be strong grounds for a later appeal to the Ministry of Transport when the company could say:- 'We collect £8,333 in fares and perform all the services in carrying these passengers and are only allowed to retain for ourselves £2,083 whilst the Corporation, who do nothing, receive £6,250'.

By early November the company had agreed to accept the same terms as it had agreed with Widnes Corporation whereby no passenger should be picked up or set down within half a mile of the outer Corporation terminus. This meant that they were prepared to give up their existing Birkenhead to Upton traffic and would not set down a passenger from Birkenhead until arriving at Bermuda Road on the Moreton route, Overchurch Road on the Saughall Massie route and the bridge over the Arrowe Brook on the Frankby route. The exception was that when the Corporation was running less frequently than half-hourly on the Upton route, Crosville would have free trade. In practice this was in the mornings and after 8.0pm. Between New Ferry and Woodside, the amount of the tram fare would be handed over to the Corporation. The Corporation's inspectors were to have the right to inspect tickets and waybills on Crosville buses in the borough.

On 22nd November 1923 Clarke met an official of the Ministry of Transport and on his return reported as follows:-

'....he made it quite clear that their policy was to allow outside buses into Towns and Cities, the only limitation being to require outside buses to charge a minimum fare of one penny more than the tram fare for passengers picked up or set down within the Borough Boundary. I put to him the question as to whether they would interfere with any agreement mutually arrived at between the company and the Corporation and he said 'No'.

'It appears that your Committee have, under existing conditions, no option but to grant the licences and, if the Crosville Co. will agree to the suggested conditions arranged between themselves, the Chief Constable and myself, these are much more favourable to the Corporation than you could hope to get if the Ministry of Transport were called on to deal with the matter'.

The Police drew up a schedule of suggested routes for Crosville buses within the borough and, in a confidential report, Clarke pointed out that the grant of these licences to Crosville would inevitably be followed by like applications from Pye, Johnston and Richardson, all of whom ran between Heswall and Singleton Avenue, and would severely damage the businesses of the local coach excursion operators who were allowed to stand at Woodside for limited periods.

However, when a draft Agreement was tabled in January 1924, the company had been induced to drop its New Ferry-Woodside application *in toto* in return for agreement on a Park Station terminus for the West Kirby services, the Woodside and Central Station extensions being refused. The picking up limits previously agreed were confirmed including the Upton exception, an empty concession, as the Corporation were soon running half-hourly at all times. Licences were granted to Crosville for New Ferry-Moreton and Rock Ferry-Raby Mere services which were not contentious. In the final Agreement, Crosville also voluntarily forfeited their right of appeal to the Minister of Transport.

In view of Clarke's November report, what happened to enable the Corporation to assert its authority in this way? The working papers for the final phase of the negotiations have not come to light if, indeed, they ever existed. The opposition of the local charabanc operators could have been given some weight as they included some influential men. Congestion at Woodside was another factor. Crosville had estimated a need for 60 licences for the New Ferry and West Kirby extensions and undertook to restrict the number of buses standing at any one time to six. But the deciding factor almost certainly lay in Crosville's conclusion of a deal with John Pye for the purchase of his Heswall services. It was probably made clear to the company that the satisfactory transfer of the licences was dependent on the company being 'reasonable' in other matters. Difficulties could be made to arise in connection with the Singleton Avenue stands as the Chief Constable had previously complained about obstruction. There was also the very important matter of additional licences to enable the service to be developed.

As it was, the same draft agreement promised the company 'full facilities at Singleton Avenue, that is to say, will license as many Buses as the Company require....' The company agreed to find room for two buses to stand on their own premises at 2-4 Singleton Avenue but retained the right to stand two buses on the roadway. A new route was granted between Rock Ferry Pier and Heswall via Storeton. This was much better treatment than Pye had received.

This Leyland LG1 Leviathan is standing at the Bermuda Road, Moreton terminus wearing the later livery with maroon upper deck panels. *D. S. Deacon*

It may be that cash flow problems made it essential for the company to obtain the revenue from the Heswall services quickly. They provided good cash receipts throughout the year whereas the New Ferry services were more seasonal. The Agreement was signed on 26th February 1924. However, the Crosville management seemed to lack the determination to pursue their objectives to the bitter end and to be overawed by large, powerful councils. In a letter to a consultant, Claude C. Taylor, managing director of Crosville, admitted that in the early 1920s, they had not pursued the extension of services to central Birkenhead 'for the sake of peace and quietness'.

Laird Street Garage

The rapid increase in the size of the bus fleet caused accommodation problems. Not only could no more buses be fitted in at New Ferry but that depot was inconveniently situated for many of the routes. A shed was erected on the west side of Laird Street tram depot in August 1925 and a washing machine was erected in the yard during 1926. This equipment was designed by the rolling stock superintendent, W.R. Shaw, and was advanced for its time. It consisted of a framework of brass tubing into which the bus was driven. Water was sprayed through 470 jets for about half a minute, followed by cleaning with soft brushes. The machine could accommodate double-deck buses and could handle eight buses per hour.

Some alterations to the depot and workshops were approved in 1927 and, later the same year, a garage extension with an entrance in Plumer Street was agreed subject to the excavation and drainage work being done by direct labour in order to reduce the cost, stated to be £11,000.

Three Guy BB type single-deck (Nos. 52-54, CM 6608-10) with bodies by the chassis manufacturer were placed in service in 1926 to provide increased capacity on the Grange Road service. Unlike No. 38 they were fitted with normal wheels but had special 6ft 3in wide bodies (one foot less than normal) which dictated the unusual seating arrangement of a long seat down one side and individual seats down the other. *D. S. Deacon*

The Town Services Expand

During 1925, Birkenhead Corporation extended and consolidated the town services. In November 1923, a service had been suggested between Charing Cross and Port Sunlight via Old Chester Road, New Ferry and Bolton Road but this could not be started because of opposition from Bebington council and Lever Bros. were not keen to have buses running through their model village. The idea developed into two new routes, the first of which, from Charing Cross to Port Sunlight via Derby Road, Bebington Road and Greendale Road, started in March. It was extended to start from Park Station in 1927 and from Claughton Village, at certain times of the day, in 1929. In June 1925, a route between Charing Cross and New Ferry via Old Chester Road and Rock Ferry Station commenced and a few days later the Shopping Bus made its appearance, running a frequent service between Market Place South and Balls Road via Grange Road and Oxton Road on weekdays. It used small one-man buses and was extended to the Half Way House, Storeton Road in August. According to *Motor Transport Year Book*, Vol. 5, a service between Storeton Road and Woodside had been contemplated in 1920 but was not proceeded with.

The last of the 1925 deliveries comprised three Leyland SG11 single-deck buses with Leyland bodywork (Nos. 39-41, CM 6046-48). They were the last of the Leylands with high straight chassis and were sold as obsolescent in 1931.
Leyland Motors

The First Tramway Abandonment

In the same month there was a bench-mark event which was not recognised as of any great importance at the time. The Claughton Road tram service, terminating at the foot of Palm Grove, had always been a loss-maker. It had never been continued to Shrewsbury Road, as originally authorised, and various later plans to extend it had come to nothing. The motor bus was now so well established in the town that the Council decided to replace the trams by buses on an extended route to St.James' Church via Egerton Road and Tollemache Road from 30th August

1925. The changeover was very successful as the buses had the benefit of traffic to and from Flaybrick Hill Cemetery. The significance of the event was that this was the first conversion of a tram route to bus operation on Merseyside and it demonstrated the ability of the bus to replace trams on urban services. However, there was no immediate change of policy in Birkenhead, large sums being spent on track renewal and improvements to trams during the 1920s. No further tram routes were abandoned for another six years and then for very different reasons.

From 30th November 1925, the Upton-Central Station and Charing Cross-New Ferry routes were combined into a through Upton-New Ferry service, the foundation of a service which was destined to grow longer and longer over the years and eventually link Eastham with Saughall Massie.

August 1926 saw the introduction of the Woodside and Kings Road service, running on weekdays up Whetstone Lane and duplicating the tram service along the full length of Church Road, Higher Tranmere. The terminus was at Cavendish Drive, within the Birkenhead boundary, until March 1930 when it was extended to Kings Lane. When expensive repairs were necessary to the track, the tram service was cut back to Whitfield Street in October 1928 but, as the outer suburbs developed, the Kings Road buses were unable to cope with the traffic, particularly at visiting times at Birkenhead Institution (now St.Catherine's Hospital) so the track was put in order as far as Allerton Road, outside the hospital, and the trams were re-extended to that point in February 1930. However, buses handled all the Sunday traffic from April 1930.

Birkenhead Corporation Act, 1926

Birkenhead Corporation deposited another Bill in Parliament for the 1926 Session asking for powers to run buses anywhere within a five mile radius of Birkenhead Town Hall which would have cleared the way for Corporation buses to run to Clatterbridge, Eastham, Greasby, Pensby and Barnston. The Crosville Motor Company prepared a Petition and this time the Corporation approached them and other objectors in order to obtain an agreed Bill, as the real objective was to purchase Arrowe Park and secure powers to run buses to it. They already had powers to run on the direct route via Woodchurch Road but wanted to be able to run from Moreton and Upton also. They also needed more powers to run in Bebington which was building up rapidly and they wanted to run further along Hoylake Road, Moreton and to the Shore (then known as the Embankment).

Crosville's view was that expansion should be on a mutual basis and any further penetration into the Wirral by the Corporation should be achieved only at the expense of concessions in Birkenhead. Eventually agreement was reached and the company withdrew its Petition. A second agreement, dated 15th March 1926, was drawn up, the principal points being as follows:-

1. In Moreton, Birkenhead buses could run along Hoylake Road to Bermuda Road, along Pasture Road to the Shore and from Moreton Cross to Upton and Arrowe Park but the restriction point for Crosville buses should be moved about 600 yds nearer to Birkenhead from Bermuda Road to Moreton Schools (effectively Rosslyn Drive). The Corporation could use the new alignment of Woodchurch Road (instead of the old road past the church) but neither route to Arrowe Park could start until the estate had been purchased and was open for public use.

2. In Upton the restriction points for Company buses should be moved eastward along Greasby Road about 300 yds from Arrowe Brook to Upton Cricket Ground and on Saughall Massie Road from Overchurch Road to the western end of the Convent wall, a concession of about half a mile on a largely unpopulated road.

3. The Corporation was to repay to the company half the money paid to Wirral RDC in 1921 for widening the Upton-Moreton road. (The Corporation paid Crosville £2,060 on 28th September 1927).

4. Crosville buses on the Rock Ferry-Heswall service could use Mount Road between Borough Road and Storeton Road instead of diverting via Prenton Road West.

5. Birkenhead Corporation buses could run in Bebington along Kings Road, Kings Lane and Town Lane; in the parish of Bidston from Ashburton Road along Boundary Road to Bidston Village (Boundary Road was just outside the borough boundary at that time); and from Prenton tram terminus along Storeton Road to Mount Road.

Consolidation in Moreton

The easing of restrictions on the Greasby and Saughall Massie roads had little practical value as these roads remained essentially rural for some years. However the Moreton concession was much more valuable as Moreton expanded westwards. In 1926 Crosville extended the New Ferry-Moreton Cross service to the Shore. Birkenhead's moves in Moreton during 1927-28 were

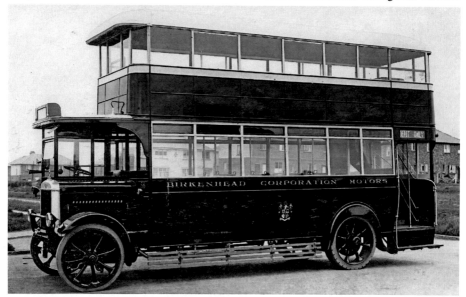

An improved version of the Leyland Leviathan, the PLSP1 model, appeared in 1927 and Birkenhead purchased 10 (Nos. 55-64, CM6611-20). The fully enclosed Leyland bodies were ahead of their time and seated 55 passengers. They were the last buses to be delivered with solid tyres but pneumatics were soon fitted all round. No.56 is pictured at Leyland before delivery.   *Leyland Motors*

essentially tactical as the Corporation was anxious to secure its position before the district was absorbed into Wallasey on 1st April 1928 after which they would need licences from Wallasey Watch Committee. As Wallasey had its own transport ambitions, Birkenhead might have had some difficulty in reaching its objectives. Both the Woodside- and Rock Ferry-Moreton services were extended from the Cross to Bermuda Road on 1st February 1927. A shuttle service using small buses commenced between the Cross and the Embankment in June, effectively putting Cole's Dinky Bus, which had previously served this route, out of business. Pasture Road was in poor condition and the railway bridge at Moreton station was only half its later width. Following negotiations with Wirral RDC, the latter agreed to accept £600 towards the cost of making the road suitable for full size buses and a through service from Woodside to the Embankment started on 1st September 1927. A second service between Upton and the Embankment, in direct competition with Crosville, started on 1st January 1928. There was little demand, particularly in the winter, and this was a direct challenge to the company which had been serving the Moreton Cross-Upton road since 1921. Both operators lost heavily and the Corporation, having established itself on the route, wisely withdrew the service for the winter on 25th October 1928.

Despite the lack of amenities, Leasowe Common and Moreton Shore became extremely popular with Liverpool people on summer Sundays and this popularity was stimulated by the intensive service of double-deck buses operated from Woodside by Birkenhead Corporation. This was the first of several services which ran daily throughout the year but experienced very heavy additional traffic at fine summer weekends. The demand was capricious and dependent entirely on the weather and off-duty drivers and conductors would report to the depot on fine Sundays and nearly always get a 'special' at overtime rates. In the evenings, there would be a continuous procession of buses loading at Moreton Shore for Woodside non-stop, returning empty for a second and sometimes a third load. An observer remembers counting 90 full buses passing Moreton Cross in one hour on a Sunday evening.

The World Boy Scout Jamboree

Meanwhile a daily service between Woodside and Osmaston Road via Singleton Avenue was started in July 1928 being extended to Arrowe Park on Saturday afternoons two months later. The World Scout Jamboree held in Arrowe Park from 22nd July to 13th August 1929 attracted crowds of visitors and thousands of passengers were carried by both Crosville and Corporation buses. Following an appeal from Birkenhead Corporation to other municipal operators, vehicles were hired from Liverpool, Manchester, Wallasey and Leigh Corporations to cope with the crowds on the busiest days. Leyland and Daimler each provided a demonstration bus. Contemporary reports suggest that Birkenhead's own buses and three Leyland PLSC Lions from Leigh were used for services to and from Arrowe Park while the other hired vehicles were used on the Moreton services. The three Leigh buses travelled 6,358 miles in 16 days, a daily average of 132 miles per bus per day, the equivalent of 13 return trips between Woodside and Arrowe Park. It is of interest to note that the motivation behind Leigh making the buses available was the likelihood of a cotton strike in the town and a desire to keep its buses profitably running. Cyril Clarke wrote to the Leigh manager after the event as follows:-

"I take this opportunity of offering to yourself and the Leigh Corporation the thanks of my Committee and myself for the very valuable assistance you were kind enough to give us and if at any future date I can reciprocate in any way, I shall be glad to do so.

"I should further like to add a word of praise and appreciation to your men and your buses. The drivers and conductors without exception were most enthusiastic in their work and won the admiration with all whom they came into contact for their willing service under trying conditions and pleasant and helpful manners and all round competence and for their pride in their work and their vehicles. Your buses ran without the slightest trouble and both your men and their buses reflected the greatest credit on yourself and your town."

On 1st June 1930 a Woodside-Upton via Arrowe Park daily service was inaugurated and within six weeks this was extended to Woodside via Park Station as a circular route, running hourly in each direction with a circular fare of 7d for those who just wanted a ride. However in October 1930 this route and the Moreton-Upton local service were withdrawn in favour of a Woodside-Arrowe Park-Upton-Moreton Shore route.

New Brighton

Leyland Lion No. 66, now painted with cream relief, is seen in Storeton Road at the Birch Road terminus of the Grange Road 'shopping bus' after being fitted with route number boxes in 1931.

T.G.Turner collection

A service which attracted a steady regular patronage with enormous holiday peaks was inaugurated, jointly with Wallasey Corporation, in October 1929. This was the New Ferry and New Brighton route which, for the first three months of its existence, was an extension at both ends of the Charing Cross and Liscard route. The mileage in Birkenhead's area was 4.462 (59.26%) and in Wallasey 3.068 (40.74%) and it was agreed that receipts should be pooled. Each operator would take out 10d per mile for running expenses and divide the balance in the same proportions as the mileage in each Corporation's area. Buses of both authorities worked on this route simultaneously. The basic frequency was every 20 minutes but it was heavily augmented at busy times. From Rock Ferry it ran along Old Chester Road and Argyle Street South then along Borough Road to Charing Cross. At the same time the Charing Cross-Liscard service commenced at 8.5am instead of 11.5am. Old Chester Road was now well served as the Woodside-Lower Bebington (Spital Cross Roads) route had started in March 1929 at the specific request of the Bebington Council. Hitherto, residents of Lower Bebington had walked to Bebington and New Ferry station and taken the train to Birkenhead or ridden by Crosville bus to New Ferry Toll Bar and then boarded a tram.

Late in 1929, there were suggestions from the public that the New Ferry-New Brighton route should be diverted via Haymarket, Hamilton Street and Cleveland Street and from January 1930 it ran along Argyle Street and Cleveland Street, providing an evening and Sunday service along the latter thoroughfare where the trams ran only on weekdays and made their last journeys before

8.0pm. A convenient link with the docks was also established. From the summer of 1930, great crowds were carried to New Brighton and many Wallasey people used the service in the other direction to reach the Crosville buses which ran from New Ferry to Chester and North Wales. After the latter were extended to Woodside, they still used the service, alighting at Hamilton Square and walking down to the ferry approach. On busy Sundays there were extra buses from St.Paul's Road and Central Station to New Brighton where long queues formed in the evenings.

The bus services made a profit of £15,000 in 1925-26, £13,000 being paid into the Rate Fund. Revenue from buses overtook that from trams for the first time in the year ending 31st March 1928 and the following year bus passengers at 18.3 million exceeded tram passengers by almost a million. Bus and tram services had different characteristics as demonstrated by usage statistics for 1928-29. Trams carried 14.27 passengers per mile at an average fare of 1.37d whilst buses carried only 8.24 passengers per mile at an average of 1.98d. Bus journeys tended to be longer and a substantial proportion of the fleet was still single-deck with a low seating capacity.

Railway Initiative

Following the passing of the Railways (Road Transport) Acts, 1928, the four main line companies purchased a number of established bus companies one of which was Crosville which became a division of the London, Midland and Scottish Railway Company from 1st May 1929. Approaches were also made by the railways to several municipalities and Birkenhead agreed to talks. The LMS wanted to get the Crosville services to Woodside reasoning that this would result in an enormous increase in traffic and made its initial approach almost within days of taking over the bus company . The Corporation's view was that expansion should be mutual; if Crosville buses were to penetrate to Birkenhead town centre then Corporation buses should push further into the Wirral villages to which many Birkenhead residents were already migrating. The Town Council wisely left the negotiations to the professionals, this time E.W.Tame, the Town Clerk, and Cyril Clarke.

The first meeting took place on 31st May 1929. After lengthy deliberations by a Royal Commission, sweeping changes in bus service licensing were proposed and the Corporation was anxious to finalise an agreement before the Road Traffic Bill became law and in time to submit a Parliamentary Bill in November 1929 as they knew they would need further statutory powers in order to achieve their objectives. There is little doubt that the Road Traffic Act 1930 would have given Crosville access to Woodside from New Ferry, Singleton Avenue and Prenton but it is unlikely that they would have been able to establish the same long distance services, including the valuable routes to Caernarfon, which the Agreement facilitated.

Birkenhead's objectives were to get their buses out to Bromborough, Eastham and Heswall and to restrict Crosville buses to traffic originating from or destined for places beyond. The Crosville negotiators were shrewd enough to realise that, in the Heswall direction, suburban development would favour the direct Pensby road and refused to concede any rights there. Eventually, in order to avoid joint working on any route, it was agreed that the service to Heswall via Irby and Thurstaston would be transferred from Crosville to the Corporation. This had a heavy summer weekend traffic but there were also two rural miles along the main Chester-West Kirby road which still remain partly undeveloped over seventy-five years later. Agreement was reached in October, in time for the Corporation to submit their Bill.

Three Leyland Leviathans led by No. 56 are seen in final form with pneumatic tyres and route number boxes at Moreton Shore. The revised livery style was introduced with the first Titans in 1928.

T.G. Turner collection

In short, company buses were to be extended from New Ferry, Singleton Avenue and Prenton tram terminus to Woodside and Corporation buses were to run out to Bromborough and Eastham; Irby, Thurstaston and Heswall; Greasby, Frankby and Thurstaston and Clatterbridge. Crosville surrendered their valuable local service between New Ferry, Bromborough and Eastham and their buses were precluded from carrying local passengers between Woodside and Allport Road, Bromborough; Marsh Lane/Mount Road, Higher Bebington; Holm Lane, Woodchurch Road (or alternatively Ivy Cottage, Thingwall or Arrowe House Farm under certain conditions); Clatterbridge Workhouse (*sic*) on journeys via Lower Bebington (again, under certain conditions) and Landican Village in the event of a new road, then planned, being built. The revenue from the Eastham-New Ferry local service alone had exceeded £7,500 in 1928 so the company paid a high price to get to Woodside.

There were a few exceptions. The New Ferry-Moreton Shore service, which was the only bus route through Higher Bebington at the time, was allowed to carry local traffic throughout and, while the New Ferry-Meols buses could, in terms of the Agreement, carry no local passengers between New Ferry and Clatterbridge, this condition was suspended so long as the service did not exceed two buses per hour (which it never did). There were a number of other provisions which will be discussed later. In the meantime, the railways had concluded a far-reaching agreement with the Tilling and BAT bus holding group covering the shareholding in bus companies country-wide and a new company, Crosville Motor Services Ltd. with LMS, Tilling and British Automobile Traction shareholding was registered on 15th May 1930, ending one year of outright railway ownership.

Birkenhead Corporation Act 1930

The Birkenhead Corporation Act, 1930 received the Royal Assent on 4th June and the Agreement with Crosville was signed two days later. The Act did much more than extend the area in which municipal buses could operate though most of its force was rendered null and void by the licensing provisions of the Road Traffic Act shortly to be passed. It set maximum fares of 1 $^{1}/_{2}$d per mile, gave the Corporation various general powers such as the right to run trolleybuses (which were fashionable at the time), to carry parcels and to fix bus stop signs on other people's lamp-posts. But it was unique in that it established 'protected routes' on which, except by agreement, other operators could not be licensed to run so long as the Corporation gave an adequate service. There were the usual safeguards for existing rights and the Minister of Transport was to be the arbiter. The general Road Traffic Act rendered these provisions redundant as it transferred licensing powers for buses from local councils to new statutory bodies known as Traffic Commissioners.

A further privilege granted by the Act was that of running express buses (or trolleybuses) at a fare equivalent to the through fare on a route. Under the old order this was a legal necessity but superfluous under the new legislation where such buses could be the subject of special

Leyland developed a 'highbridge' version of the TD1 and this demonstrator was tried in 1929 but, although more TD1s were ordered, all were of the lowbridge type. TE9855 is seen at Woodside on the Kings Road service. Note that the destination equipment is not being used, route details being shown on window labels.   *D.S. Deacon*

37

conditions. Nevertheless, it showed remarkable foresight and Birkenhead was to be the first operator of limited stop buses over local routes in Merseyside. General powers to operate electric trolleybuses were included in the Act. This mode had been considered for replacement of the Claughton Road trams in 1925 and a 36-seat AEC had been demonstrated over that route on 27th December 1923 by Mr C. F. Rymer of Wallasey who was the AEC agent. However, the mode was never adopted by Birkenhead. The 1930 Agreement was the culmination of Birkenhead Corporation's transport empire-building ambitions of the 1920s. It set the stage for the prodigious growth of the bus fleet in the 1930s and indirectly condemned the tramway system to extinction. Most, but not all, of its provisions were beneficial to the public. Inevitably it led to some wasted resources and killed competition as Crosville buses were unable to carry local passengers in Birkenhead and over lengthy stretches of road in Bebington. However, despite numerous attempts to have them set aside, its provisions were destined to remain in force with very little modification until 1972.

Both the Birkenhead Corporation transport undertaking and the new Crosville company were on the threshold of an era of enormous and exciting expansion.

The local motor coach operators were dismayed by the effect they believed the Agreement would have on their businesses. They deplored the facilities given to Crosville at Woodside and asked that they be allowed to stand and load from two boats instead of one, as laid down by the Watch Committee in the past. They also requested that the loading time be extended from 1.0pm to 2.30pm. The Council was unsympathetic and the Watch Committee, at their meeting on 16th June 1930, fixed standing time as 30 minutes between 8.0am and 1.0pm and 15 minutes between 1.0pm and 8.0pm. The more resilient operators turned to regular express operation or developed stands in other parts of the town. The speculative excursion could not compete with a frequent regular service and Woodside became much less important as an excursion coach stand.

Leyland Titan TD1 No. 88 is seen in its post-1933 blue livery on the one way road at Moreton station in the summer of 1937. *T.G. Turner collection*

3 – The Prosperous Years: 1930-39

The route licensing provisions of the Road Traffic Act 1930 came into force on 9th February 1931 after which no alterations of routes, times or fares could be made without the approval of the Traffic Commissioners. It was important to implement the services agreed with Crosville as soon as possible and it was agreed to do this in two stages - on 1st August 1930 for New Chester Road and 1st October for Heswall. As the relatively infrequent Crosville service between New Ferry and Clatterbridge was adequate, the Corporation did not exercise its rights on that section.

Buses to Bromborough and Eastham

On 1st August 1930 the Corporation's Upton-New Ferry service was extended to Bromborough Cross and a new service commenced running between Woodside and Eastham Village; these two services were timed to give a combined 10-minute frequency between Bedford Road and Bromborough Cross. A few trips ran between Woodside and Eastham Ferry in summer. The trams between Woodside and New Ferry were not protected by minimum fares and there were 1d, $1^1/_2$d, 2d and 3d fares on the bus route throughout but for shorter distances than on the trams. The through bus fare between Woodside and New Ferry was 3d compared with $2^1/_2$d by tram.

The infrequent route between New Ferry and Bromborough via Trafalgar had been covered by Crosville's seasonal Rock Ferry-Raby Mere route which finished running at the end of September and, under the new arrangements could not set down until reaching Allport Road. Even though there had been no winter service for some years, the Corporation decided, in November, to put a bus on between the New Ferry Hotel, New Ferry Road and Allport Road via Lower Bebington, Bromborough Road and Allport Lane. The route was soon shortened at both ends to run 3-4 trips between Toll Bar and Bromborough Cross; it was restricted to single-deck buses because of the low bridge in Bromborough Road.

At the same time, the Eastham Ferry trips were detached from the Woodside-Eastham route and a new hourly single-deck route commenced on weekday afternoons and evenings between St.Paul's Road (Old Chester Road) and Eastham Ferry via Bedford Road and New Chester Road. The inner terminus was probably selected because there was a convenient place in Well Lane for the bus to stand. Eastham had lost its attraction as a resort, the ferry having closed in 1929 and, while some buses ran between Woodside and Eastham Ferry in the summer of 1931, they were not repeated in later years. A 1/2d bus and ferry return ticket between Liverpool and Eastham Ferry was available. The service between New Ferry and Bromborough Pool Village was not advertised though it appeared in the fare list dated November 1930 and it is assumed that the Corporation continued to run the service as provided by Crosville. From 1932, a service on Friday and Saturday evenings was advertised and this is probably what ran from the start.

Irby, Thurstaston and Heswall

On 1st October, all the Crosville Heswall-Singleton Avenue via Pensby and Barnston services were extended to Woodside and the route via Thurstaston and Irby was taken over by the Corporation. The route was the least frequent of the three services between Birkenhead and Heswall and was maintained by two buses running every 45 minutes with extra trips to Irby and Thurstaston. Crosville's kiosk at Thurstaston was bought for £25 and the telephone transferred.

The last Titan TD1s to enter the fleet came in 1931 (Nos. 159-163, BG 472-6). Like the Daimlers, they were fitted with Leyland designed bodywork by Massey Bros. No. 160 was caught by the camera at Spital Cross Roads in 1932. *F. Kehoe*

The Corporation provided frequent local facilities along Woodchurch Road from the outset so the restriction point for Crosville buses was fixed at Ivy Cottage (which stood opposite Landican Cemetery). This was done by extending the Osmaston Road service down Swan Hill to Prenton Dell Road and, later in the month, as already mentioned, the Woodside-Upton service was reorganised to run between Woodside and Moreton Shore, absorbing the Upton-Moreton local service. The lost facility between Park Station and Arrowe Park was replaced by a direct Sunday service (16) in July 1931. From June 1936 the service was extended to New Ferry via Woodchurch Lane and Bedford Drive and ran also on weekdays in the summer, every 80 minutes, doubled during the school summer holidays.

Route Numbers

Route numbers had been shown in time-tables and were displayed at the rear of certain buses from 1926. They are said to have originated from a code identifying the position in the garage where the bus had to be parked. Although they continued to be allocated up to October 1930, it is doubtful if any of the modern Leyland buses displayed them. The extended route network required a more comprehensive scheme to assist the public to identify the buses on the various services. New route numbers were officially adopted from 1st January 1931 but in practice were phased in over several weeks. Polished wood boxes were mounted in the front upper saloon windows or, on the older buses, supported by stays above the front destination box. Separate tracks were provided for tens and units and for several years no numbers below 10 were used. Regular short workings were given their own numbers and groups were allocated to particular districts. At first, no numbers in the thirties or eighties were used. (See Appendix 2).

The End of the New Ferry Trams

The New Ferry trams lost thousands of passengers to Corporation and Crosville buses; the New Chester Road track was nearing the end of its useful life and trams were replaced by buses on 27th December 1931. None of the regular passengers was really sorry to see the end of the antiquated cars with their awkward knifeboard seating upstairs. There is some evidence that an extension of the New Ferry bus service to Port Sunlight, probably via Bolton Road, was contemplated as 'PORT SUNLIGHT via NEW FERRY' was added to some side destination blinds. But Lever Brothers had made an agreement with the railways for the conveyance of their workers at special rates and one of the conditions was that no competitive arrangement should be made with a bus operator. As the roads within the Model Village were all private, permission for the buses to be extended from New Ferry was withheld. The area between New Ferry and Eastham was developing rapidly and greater flexibility was now possible. In 1933, the tram replacement service (49) was extended to Bolton Road (39) and to Pool Lane (38) in peak hours; by 1936 or 1937 Pool Lane had become the terminus for most of the day on weekdays and there was a 10-minute service through to Eastham Village on summer Sundays. Further service beyond New Ferry was supplied from June 1932 by the diversion of the Moreton-Rock Ferry (26) buses to Bromborough Cross after 11.30am. On Saturdays a supplementary service (27) ran between Hurrell Road and Rock Ferry Pier. Following the demolition of some shops. the Tramways Committee had paid £380 for the provision of a turning circle for buses at Rock Ferry but the ferry had been decaying for some time and the Port Sunlight (54) service was well able to cater for ferry traffic. The 26 and Upton-Bromborough (43) routes were timed to provide a combined 10-minute service between Bromborough and Park Station though by different routes from Rock Ferry Station, 26 via Bebington Road, Derby Road and Exmouth Street and 43 via Old Chester Road, Central Station and Park Road East. To serve new housing the 26 service was rerouted via Bedford Drive and Borough Road instead of Derby Road and Bebington Road from September 1933.

Anticipating the demise of the trams, radical alterations to New Ferry depot had been started by August 1930 and, within three weeks of the through bus services starting, it was decided to reduce the tram service and dispose of five cars and the bodies of two others, thus relieving congestion in the depot during rebuilding. Adjoining property was bought for £2,000 in October. In June 1931, the tender of J A Milestone & Son Ltd. was accepted to build a new bus garage and, as soon as the trams had gone, the New Ferry tram depot facade was rapidly demolished and a new combined bus depot and station with accommodation for 50 vehicles was integrated with the altered premises at a cost of £14,488, equipment bringing the total up to £18,500. This sum was raised by a loan, half the interest on which was paid by the Unemployment Grants Committee for 15 years. On completion, about August 1932, buses terminating at New Ferry Toll Bar used the depot as a bus station instead of terminating in nearby Grove Street. Dead mileage to and from Laird Street depot was substantially reduced. All maintenance work, other than minor adjustments, continued to be done at Laird Street, and New Ferry never had a dedicated allocation, buses being changed over as necessary.

Nos. 164-170 (BG 739-45) introduced the Leyland TD2 model to the fleet, entering service in May 1932. Nos. 164-8 were the last petrol-engined Leylands to be received and, like others of their kind, were painted blue and black during the 1939-45 war. Nos. 164/167 were converted to producer gas propulsion from 1943 to September 1944 but, unlike the converted TD1s, reverted to petrol operation, running until May 1947. No. 168 was destroyed in 1940 and 169-170 were the Corporation's first diesel-engined buses.

Leyland Motors

More New Services

By 1933 the spread of housing in Bromborough justified the diversion of the St.Paul's Road-Eastham Ferry (44) service along Allport Lane, Allport Road, Raeburn Avenue and Heygarth Road and a year later this service was further diverted via Lower Bebington and Trafalgar absorbing the local evening service (46). The extra running time needed resulted in an awkward 70-minute frequency so that the times of the bus were difficult for the public to memorise.

Building development in Higher Bebington required new facilities which were provided by extending alternate buses on the Woodside-Kings Road (60) route through Higher and Lower Bebington to the Great Eastern Hotel, New Ferry as 64 from August 1932.

The Corporation's powers to run to Greasby and Frankby were not exercised until April 1932 when a lengthy but infrequent route (85) was started between Woodside and Thurstaston via Park Station, Upton, Greasby, Frankby and Montgomery Hill. To avoid standing on the main road buses terminated at Thurstaston Church. The 85 service ran only every $1^1/_2$ hours and, except at busy weekends, it was usually worked by one of the 1930 Lion single-deckers.

In the summer months, traffic to Thurstaston was very heavy as the Common with uninterrupted views across the Dee estuary, was very popular with Liverpool and Birkenhead people. The 72 service carried most of the traffic but the 85 supplied a useful facility from North Birkenhead in addition to establishing a link between Frankby, Greasby and Woodside though the bulk of the local traffic was carried by the frequent Crosville service terminating at Park Station.

Limited Stop Buses

The limited stop provisions envisaged in the private Act were soon implemented in the form of selective loading rules. They were already in force on the Osmaston Road route in 1929, only passengers for beyond Singleton Avenue being accepted on the outward journey in the evening and Saturday midday peaks, until reaching Whetstone Lane. By 1932, after some experimentation, the arrangements were as follows:-

1. MORETON Three limited stop buses from Moreton Cross (later extended from Bermuda Road) each morning and some afternoon return journeys which were not advertised in the time table. These deviated from the normal route via Cleveland Street, and either Old Bidston Road and Brassey Street or Corporation Road.

2. EASTHAM After trying out various arrangements, all inward buses from Eastham before 9.0am did not stop to pick up after leaving New Ferry.

3. HESWALL Between 12 noon and 6.40pm weekdays and 1.30 and 4.30pm Sundays, the service from Woodside was available only for passengers travelling to Landican Lane or beyond. One morning bus from Heswall did not pick up after leaving Storeton Road and one from Thurstaston after leaving Landican Lane. By 1935 there were six limited stop buses in the mornings with designated setting down points in Birkenhead.

4. PRENTON DELL ROAD & MORETON via ARROWE PARK adopted the restriction previously imposed on Osmaston Road buses, i.e. no setting down before Singleton Avenue. There were also two limited stop buses from Arrowe Park each morning.

These arrangements were very popular with regular travellers who were given faster journeys to work. On the return journey, they segregated the long and medium distance passengers and on some sections of route such as Borough Road there were three strata of service - trams for short journeys to Singleton Avenue; Prenton or Moreton buses for points between Singleton Avenue and Prenton Dell Road; and Heswall buses for Landican Lane and beyond. Various amendments of detail were made from time to time and the scheme was extended to the 64 and 85 routes with restrictions to Prenton Road West and Noctorum Lane at certain times. The available accommodation was used very efficiently indeed and Birkenhead was a pioneer of limited stop operation on Merseyside. At first, boarding passengers were warned by card notices displayed near the entrance; later special displays were added to the side route blinds. Buses working trips with special setting down arrangements at first showed 'Express' on the upper blind; later this was changed to 'Limited Stop' displayed on the lower blind.

Higher Tranmere and Prenton

In January 1934, the abandonment of the Tranmere and Prenton tram routes was discussed. The former was, of course, already partly covered by the Kings Road buses. It was proposed that both routes should go round loops at the outer ends; in the case of Tranmere it was to be formed by Bebington Road, Bedford Drive and Mount Road and would be traversed in each direction alternately whilst at Prenton, buses would run via Woodchurch Lane and Storeton Road and return by way of Prenton Road West. These arrangements on their own would probably have worked reasonably well but, with the determination of inexperienced amateurs, the councillors proceeded to embroider the plan with alterations to other services. The Kings Road services 60 and 64 were to be diverted from Church Road to Borough Road and the Port Sunlight services 51 and 52 from Derby Road to Church Road. As the Bromborough-Moreton (26) service had been diverted from Derby Road to Borough Road a few months before, this would have left Derby Road and Greenway Road without any buses. It was further proposed that the 'shopping bus' (79) should be diverted from Birch Road to Carlaw Road.

At the February Council meeting the Prenton, Bedford Drive and Kings Road proposals were confirmed but the others were thrown out thus leaving a serious gap for, with the Tranmere buses using the tram route up Argyle Street South and the steep incline of Pearson Road, there would no longer be a connection between the Charing Cross district and Church Road. The Council stuck to their decision and licences to this effect were duly granted by the Traffic Commissioners.

Buses took over to Tranmere and Prenton on 1st October. The Bedford Drive loop was given number 65 and there was no means by which intending passengers could tell which way round the loop the bus was going. This was a nuisance as the terminus was fixed half way along Bedford Drive at a place where no one wanted to go. At peak hours, extra buses ran between Thornton Road and Central Station (62) or Woodside (61). The whole service ran via Pearson Road and the former 'Board of Trade' tram stop outside Holt Hill Convent was replaced by a compulsory bus stop with a board which gave drivers strict instructions to engage low gear. The Kings Road (60 and 64) buses ran via Borough Road as planned and the 60 was extended from Kings Lane to Village Road, Higher Bebington.

The public was very unhappy with the new arrangements, some passengers feeling that Pearson Road was unsafe for buses, particularly in wintry conditions, as it was still paved with granite setts and the slippery tram track remained in position. Within six weeks, the Bedford Drive loop was abandoned in favour of all day operation to Thornton Road and after another three months of complaints, the Kings Road (60) service went back to the Whetstone Lane and Church Road route, leaving the 64 on Borough Road. Any trips on the latter route which terminated at Village Road were numbered 63. The Pearson Road route was now used only by the 61 and 62 buses at peak hours and in 1936 they were withdrawn altogether as they taxed the buses to the utmost and served no useful purpose which could not be better achieved by the Whetstone Lane buses. Buses to Thornton Road by the latter route became 66 from Woodside and 67 from Central Station. As the population of Higher Bebington grew, the 60 was further extended, at first to Gorsey Hey and eventually down Heath Road to Pulford Road in 1937. A request for Sunday buses down Town Lane to Bebington Cemetery was rejected by the Council. Despite these extensions, buses continued to show 'Kings Road' as a destination.

At Prenton, the loop arrangements worked well, Woodchurch Lane being given a service for the first time. The buses carried numbers 80 from Woodside and 81 from Central Station and morning peak hour trips from Singleton Avenue to Woodside were numbered 82. In October 1937 the 80 service was extended to Prenton War Memorial using Prenton Road West both ways though after a time the loop workings were changed being used anti-clockwise in the morning and clockwise in the afternoon. Woodside-Storeton Road trips now showed No.83. Just before the outbreak of war, half the 80 service was diverted southwards along Storeton Road and Mount Road to the top of Thornton Road (Lever Causeway) and these buses showed No.84.

The End of the Trams

From 1st November 1934 the Tramways Committee was renamed the Transport Committee and new title 'Birkenhead Corporation Transport' was adopted in place of 'Birkenhead Corporation Tramways and Motors', the legend on the waistband of the buses was gradually changed from 'Motors' to 'Transport'. There now remained only the Line of Docks and Circle tram routes but subsequent abandonment was related to track condition as large sums had been spent on renewals in the 1920s. The Docks trams ran on weekdays only until about 8.0pm so the service was greatly improved from 1st April 1935 when the North Circle bus route was substituted. The buses continued up Ilchester Road to St.James' Church where a link-up was made with the 90 service to Woodside via Claughton Road. Buses showed 94 all the way round anti-clockwise and 90 clockwise. No.92 was used for part-way buses covering the former 90 and there was a peak hour service numbered 95 between Woodside and Station Road via Cleveland Street. On Sundays, a 15-minute supplementary service (91) continued to run between Haymarket and Flaybrick Hill Cemetery and there were morning peak hour buses from Forest Road to Woodside.

At the same time the New Ferry-New Brighton No.10 joint service was rerouted via Grange Street, Chester Street and Bridge Street instead of Argyle Street and the fares along Cleveland Street were brought into line with the North Circle buses. This was a boon for Wallasey people who had complained about the uphill walk, often with a heavy suitcase, from Woodside station to Argyle Street. The change of route probably owed something to an application to the Traffic Commissioners by C.F. Rymer, a Wallasey alderman and former coach proprietor, for permission to run an express service between New Brighton and Woodside. At a Public Sitting in November 1933, Rymer's attempt 'to turn the Wirral cul-de-sac into a main line route' was refused on the grounds that there was insufficient evidence of public demand or of any deficiency in the services of the existing operators. The service was to have run every 20 minutes on weekdays and hourly on Sundays from May to October. The Chairman of the Commissioners called Mr Rymer 'a marvel' when he learned of his plan to run six vehicles on expected receipts of 1/2d per mile and costs of 8.25d.

The Oxton and Claughton Circle trams were withdrawn with appropriate ceremony at midnight on 17th July 1937. The following day, a fleet of new Leyland Titans started running on the Oxton Circle, numbered 2 anti-clockwise and 6 clockwise. Short journeys took the numbers 3 to Upton Road and 4 to Laird Street via Conway Street and 7 to Laird Street via Borough Road. 'Upton Road' was the same place that the buses had always called 'Claughton Village' but, nevertheless No. 3 was always described as 'Upton Road' which was included on the destination blinds. Several early morning buses ran from Upton Road to Woodside via Chester Street and, many years later the number 5 was allocated for these. There was never a number 1 in Corporation days. In due course, 'Laird Street 4' tended to be displayed whenever running into depot from anywhere, a source of confusion and complaint during the wartime blackout years when depot bound buses from Moreton showed No.4 which was the number of the principal Wallasey Corporation service over the same road.

Laird Street Depot Improvements

Laird Street depot had been described as 'not fit for men to work in' and the Council voted £71,000 for extensions and modernisation in 1938. As the trams had been withdrawn, buses had encroached further and further into the tram shed and, in 1937, the final four tracks were adapted. The depot had been built on stilts on sloping ground and the cramped space below the garage floor was no longer suitable for maintenance work. Extensions were planned at the rear and a parking area was surfaced as an interim measure. Whilst some improvements were made to the workshops, the outbreak of war prevented the full plan going ahead.

One plan that failed was the proposal in late 1937 to run a joint service with Wallasey Corporation over Poulton Bridge, which had been freed from tolls in 1936. Route 11 had been experimentally diverted over the bridge instead of the Four Bridges during the closure of Duke Street bridge and Wallasey, in particular, thought a permanent service was desirable. Several routes were suggested, Harrison Drive-Prenton, Egremont (Trafalgar Road)-Prenton, Harrison Drive-Bidston Hill and Harrison Drive-Central Station via Sumner Road, Park Road West and Claughton Road, but eventually a route between the last two points via Beaufort Road and Price Street was selected. The Corporation was so confident of getting a licence that they included the fares in the new issue of the fare list and added 'Harrison Drive' and 'via Poulton Bridge 13' to the destination blinds of the new buses. On this occasion the number 13 was truly unlucky as the Mersey and LMS Railway companies successfully opposed the application on the very adequate grounds that both termini were on their network which was then in course of electrification. The Traffic Commissioners acknowledged the need for a service across Poulton Bridge and said that they would have granted the application if the Wallasey terminus had been elsewhere. Poulton Bridge continued to be used by route 11 whenever Duke Street bridge was closed to traffic.

Mersey Tunnel Buses

When the first Mersey road tunnel had been planned in 1924-25, there had been a scheme to run trams through the lower half of the tube but this was abandoned at an early stage. The tunnel was opened with considerable pomp by King George V and Queen Mary on 18th July 1934 and it was not long before the question of buses through the tunnel was brought up. The Mersey Tunnel Joint Committee, made up of representatives of Liverpool and Birkenhead Corporations, was unenthusiastic as it had a duty to cover the losses of the Birkenhead ferries, and the Mersey Railway, although it enjoyed some protection under the Mersey Tunnel Act 1925, was hostile. The ball was set rolling when Crosville proposed to extend their Loggerheads and Mold to Woodside service through to Liverpool and at the Traffic Commissioners' hearing in December 1934, the Joint Committee, the Corporations and the Mersey Railway strongly opposed the proposal on the grounds that bus services should be planned on a regional basis. The Councils purported to be in favour of such services and the Commissioners reserved their decision to give them time to come forward with their ideas. In May 1935, councillors from Liverpool,

Birkenhead, Wallasey and Bootle met and decided that applications for a network of joint municipal services linking various districts of Liverpool with places on the Wirral side of the Mersey would be submitted and, if licences were refused, they would oppose any applications by the companies.

When the matter was passed from the politicians to the professionals, the general managers of Liverpool and Birkenhead transport undertakings, in a joint report, pointed out the impracticability of tunnel bus services on financial grounds. The tunnel toll for a bus was 5/- (25p) each way plus 2d for each passenger so the return fare by bus between Birkenhead and Liverpool would need to be at least 1/1d compared with 6d by rail or 4d by ferry. The ferry contract rate was 1.48d per day and the rail contract 3.65d per day. Many contract holders went home to lunch and so had four daily trips for these amounts. The managers chose one route on each side of the river of similar length and earning power and hypothetically linked them through the tunnel to create a route between Childwall and Moreton. The through return fare would have had to be 2/8d (13.3p) instead of 1/6d (7^1/$_2$p) by the existing bus and boat facilities. Their calculations are set out in Table 3 at the end of this chapter.

They further pointed out the physical difficulties as, due to the curvature of the tunnel roof, double deck buses could use only the middle or 'fast' lane with a speed range of 21-35 mph. There could have been serious problems in the event of an obstruction in the fast lanes as there was insufficient height for a bus to manoeuvre into the 'slow' lane. The plan was then abandoned. The Loggerheads application was eventually refused but the matter was revived in March 1936 when Crosville and Ribble Motor Services Ltd. of Preston applied jointly for a through Chester-Southport service with a condition that no local passengers be carried between Seaforth and Overpool Cemetery Gates, near Ellesmere Port, thus giving local operators and the Mersey Railway complete protection.

Counsel for the two bus companies appealed to the Commissioners not to prevent the use of the tunnel in the way intended by Parliament because of the indecision of the local authorities, pointing out that co-ordination had been talked about for two years and suggesting that no plan existed. Two very eminent Counsel, both destined to become cabinet ministers, David Maxwell-Fyfe (later Lord Kilmuir) and Mr (later Sir) Hartley Shawcross appeared for the Corporations and reaffirmed at various hearings that a scheme was being prepared and would be ready within three years! The Merseyside Co-ordination Committee, on which all the local authorities in the area were represented, agreed to consult with the bus companies if the Chester-Southport application was withdrawn but the companies would not agree. However, it was refused by the Traffic Commissioners and subsequently turned down by the Minister of Transport on appeal.

Increasing Prosperity

The early 1930s were years of economic depression with high unemployment. In Birkenhead, buses and trams combined carried 38.9 million passengers in the year 1929-30 and about 1.5 million additional passengers were carried in the next year as a result of the Crosville Agreement. Passengers remained around the 40 million mark until 1934-35, declining slightly in the previous two years but thereafter conditions improved year by year with a 4.47% increase in 1935-36, 6.25% in 1936-37, 7.98% in 1937-38 and 4.9% in 1938-39 when 50.9 million passengers were carried.

The normal working day started between 7.0 and 8.0am for blue-collar workers and at 9.0am white-collar workers, Saturday being a half day when work ended between 12.0 noon and 1.0pm. All but the most senior workers were paid weekly, usually on a Friday, so there was a great demand for public transport on Friday evenings when people went to pubs, cinemas, dance halls or visited their friends. As most married women were housewives, the demand for bus services was low during weekday mornings as most shopping was done locally. On Sunday, many people attended church services and many bus services did not start until after lunch.

As employment increased at such places as Cammell Lairds and the ship-repairers' yards, there was a demand for special workers' buses. During the years of depression many work journeys consisted of combined walk and bus or tram trips, designed to get the best value for a penny fare. More and more people were finding transport affordable, helped to some extent by the fare reductions which were made during the 1930s (See chapter 9).

New Workpeople's Services

In 1933, licences were granted for special services from Laird Street to Green Lane (for Cammell Lairds) via Conway Street and Market Place South and from Claughton Village to Green Lane via Park Road West, Claughton Road and Market Place South. The railway bridge in Green Lane was (and still is) too low for a double-deck bus to pass beneath and, after a time, it was decided to ease congestion on the main road by working special buses to the west side of the bridge, via Argyle Street South and Hinderton Road. A special service between Hurrell Road and The Wiend, Lower Bebington via Park Road East and Derby Road was also applied for but does not seem to have run for very long, if it ever started. It got close to Port Sunlight works without having to negotiate the low bridge at Bebington Station. In later years it followed the normal route to Port Sunlight, showing No. 52, but returned via Borough Road, showing No. 27. However, from about June 1935 until the end of 1945, three early morning route 50 buses from Woodside to Lower Bebington were diverted via Bromborough Road and The Wiend for the benefit of Port Sunlight workers who then walked through the subway.

The No. 10 service from New Brighton did not start running until about 8.0am and, in 1935, there was agitation in Wallasey for earlier buses as many more men were working in Birkenhead. An early bus at 6.45am was put on in October 1935 and this proved so popular that the whole service ran at 20-minute intervals from 6.16am soon afterwards; this had doubled by 1939. Various routes had early buses, mainly unadvertised, that ran inward to Woodside via Chester Street for the convenience of shipyard workers. Originally the Moreton services (and 85) had travelled in and out via Chester Street at all times, presumably to keep clear of tramway traffic. The Woodchurch Road services left Woodside via Chester Street but approached via Argyle Street; other services travelled out via Hamilton Street and in via Argyle Street. Crosville services left via Chester Street and ran inward via Hamilton Street. Changes in the street layout because of the construction of the Mersey Tunnel entrance led to a reappraisal of these rather confusing arrangements and from 1933, the Moreton services changed to the out Hamilton Street, in Argyle Street routing, being followed by the Woodchurch Road services in May 1936.

In July 1936, a service commenced between Hurrell Road and Stork Margarine Works (known at the time as 'Planters') via Park Road East and Old Chester Road, showing riute number 00. Some of the Laird Street-Green Lane journeys were also extended to commence at Hurrell Road and showed the number 99. More journeys on the Bromborough and Eastham services deviated via Port Causeway and Magazine Road at factory times. In 1938, the Port Sunlight services were extended to the factory gate at peak hours.

Recreational Facilities

Improving economic conditions led to an increased demand for special buses for football matches at Prenton Park. In 1933, licences were granted for services from Woodside (previously served exclusively by trams), St. James' Church via Park Station and Charing Cross, Port Sunlight via Bebington Road and Bedford Drive and Rock Ferry Station via Bedford Avenue. After the Prenton trams were withdrawn, it was customary to run a shuttle service from Whetstone Lane via Borough Road, returning empty via Prenton Road East and Derby Road for a further load. From 1938, another service was added from Claughton Village via Shrewsbury Road. Extra buses also ran on services 26/27 and 63/64 which passed the ground.

Birkenhead Corporation's policy of providing recreational facilities, even at a loss, was continued. Arrowe Park was an object of special municipal pride and everything possible was done to put it within easy reach of every resident. The Sunday service No. 16 from Park Station to Arrowe Park which was enigmatically described in the timetable as running 'every 40 minutes until one hour after sunset' was given a daily service in the school holidays of 1936 and extended from Arrowe Park to New Ferry via Prenton and Rock Ferry; in the following year it was rerouted via Laird Street and Tollemache Road to serve the north end municipal housing estates. Football specials were also run on Saturdays for amateur matches at pitches adjoining Arrowe Brook Road.

Recreation of a different kind was facilitated by a series of experiments in 1938-39 involving running buses between Laird Street depot and the Plaza Cinema and Ballroom, Borough Road on Friday and Saturday evenings and to Tranmere Rovers Ground on Saturday afternoons. These buses ran via Shrewsbury Road, Bessborough Road and Singleton Avenue, returning via Kingsland Road and, after discontinuation of the Friday trips in July 1938, continued unnumbered and virtually unadvertised until the advent of war put an end to them.

A New Crosville Agreement

New housing was going up in the area between Bromborough Cross and Eastham which was served only by the infrequent 44 service between St. Paul's Road and Eastham Ferry. A service was needed from Woodside and in 1937, the Corporation applied to extend the Woodside-Pool Lane intermediate service to Manor Road, Bromborough via Allport Lane, Allport Road and Raeburn Avenue with one or two peak hour trips to Heygarth Road. As the terminus was in the free trade area beyond Allport Road, Crosville was somewhat uneasy about this incursion, but the licence was granted and the service, still numbered 38, started in July 1937. The seven year Agreement between the two operators was coming to an end and both parties were jockeying for position. In June, Birkenhead Corporation sought a licence for the Wirral Circle, a combination of the 72 and 85 routes, via Upton, Greasby, Frankby, Thurstaston, Irby and Arrowe Park. The service was to run daily throughout the year from 6.15am (1.15pm Sundays) to 11.15pm with a 20-minute service in both directions. This was qualified in the application to the Traffic Commissioners by the condition that 'this being a pleasure route, extra journeys will be run during summer weekends, according to weather and traffic requirements. Services were to be augmented or curtailed according to traffic requirements'.

Crosville, having increased their Woodside-Meols via Irby Mill Hill and Caldy service to hourly (half-hourly at peak hours and on Saturday and Sunday afternoons), applied for an alternative route between Arrowe Bridge and the Farmer's Arms, Frankby via Greasby and Frankby villages instead of Irby Mill Hill, an hourly service to run by each route. The district between Arrowe Bridge and Greasby village was being developed for housing and there would be a need for a service within the next few months.

The Wirral Circle was potentially damaging to the excursion operators as well as to Crosville and, when the absurdity of the 20-minute service is considered, one can only assume that it was applied for as a bargaining counter. The 85 service through Greasby and Frankby to Thurstaston was a financial disaster, most of its passengers being people who happened to be standing at a bus stop waiting for a Crosville bus when the 85 came along. During the winter, the bus trundled its way to and from Thurstaston more or less empty. The route could not be cut short because the Agreement stipulated that buses must be proceeding to Irby or Thurstaston.

Both the Corporation and the company wanted some changes to the Agreement in the light of the urbanisation of the Wirral villages which was proceeding apace and hearing of these applications was delayed whilst negotiations took place. It was agreed that Crosville would be entitled to all the traffic between Park Station, Greasby and Frankby village while the Corporation would have a monopoly of traffic between those places and Woodside. It was also agreed to share running rights on Saughall Massie Road between Upton and Saughall Massie Hotel and, in the event of a service becoming necessary, along Wood Lane, Greasby on the same basis as the 85 route, the Corporation looking after Woodside traffic and the company providing services to Park Station. Wood Lane never merited a service and development towards Saughall Massie was delayed by the war. The Corporation also surrendered the right to run on Arrowebrook Lane and Hillbark Road, between Arrowe Bridge and the Farmer's Arms, Frankby via Irby Mill Hill, which they had never exercised. The Wirral Circle was also approved in principle (but not via Park Station) but was never put into operation.

The company also conceded the Corporation's right to extend its Woodside-Pool Lane (38) service to Raeburn Avenue, Bromborough which had already been done but, in the event of Allport Lane being extended southwards, Crosville was to have the right to use the new road. This was not done for many years, becoming Bridle Road in due course.

A Supplemental Agreement covering all these points was signed on 22nd April 1938 but there were no immediate developments as there were various matters of detail to be settled. Crosville wanted several fare revisions, in particular through bus and ferry tickets from West Kirby, Caldy, Frankby and Greasby which were eventually conceded. Reduced return tickets between Liscard and Upton or Arrowe Park were also agreed.

Both the Wirral Circle and Woodside-Meols via Greasby applications were withdrawn but it was 2nd July 1939 before services were changed. The 85 service was diverted via Claughton Road and Tollemache Road, shortening the journey time to the extent that two buses could maintain a 40-minute service between Woodside and Thurstaston, and a new route (78) was started between

Woodside and Greasby via Arrowe Park, Arrowe Brook Road and Arrowe Bridge every hour during the day, increasing to half-hourly during the evenings and on Saturday afternoons. On the journey from Woodside, the 78 service buses ran through the village and then most of the length of the by-pass, terminating at the Upton end. They then re-entered the old road, completing the circuit of the village before returning via Arrowe Road. This soon became a popular service with Greasby people.

The growth of Greasby was typical of the spread of suburbia over the Wirral countryside in the thirties. Bebington was given borough status in 1936 and expanded its boundaries to take in large tracts of rural territory. Irby, which was in the Wirral UDC area, considered itself a very select community and complained to the Corporation about the 'ramshackle buses' serving the village. In a strong reply, Clarke said that the roads in Irby were in a very poor state and were damaging his buses. The ratepayers should direct their efforts at raising the standard of road maintenance.

A Joint Board

In April 1938 the chairman of the Co-ordination Committee, Alderman A.E.Shennan of Liverpool, suggested the formation of a Merseyside Joint Transport Board, a form of organisation which had been proposed in various metropolitan areas since the establishment of the London Passenger Transport Board in 1933. A special meeting of Birkenhead Borough Council voted to oppose the scheme. They felt that only Birkenhead stood to lose as the bus undertaking was highly profitable. They had already lost a consistent contributor to the rate fund when the goods ferry lost its traffic to the Tunnel and did not want to repeat the experience.

Three eminent consultants were appointed by the Co-ordination Committee, one of them being A R Fearnley, Birkenhead's first tramways manager who had left the town over 30 years earlier. In their report, made in January 1939, the experts made various recommendations about cross-river facilities including the closure of Rock Ferry (which was implemented very quickly) but they pointed out that the Corporations could not afford to allow the companies to develop medium distance tunnel bus services even under protective conditions as this would generate public agitation for similar local facilities which, in turn, would undermine the ferries. The idea of an experimental tunnel bus service was encouraged, the suggested trial route being from Bromborough, surprisingly as it was paralleled by rail. A shuttle service through the tunnel was also suggested with short loops at each end; in Birkenhead it was to be via Grange Road, Borough Road, Central Station, Argyle Street, Conway Street and Market Place South. They did not agree with the proposed Joint Board, but recommended the amalgamation of the Birkenhead and Wallasey Corporation transport undertakings. War broke out six months after the report was made and nothing was done for another thirty years.

The Traffic Pattern

The pattern of bus traffic in the immediate pre-war period was quite different from that of today. After the morning peak hour, many services ran at reduced frequencies as the majority of women stayed at home doing their housework or shopped locally. Demand increased after lunch but evenings, particularly at weekends, were the times of greatest activity. Cinemas and ballrooms were well patronised and people used the buses to visit their friends. At weekends, Grange Road, the principal shopping street, was thronged until late in the evening and Birkenhead market

The ten Northern Counties-bodied 1938 buses (Nos. 269-78) were of a very curvaceous design with curved end windows on both decks. The torque converters of Nos. 275-78 were replaced by gearboxes taken from withdrawn buses in the 279-318 series, in 1950-52. A superb view of No.269 when newly in service provided a dramatic contrast in body styles with eight-year old TDI No. 146 alongside. *T. Lawson*

attracted much interest on Saturday evenings as, in the days before widespread refrigeration, a chicken or duck could often be picked up for next to nothing, as it was better to sell it for a shilling or two than let it rot over the weekend.

By 1939 the Birkenhead transport network was like a well-oiled, highly efficient machine incorporating three major interchanges and three others of lesser importance. The inter-modal transfers at Woodside were considerable but the 10-minute frequency of the ferry service and the high capacity of the boats enabled peaks in demand to be absorbed without difficulty. There was a large volume of rail/ferry traffic but the main interchange was between buses and boats; bus/rail transfers at Woodside were important but not comparable with the other flows. Woodside was the largest bus terminus in Wirral but there were no formal stands or queue rails. All the buses unloaded on the north side and there were regular positions on the ferry approach at which the buses on the various routes stood, some at the kerbside but others in the middle of the roadway. The Crosville buses stood at the kerb on the Chester Street approach or in Church Street.

The bus routes serving Woodside also catered for the needs of traffic to and from Hamilton

Square station, a mere 400 yards from the ferry approach. Some rail passengers on the journey from Liverpool had the option of alighting at either Hamilton Square or Central and their choice was influenced by their ultimate destination or whether their bus route had a supplementary service originating at Central Station.

Park Station was busy at peak hours though its traffic volumes did not approach those mentioned above. Even after electrification of the Wirral lines in March 1938, large numbers of Moreton passengers transferred to and from buses at Park as the station at Moreton was badly situated well to the north of most of the urban development. The Corporation ran a local service (15) between Park station and Upton in the peak hours and the afternoon extension of the Port Sunlight - Park Station (52) service to Claughton Village (51) provided additional accommodation along Park Road North. This service was extended to the corner of Bidston Road and Ashburton Road (57) in 1939 to improve the road/rail transfer facilities though there was no comparable morning service. In the opposite direction, the two Bromborough services (26 and 43) and the Port Sunlight services (51 and 52) gave convenient access from Park Station to the Grange Road shopping area for passengers from the West Kirby and New Brighton lines. Most services gave direct access to the station, using Beckwith Street and Aspinall Street towards Woodside or Charing Cross and Arthur Street, Beckwith Street and Duke Street in the other direction.

The End of Rock Ferry

Rock Ferry traffic dwindled slowly in the years between the wars and the importance of bus feeder services was reduced accordingly. After the Rock Ferry boats were withdrawn, on 30th June 1939, the morning journeys on 26 and the 54 from Port Sunlight continued to run aimlessly to and from the pier. The Transport Committee seemed to be uncertain of what to do with the bus services and licence applications were submitted only two weeks before the ferry closed. The 26 was diverted to New Ferry at the end of July and it was intended to run 54 along New Chester Road to King's Square, with journeys to and from Woodside when required. This did not please the railways, who carried substantial numbers between Woodside and Port Sunlight, and Lever Bros. were not prepared to waive the clause in their agreement with the railways. The necessary application for a licence had not been heard before the service was withdrawn to save fuel at the outbreak of war and never reinstated. Passengers with unexpired ferry contracts were allowed to use them by bus between Bedford Road and Woodside, the ferries department paying the transport department 1d for every trip made.

Supplementary Services

Unadvertised supplementary services abounded in Birkenhead and they were not confined to peak hours. There had been a regular tram service between the Argyle Street/Conway Street junction and Laird Street depot which was sometimes extended to Upton Road. Some time after the trams were withdrawn it was replaced by the 25 bus running between Market Place South and St.James' Church, a route which was absolutely straight for its entire length except for turning at each end; it was eventually extended to Hurrell Road as 24 and during the morning peak and on Saturday evenings there was enough traffic to run between Woodside and Hurrell Road as 23. Although these workings were classified as short workings on the 21/22 Moreton services, the 24/25 workings, like the Oxton Circle, ran throughout via Park Road North and did not deviate via Park Station.

The 27 service between Rock Ferry (later New Ferry) and Hurrell Road has been previously mentioned and there was a comparable working on the 43 Bromborough-Upton route. This originally took the form of New Ferry-Charing Cross journeys (48), later extended to Bromborough (47) as the population of that district increased. Eventually some of these trips were extended at the other end to Park Station. When both these workings were operating there was a 10-minute service over the busiest parts of both the 26 and 43 services.

Lengthy lunch hours of at least one hour and sometimes longer, coupled with greater urban population density, created a minor midday peak. Workers in the town centre and dock areas and many clerks whose offices were close to Liverpool Pier Head travelled home to lunch and it was only good, reliable transport with no time wasted at interchange points that made this possible. In many cases the ordinary services, running on 7-10 minute frequencies, could absorb this traffic but some extra buses were provided, notably between Woodside and Higher Tranmere (66), New Ferry (49), Station Road (95) and, after 1938, Storeton Road (83).

In the evening peak, there was a wide range of short workings from Central Station - to Tranmere, Storeton Road, Kings Road, Town Lane and, for a time, the shortest of them all, to St.Paul's Road (45). Buses took any layover in Wilbraham Street, pulling on to the stop only

Northern Counties supplied the bodies for six Leyland TD3c buses delivered in time to replace the trams on the Tranmere and Prenton routes in September 1934. They were fitted with torque converters and bore the inscription 'Gearless Bus' on the radiator. This form of transmission became standard up to No. 318 of 1939. Three buses, (Nos. 186-8 BG 2651-3) had metal-framed lowbridge bodies, the last to join the fleet, and three (Nos. 189-91, BG 2654-6) had 'highbridge' bodies; all six were fitted with blue and beige moquette seats. A rear view is shown of No. 188 with No. 192 of the Massey 1934 batch whilst furthest from the camera is No. 214 carrying its 1942 replacement East Lancashire body in the Laird Street parking area in 1946.

T.G.Turner

Ten Leyland TD4c buses (nos. 198-207, BG 3423-32) arrived in 1935, five with Massey bodies and five from Northern Counties. Nos. 198, 204 and 206 received replacement bodies in 1942 following air raid damage and 199 was painted in wartime blue and black livery. Northern Counties-bodied 203 is seen at Woodside in March 1948 by which time, in the course of body repairs in 1947, it had been fitted with a front destination and number equipment similar to that adopted from 1936, the rear arrangement remaining unchanged.   *I. Kennedy*

when it was time for departure. The glass awning covering the pavement outside the station was then much more extensive than it is today and passengers from the trains could wait for buses under cover. On Saturdays it was customary to run extra buses between Central Station and Irby (74) and Arrowe Park (76). At busy shopping times, the Central Station workings would be extended to start from the Haymarket.

Fine summer Sundays and Bank Holidays were hectic with crowds streaming off the boats bound for Moreton Shore, Bidston Hill, Arrowe Park and Thurstaston to swell the hordes of local people in search of open spaces, many of them bound for New Brighton. In those days, a few day trips were the full extent of family holidays as thousands of ordinary people could not afford to go away. Hiking was a popular pastime but many walkers would start and finish the day with a bus ride.

The combined revenue of trams and buses in the year ending 31st March 1930 was £271,724. 38.9 million passengers were carried over 3.84 million miles at an average fare of 1.67d per passenger and an average density of 10.14 passengers per mile. It will be apparent that short

The last new vehicles to be delivered before the outbreak of war in September 1939 were 40 Leyland TD5c buses with Massey bodies. (Nos. 279-318 BG 7701-40). Although not as curvaceous as the 1938 Northern Counties bodies, they were of an attractive design with upper and lower cream bands edged with polished mouldings, adding to the pleasing overall appearance. All eventually had their torque converters replaced by gearboxes starting with 315 in November 1947 and ending with 312 in 1950. A brand new No. 287 awaits delivery, complete with proud poster in the front window. The white roofs and cream wheels were painted blue during the war, both changes becoming permanent.   *Massey Bros.*

distance passengers were the backbone of the undertaking's success and, indeed, economic circumstances were such that many journeys were a combination of walk and ride. Bus revenue in the year ending 31st March 1939 was £341,160, an increase of 25.55% in nine years with a lower fare scale. Passengers carried, at 50.9 million, had increased by 30.85% but mileage of 6.3 million had increased by a massive 65.76%, reflecting the longer routes and the much greater frequency of services which was pitched at a level at which waiting time was so short that ridership was encouraged, even over the shortest distances. Despite the longer routes operated, the average fare had fallen to 1.61d at a 21% lower utilisation of 8.01 passengers per mile, because of the lower residential density in the newer suburban districts. It was clear that, even with higher employment and increased prosperity, it was still the short distance passenger, paying the highest rate per mile, who put the surplus into the rate fund each year.

The busman's alleged insatiable appetite for cups of tea was recognised by the management and special arrangements were made at places where there were no public refreshment or toilet facilities. Thus a small temperance bar in the Haymarket supplied hot water and the use of a toilet for the crews working the No. 79 'Shopping Bus' and a retired employee recalled how he was sent each month to pay the proprietor eight shillings and was always given a soft drink. There was a similar arrangement with a private householder near Charing Cross for the crews on the cross-docks services 11 and 12.

Post Boxes on Buses

One ancillary service provided by the buses was the late posting box facility for letters on Mondays to Fridays. This had been introduced in Birkenhead on trams only on 28th March 1927 and it was not until the trams were replaced by buses that that the scope of the service was widened. The Post Office paid the Corporation £4 per box per annum. In those days, last collections were generally at 8.30pm from suburban street boxes and 9.30pm from the General Post Office. The mobile service gave a later collection in the suburbs up to about 9.45pm. Boxes were hung from a bracket on the rear panels of buses; not all vehicles were fitted and control staff had to be certain that a suitably equipped bus was on each duty. By 1934, boxes were carried on the remaining trams on the Prenton and Circle routes and on the 39 bus leaving New Ferry at 9.45pm, the 64 from Lower Bebington at 9.44pm and the 71 leaving Heswall at 8.45pm. At Woodside, the boxes were collected by a postman who emptied the contents into a sack, ran down to catch the next boat, hurriedly transferred them to another postman at Liverpool Pier Head, and endeavoured to catch the same boat back. The boxes were stored in the inspector's office. The facility was discontinued at the end of August 1936 when 9.30pm collections were introduced at selected suburban post-boxes.

The 1936 body order for 11 Leyland TD4c buses (Nos. 208-18, BG 4381-91) went to Massey, one extra being added to the original order for ten to cover the loss of No.183 by fire earlier in the year. The outline was similar to the previous Massey batch but larger route numbers were carried alongside, instead of above, the destination boxes. Another new feature was the fitting of rear bumpers, repeated on all buses up to 1939 and reintroduced on the post-war PD1 deliveries. No. 214 received a new East Lancashire body in 1942 and 217 received a similar one, taken from 182, in 1947. No. 208, photographed with rear tyre on fire in Woodchurch Road in April 1939 demonstrates the new larger route numbers and the bumpers.   *T.G. Turner collection*

With an attractive modern fleet, a docile labour force, ever increasing passengers, a buoyant demand throughout the day and a complete absence of obstruction from motor traffic, the Birkenhead transport undertaking in August 1939 would have been the envy of present-day bus managers.

Table 3 - Mersey Tunnel Buses

Summary of Calculations in Combined Report by W G Marks, General Manager, Liverpool Corporation Passenger Transport and C. Clarke, General Manager, Birkenhead Corporation Transport, 17th April 1935.

COST TO CARRY EACH PERSON (RETURN)

Operating Cost for the tunnel section @ 1/- per bus mile	3/11d
Toll (including conductor)	10/4d
Passenger toll	4d
TOTAL	14/7d

AVERAGE COST PER PERSON

10 passengers	1/9.5d
15 passengers	1/3.7d
20 passengers	1/0.7d
25 passengers	11.0d
30 passengers	9.8d

EXAMPLE: CHILDWALL (TAGGART AVENUE) to MORETON. Distance 20 miles return.

Present receipts (City-Taggart Avenue)	13.43d per mile
(Woodside-Moreton)	13.89d per mile
Anticipated receipts	
10 miles @ 13.43 + 10 miles @ 13.89d	£1. 2. 9d
Running cost 20 miles @ 1/- per mile	£1. 0. 0d
Distance increased to 25 miles via Tunnel.	
25 miles @ 1/- per mile	£1. 5. 0d
Toll	10. 4d
Passenger Toll (average 15 persons)	5 .0d
	£2. 0 .4d

So to run the 5 miles through the tunnel would cost £1. 0.4d or as much as the present 20 miles and to cover the actual cost, if 15 passengers per journey were realised, an average fare for the tunnel of 1/4d per passenger would need to be charged.

Thus Taggart Avenue to Moreton Return Fare	2/8d
Existing Bus-Boat-Bus Return	1/6d

NOTE: The arithmetic is difficult to reconcile. The toll for a bus and driver was five shillings (25p) plus two pence (d) for each passenger per single journey.

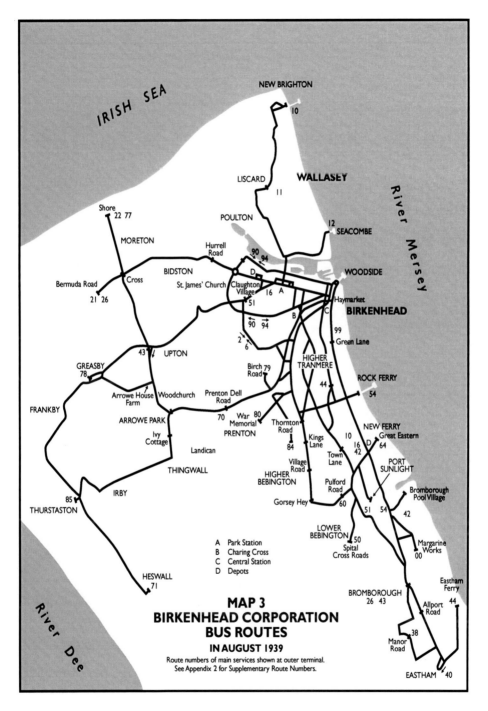

IRISH SEA

NEW BRIGHTON

10

LISCARD   **WALLASEY**

11

POULTON   12 **SEACOMBE**

Shore
22 77

MORETON

Hurrell
Road

90 94

BIDSTON   St. James' Church   Claughton
Village   D

Cross   16 A

Bermuda Road   51

21 26   90 94   B

2   99
6   Green Lane

43   UPTON   HIGHER
TRANMERE

GREASBY   Birch 79
78   Road   44   ROCK FERRY
54

FRANKBY   Arrowe House   Woodchurch   Prenton Dell
Farm   Road   War 80
70   Memorial   Thornton   NEW FERRY
ARROWE PARK   PRENTON   Road   Great Eastern
Ivy   84   Kings   10
Cottage   Lane   16   D 64
Landican   Village   Town   42
Road   Lane   PORT
THINGWALL   HIGHER   SUNLIGHT
BEBINGTON   Pulford   Bromborough
Road   Pool Village
85   IRBY   Gorsey Hey   60
THURSTASTON   51 54   42

LOWER
BEBINGTON   50
Spital   Margarine
Cross Roads   Works
00

A   Park Station
B   Charing Cross
C   Central Station   BROMBOROUGH   Eastham
D   Depots   26 43   Ferry
Allport   44
HESWALL   Road
71   38
Manor
MAP 3   Road
BIRKENHEAD CORPORATION   EASTHAM   40
BUS ROUTES
IN AUGUST 1939
Route numbers of main services shown at outer terminal.
See Appendix 2 for Supplementary Route Numbers.

River Mersey

WOODSIDE
Haymarket
C **BIRKENHEAD**

River Dee

4 – The Bus Fleet 1919-39

The first ten years of bus operation in Birkenhead saw a revolution in bus design spurred on by a tremendous demand as road transport activities expanded and by the forces of competition as the many different manufacturers struggled for ascendancy. The models available in 1919 were largely derived from vehicles developed during the 1914-18 war when research and development had accelerated at a rate which would have been unsustainable under the commercial conditions of the times. The enforced delay in starting municipal bus services therefore resulted in the availability of more advanced and reliable vehicles than were obtainable in 1914. Nevertheless, they were crude by the standards of the end of the decade. Competition kept the cost of new vehicles down which is fortunate as obsolescence shortened the effective lives of many buses.

The first ten Birkenhead Corporation buses (1-10) have been wrongly described as RAF type Leylands. The origin of the RAF type is clear from its name and Leyland Motors recovered over 900 of the type from France and reconditioned them for civilian use, at the same time producing new chassis of similar design known as the G type. At this time the same chassis designs were used for both passenger and goods vehicles, resulting in a high floor level, usually reached by three steps. The O type ordered by Birkenhead was a longer derivative of the RAF model with a 16ft 3in wheelbase and a body length of 25ft 4in. The bodywork was also a Leyland product with a 32-seat rear entrance layout including accommodation for three passengers alongside the driver. The design was 'normal control' i.e. with a bonnet in front like a motor car.

Bus No. 3 is seen at the Moreton terminus soon after the route was extended from Park Station in 1920.

D S Randall

The first double-deck buses were two AEC 34-seat B types obtained second-hand from the London General Omnibus Co. Ltd. where they were numbered B2414 (LF 9888) and B 2026 (LF 9345). However, they were re-registered CM1711-12 (Nos. 11-12) before entering service at Birkenhead. *AEC*

The power unit was a 36/40hp four-cylinder petrol engine though, at least for a time, Birkenhead used benzole, a less refined product, which is said to have given a quite creditable consumption of 9 mpg. Gear boxes were four-speed sliding mesh, a design which was to be normal for the next ten years or so. They were equipped with paper label destinations displayed in the front and side windows; they were later equipped with roller-blinds and No. 3 was fitted with a Klaxon horn. They were all withdrawn by May 1927 and sold to the Mersey Railway, for what purpose is not known though No. 1 had been the first bus to be equipped with an air-operated self starter, designed by the general manager of that company. They all turned up elsewhere, converted to lorries, No. 10 running in the service of Liverpool City Engineer until January 1945.

The next purchases were two AEC B-type double-deckers (11-12), second hand from the London General Omnibus Co., for whom they had carried the registrations LF 9888 (B2414) and LF 9345 (B2026). They were re-registered CM 1711-2 in Birkenhead. About 3000 B type buses were built and the General was replacing them with a newer type. It was this type which had been brought to Birkenhead in July 1914 but why it should have been bought in 1921 is a mystery as it seated only two more passengers (18 on top and 16 inside) than the existing type of single-decker, the result of the Metropolitan Police rule that a fully-laden double-decker should not exceed 6 tons. The unladen weight of the B type was only 3t 10cwt. Its 5.3litre swept volume engine was of typical Edwardian T-head layout with inlet and outlet valves on opposite sides of the engine. The 30bhp output was less than a Mini but the vehicle was designed to pull well at low speeds. These two vehicles had been new in 1913 and 1912 respectively and were withdrawn in 1925-26 after which both were sold and converted to lorries.

In March 1922, the Corporation bought five two-year old Straker Squire 34-seat model A buses from Plymouth Corporation. Two were dismantled for spares (a shrewd move as Strakers went into liquidation in 1925) and the other three, registered CO 3398-3400, were reseated to 32 and numbered 13-15. They had an early design of overhead valve engine but such a difficult clutch and gear box that contemporary observers say that it was customary to start in top gear whenever possible. In July the same year a fourth similar vehicle was bought, also second-hand, from a local dealer-cum-charabanc operator, W.B. ('Barney') Horn. This is said to have been ordered and cancelled by J. Pye of Heswall, who operated five of this type. It had certainly been used by Horn as a picture exists of it at Raby Mere. It was numbered 16 and remained in the blue livery in which it arrived for some time. All four Strakers were withdrawn in 1927, though No. 14 was retained by the Corporation and converted into a tower wagon. As such, it was seen round the town for many more years, its bodywork revealing its bus origins. No. 13 was used experimentally as a mechanical street sweeper and then dismantled, possibly to provide a source of spares for its sister vehicle; the others were sold and converted to lorries.

The next acquisition, in February 1923, was No. 17, a diminutive Thornycroft BT with 20-seat

This 20-seat Thornycroft, No.17 (CM 4686) was bodied by Strachan and Brown. Note the incorrect number plate in this February 1923 photograph. *Thornycroft*

front entrance Strachan and Brown body. It was one-man operated and had a change dispensing machine to speed up ticket issue. This was loaded with all denominations of coins and the driver pressed shilling and pence keys to deliver the correct amount into a tray. The folding door was controlled by a lever mounted beside the driver. This bus ran originally on the Upton service later serving as the Grange Road shopping bus and latterly appeared on the Moreton Shore-Upton route. It ran until August 1928, its ultimate fate being unknown.

After the brief flirtation with Straker Squire, the Corporation went back to Leyland for its full-size buses. The six G7 models delivered in July 1923 (Nos. 18-23) were of very similar design and appearance to 1-10 but five inches shorter in both body length and wheelbase. This was because many licensing authorities would not approve buses over 25ft long so Leyland produced a design 24ft 11in long to be on the safe side. A roller blind destination indicator was fitted at the front nearside and probably also in the saloon windows each side. No. 21 was withdrawn in 1928, becoming a lorry for the local wine and spirit merchants, Mackie and Gladstone, and all the others were sold in 1929, to become lorries, No. 19 running for a Hull owner until 1942.

There was now a demand for a larger chassis and Leyland came up with a design where the driver sat alongside the engine. Nos. 24-29 of 1924 were of model SGH7 with a full-width cab and seats for 40 passengers. Although they gave the appearance of greater length, this was an illusion caused by the absence of the usual long bonnet and their dimensions were exactly the same as their G7 predecessors from which the design was derived. The engine was the same too, though the rear axle was worm driven. Nos. 28 and 29 were later re-seated to 39 and No. 29 was the subject of early spray painting experiments. All were withdrawn in 1930 to end their days as lorries. Nos. 18-29 were delivered with rear doors but these were eventually removed.

The principal deliveries in 1924 were six all-Leyland 40GH7 buses which had as many as 40 seats, an arrangement facilitated by moving the driving position forward to beside the engine. No. 29 was photographed before registration plates were fitted. *Leyland Motors*

Allocation to Routes

It was customary to keep the old buses on the same routes a practice at first dictated by the paper destination labels which could not easily be changed. The following is believed to be the original allocation of duties:-

> Rock Ferry-Moreton Nos. 1, 2, 3, 18, 19, 21, 23, 24, 26, 29
> Woodside-Moreton Nos. 13, 14, 16, 30, 31, 35, 42.
> Central Station-Upton Nos. 4, 8, 9, 17.
> Cross Docks Nos. 10, 11, 12, 22, 33.
> Rock Ferry-Port Sunlight Nos. 6, 20, 25, 27
> Charing Cross-Port Sunlight Nos. 15, 39-41
> Woodside-St. James' Church Nos. 32, 34, 37
> Woodside-Kings Road No. 36
> Shopping Bus & Moreton-Upton Nos. 17, 38
> Spare Nos. 7, 28

Nos. 11-12 are also said to have worked between Charing Cross and Moreton. The first buses to run on various services are quoted as No. 3, first to go beyond Park Station to Moreton, No. 5, Rock Ferry-Port Sunlight and No. 36, Woodside-Kings Road.

Birkenhead was a major operator of Leyland Leviathan double-deckers. There were 18 of this early open staircase model, the LG1, placed in service in 1925-26, Nos. 30-37 and 42-51. No. 43 (CM 6050) is seen descending Tollemache Road on the Woodside-Claughton Road-St, James' Church service, an extended version of the first Merseyside tram route to be converted to bus operation. *T.G.Turner collection*

In 1925, Leyland introduced the L range which included a double-deck version styled the LG1 'Leviathan'. This had an 8-litre four-cylinder side-valve engine with 5in bore and $6^1/_2$in stroke. The wheelbase was 15ft $11^1/_4$in with an overall chassis length of 24ft $7^1/_2$in. An open staircase 52-seat body with protruding half-cab was fitted. Birkenhead took the first eight off the production line which became Nos. 30-37 in the fleet and the first covered-top double-deck bus to run in the town took to the road on 27th May 1925. They replaced the Claughton Road trams and were used on the Woodside-Moreton service on which loads of 100 passengers were not unknown. A repeat order for a further 10 similar LG1s (Nos. 42-51) was received in 1926 in which year Leyland announced an overhead-valve version of the same engine, the model being designated LSP1. Ten of these (Nos. 55-64) were acquired in 1927 with an advanced (for the time) fully enclosed body. Less than 100 Leviathans were built and 40 of them operated in Wirral, the 28 owned by Birkenhead Corporation being augmented by 12 Crosvilles working the Park Station or Liscard-West Kirby and New Ferry-Bromborough services.

Bus No. 38 (CM 6045) was a 20-seat Guy J type with Buckingham body specially ordered for the Grange Road 'shopping service'. It had small diameter wheels and low steps to facilitate easy access for shoppers. It was sold in 1930, together with Nos. 52-54. *T.B. Maund collection*

The intervening numbers were filled by a variety of single-deck vehicles. No. 38 was an 18-seat Guy J with Buckingham body supplied with small solid tyred wheels similar to those fitted to SD Freighter refuse collection vehicles of the time. It was used on the Shopping Bus in its earlier days but after being re-seated to 20 and fitted with balloon tyres in 1928, it joined 17 and 52-54 on the Moreton-Upton road. It was sold in 1930. Nos. 39-41 were in one respect the last of the old style of high floored chassis being SG11s which, with a body length of 26ft 1in, were larger than their predecessors. However, in another respect they were quite up-to-date as they were fitted with a half-cab style body which, with a little modification, was to be mass-produced for later models. The absence of seats alongside the driver kept the capacity down to 38 (36 by 1927); there was a long rearward facing seat for five passengers along the front bulkhead and Birkenhead specified twin doors, the front one being for occasional use as it opened outwards and had folding steps.

65

Nos. 52-54 which came into service in April 1926 were of the Guy BB type with a 30-34hp engine. They were the last normal-control buses to be purchased and the first to be delivered with pneumatic tyres. They were bought because larger vehicles were now needed on the Shopping service but the Council would not permit full-size buses to be used along Grange Road so Guy Motors built the 27-seat bodies to the special width of 6ft 3in, a foot less than normal. This necessitated a special seating arrangement with a long seat down the nearside and the usual pairs on the offside. There were twin doors, rear entry and front exit. They ran for less than five years being withdrawn as obsolescent towards the end of 1930. No. 52 saw further passenger service with the South Notts Bus Co. Bus 53 became a lorry and 54 was broken up at Birkenhead.

One of the great developments of the 1920s was the progressive improvement of pneumatic tyres. Such equipment was quite impossible for really heavy vehicles at the beginning of the decade and a light Leyland charabanc so fitted in 1920 carried two spare wheels. But the spur of competition accelerated technical progress and by 1925, buses were having spoked wheels and solid tyres replaced by disc wheels with pneumatics. For a time, solid-tyred vehicles had their front wheels painted yellow. Birkenhead seemed to have no settled policy on conversion. Of Nos. 1-10 only No.10 was fitted, 11-17 remained on solids; 18-29 went pneumatic except 25 which retained solids on the rear axle. The LG1 Leviathans were similarly treated and possibly the SG11s though some sources say the latter were fully converted. No. 38 and the LSP1 Leviathans had pneumatics all round. Conversion was quite expensive as it involved modifications to the axles and new front mudguards as well as new wheels and tyres but the ride was enormously improved as was the ease of steering. The earlier solid-tyred models had smaller wheels on the front axle as it was otherwise difficult to steer them.

Another area in which great technical strides were made during the 'twenties was lighting. No.10, which always worked on the cross-docks services, was fitted with a Stewart spotlight after narrowly avoiding running into the dock in a fog. Later all buses up to No. 51 (except 11, 12 and 38) were similarly equipped. All vehicles up to No.29 were fitted with oil lamps in the rear interior in case the electrical equipment failed. The side-lamps of all buses up to 54 were of the oil burning type, wired for electrical operation so that the bulb could be removed and the wick turned up and lit. No.42 arrived with electric sidelights but the dual type was soon substituted. The rear saloon light acted as the rear light being on the same circuit as the side lights, shining through ruby glass and, as voltage regulators were still in the development stage, some drivers would switch out the remaining interior lights when driving on unlit roads such as between Bidston and Moreton, to give more power to the headlights.

Trafficators were tried out from an early date, taking the form of an arrow in the cab, illuminated at night, which the driver could turn to show which way he was turning. Connected to this was a triangle at the back with two arrows and a red triangle which lit up when the brakes were applied. For many years after brake lights were compulsory, the red triangle was still painted on the rear panels with the legend 'Dewandre Vacuum Brakes'.

The most popular single-deck version of the Leyland L range was the Lion forward control saloon. The original version which was a little under 24ft long was designated PLSC1, the P prefix denoting pneumatic tyres which were fitted as standard. Birkenhead bought none of this model but waited for the longer PLSC3 model which appeared late in 1926. This had a 16ft5in wheelbase permitting bodywork up to 26ft long and 36 passengers were comfortably seated. The

The Leyland PLSC Lion revolutionised bus design, having a cranked chassis so that the floor was nearer the ground and was built in large numbers. Birkenhead bought 14 of the longer PLSC3 model with standard Leyland 36-seat body. They came in two batches (Nos. 65-74 (CM 7384-93) and 75-78 (CM 8060-3). The bus shown is either 75 or 78 and is seen at St. James' Church in original all-maroon livery.

T.G.Turner collection

Lion engine had a $4\frac{1}{4}$in bore and $5\frac{1}{2}$in stroke, giving a capacity of 5.1 litres producing, in present-day terms, 62bhp at 1800 rpm. The drive was taken through the usual single-plate clutch and sliding mesh gearbox to a double reduction spiral bevel rear axle. This feature was unusual on buses and gave rise to the distinctive whine associated with the PLSC Lions.

The most advanced feature was the much lower chassis achieved by redesigning the method of attaching the axles to the frame. This made boarding and alighting much easier, especially for elderly passengers. The standard Leyland body which was fitted to over half the PLSC Lions built, obviously owed its ancestry to the bodies on the SGs. Front, rear or dual entrances were optional and Birkenhead chose rear entrances for the 19 PLSC3s ordered in 1927-28 of which only 14 (Nos. 65-78) were delivered as the order for the last five was changed to double-deckers.

The Lion was an enormous improvement on everything that had gone before and was the turning point in the fortunes of Leyland Motors. Whereas the Leviathans were all withdrawn as obsolescent in 1930-31, most becoming lorries, the Lions continued in service until 1935, most seeing further use as buses. No. 74 went to Jersey where it ran for many years while 75 and 76 went into the Crosville fleet as Nos.B99 and B100 for a short time via a Caernarfon operator which the company acquired; Nos. 65 and 69 were still being used by showmen as fairground vans in the 1950s. It is of interest to note that Leviathan No. 55, in its later lorry form, actually found itself in the British Road Services fleet in West Yorkshire when road haulage was nationalised in the post-war era and was not scrapped until 1950.

Enter the Titan

In October 1927, Leyland Motors clinched their success by unveiling the T range - the Titan double-decker and the Tiger single-decker. The Titan was to do more than anything else to influence the spread of double-deck bus operation in Britain and to facilitate its use on longer interurban routes.

The two sides of the Leyland organisation - chassis and body - had collaborated to produce a perfectly matched design of lightweight double-deck bus of low overall height on a much lower

67

built two-axle chassis. The chassis was cranked between the axles and tapered inward at the front end, allowing a platform height of only 1ft 2in, and an 8in step to the lower saloon which was ramped over the rear axle to give a maximum floor height of 2ft 4in - 9in lower than the PLSC Lion, itself considered a low-loader at the time. The upper deck was reached by an open but fully panelled staircase from the open rear platform and access to the seats, arranged in rows of four, was given by a sunken offside gangway which protruded into the lower saloon. This was not an ideal arrangement but it reduced the overall height to almost exactly 13ft, two to three feet lower than a Leviathan. The composite body was panelled with aluminium sheeting, reducing weight to $5^1/_2$ tons of which $3^1/_2$ tons was chassis. This was low enough to enable pneumatic tyres to be fitted all round without restriction.

The TD1, as it was designated, took the bus engine into the six cylinder era. Its 6.8 litre overhead camshaft engine with 4in bore and $5^1/_2$in stroke developed 90hp at 2000rpm; it was of monobloc construction with detachable head and had undergone 80,000 trial miles during an 18-month development period. The body design introduced the 'piano front' which took the upper deck over the driver's cab instead of stopping short over the lower deck bulkhead as was usual on

The first of the famous Leyland Titan TD1s (Nos.84-93 CM 8069-78) arrived in May 1928. They carried Leyland 'lowbridge' bodywork with open staircases and introduced the revised livery with three cream bands. They were joined in December by five more, (Nos. 79-83, CM 8064-8) which replaced a cancelled order for further PLSC3 Lions. Nos. 79-83 were fitted with twin destination boxes, front and rear in place of the standard Leyland single aperture at the front only. In 1933 all 15 were rebuilt by Massey Bros. with enclosed platforms and twin destination boxes. Nos. 81 and 105, seen at Woodside in August 1929, provide a comparison of the open and closed versions of the standard Leyland body type which were adopted by Birkenhead because of bridge height restrictions in Chester Street and at Bebington station.

Leyland Motors

earlier models. The Titan was years ahead of its competitors and the range continued in production with various modifications for 40 years.

One of the model's advantages was that it increased the mobility of double-deck buses, making them accessible to places where low bridges or overhanging trees were hazards. Birkenhead had two problem railway overbridges, one at the foot of Chester Street, which had dictated the use on the New Ferry route of trams of unorthodox design, and another at Bebington and New Ferry station on the Port Sunlight routes.

Birkenhead Corporation immediately ordered 10 TD1s (Nos. 84-93) which arrived in May and June 1928 and, at the same time, altered an order for five more PLSC3 Lion single-deckers to Titans. These (79-83) arrived in December. The original 10 had a standard Leyland single line destination indicator at the front, the rear destination box being occupied by the number plate while 79-83 introduced a new twin destination display, front and rear, the number plate being repositioned at roof level. They were the first Birkenhead buses to have a destination display to the rear. These buses also had a new livery style, a very dark chocolate (officially 'scotch purple') with three cream bands and a white roof. "Birkenhead Corporation Motors" in elaborate shaded lettering was placed in the lower band at waist level. The Lions and LSP Leviathans were subsequently repainted in similar style.

Twenty-five more Leyland TD1s were purchased in 1930, (Nos. 132-146, CM 9756-70) and 1931 (Nos. 147-156, (CM 9771-75/BG 200-4). These Leyland-bodied vehicles were similar to the previous series but had opening and lower rear windows as emergency exits. Nos. 147-156 could be distinguished by their lower fitted headlamps and front wheel guard rings. Nos. 132-5 and 142 towed producer gas trailers from 1943 to September 1944. No. 151 is seen at the Prenton Dell Road terminus of route 70 when new in May 1931. *Commercial postcard*

Having operated 10 fully enclosed Leviathans since 1927, Birkenhead thought that the open staircase arrangement was rather regressive and suggested to Leyland Motors that they should design a fully-enclosed Titan. An experimental body was built in January 1929 and inspected by Corporation officials. An order for 32 was placed, being delivered in April-June 1929 (Nos. 94-108) and February-March 1930 (Nos. 109-125). The awkward gangway and seating arrangement on the upper deck was improved slightly by installing alternate rows of three and four seats, thus providing three passing-places but reducing the seating capacity from 51 to 48. Passengers complained of bumping their heads when leaving their offside lower deck seats and warning notices were displayed on the seat backs - 'Please Lower Your Head When Leaving Your Seat'. However, the design was tolerated for many years because of the comfort of the ride and the ubiquity of the Titan. It was the backbone of the Birkenhead fleet until the mid-thirties. Technical advances in motor bus design during the 1920s are highlighted by comparing the O type of 1919-20 with the TD1 of 1928-29. The fully enclosed Titan became the standard model which could be found throughout the country but it is not generally known that it was inspired by Birkenhead's management.

The new LT series Leyland Lions bore little resemblance to their predecessors, having an even lower floor; Birkenhead now had very limited use for single-deck buses but bought six of the LT2 model in 1930 with Leyland rear-entrance bodies seating 35 passengers (Nos. 126-131 CM 9387-92) No. 126 was withdrawn in 1939 and 128 was destroyed in a 1941 air raid but the remaining four were converted to perimeter seating to provide room for extra standing passengers during wartime. The crew pose with No. 126 at the Haymarket terminus of the Grange Road 'shopping bus'.   *T.G. Turner collection*

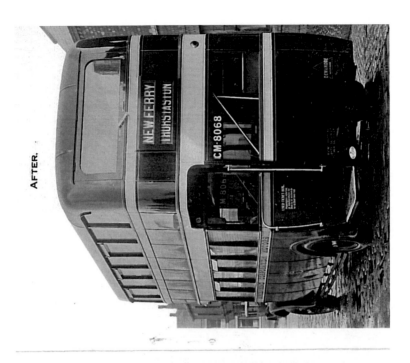

AFTER.

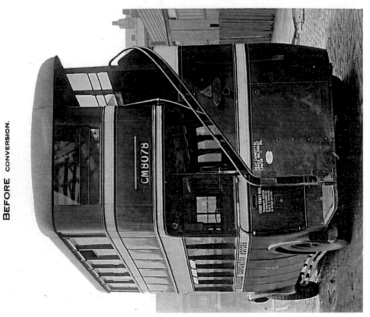

BEFORE CONVERSION.

71

The Buses of the 1930s

By March 1930, Birkenhead Corporation's bus fleet comprised 73 double-deck and 21 single-deck buses, all but four (Guys due to be scrapped within two months) being of Leyland manufacture. The most numerous type was the Titan TD1 of which there were 45. A further 15 (Nos.132-146) were added in the summer together with six examples of the updated Lion LT2 with sleek, rear entrance 35-seat bodies (Nos.126-131). These replaced the ageing Guys and, as the usefulness of single-deckers was rapidly diminishing with increasing traffic, they were to be the last of the type purchased for 18 years.

A further 15 TD1s came into the fleet the following year. The first 10 (Nos.147-156) were remarkable only in that there was a changeover from the old 'CM' registration numbers to the new 'BG' mark in the middle of the batch, 151 being CM 9775 while 152 was BG 200. The last five, Nos.159-163, had bodies built by Massey Bros. of Wigan to Leyland specifications, the start of a long association between the Corporation and this body-builder. A surprise was the appearance of two Daimler CH6 buses with Massey 53-seat lowbridge bodies to the new permissible length of 26ft (Nos.157-8) and fluid flywheels. They had 5.76 litre 6-cylinder sleeve valve engines, said to have a higher compression ratio than poppet-valve engines, thus giving fuel economy and absence of pinking; there was also no need to adjust tappets or grind valves. Whether this order was placed with a view to keeping Leyland on their toes is not known but it was followed by a further order for five similar vehicles, delivered in May 1932 (Nos.171-5).

There were surprise additions to the fleet in 1931 in the form of two Daimler CH6 buses with bodies by Massey Bros. of Wigan from whom many more bodies would be supplied over the years. (Nos. 157-8, BG 205-6). No. 158 is seen when new showing the Leyland design of bodywork fitted. *Massey Bros.*

The drivers did not like them and, on the straight stretch from Bidston to Leasowe, some men would change from top gear to first in one swift move with disastrous results.

However, while the Titans of the early 1930s mostly survived into the wartime or early post-war years, all seven Daimlers were sold off in 1938 as soon as they were fully depreciated, though they all saw further service in districts as far apart as Cumberland, Staffordshire and South Wales. In their later Birkenhead years, they were concentrated at New Ferry depot from where the flat terrain of New Chester Road made the least demands on their underpowered engines.

The seven Titans (Nos.164-170) delivered in 1932 were of the new TD2 model, one foot longer than the TD1 and incorporating several technical improvements such as fully floating rear axle, triple- instead of single-servo brakes and front springs anchored at the front end and shackled at the rear instead of vice versa as had been previous Leyland practice. The Leyland bodies were the last bought until 1951.

Nos.169-170 were fitted with 8.6 litre diesel engines, then known as 'oil engines', instead of the 7.6 litre petrol engine which was a larger version of the TD1 engine. This engine was to remain Leyland's basic power unit for buses until 1948. Experimental diesel engines had been developing for several years but were not regarded as a practical proposition for buses, bearing in mind the high reliability factor needed, until 1930-31. The engine noise was much greater than

Further Leyland TD2s, (Nos. 176-184 BG 1500-8) fitted with Leyland-style Massey Bros. bodies arrived in 1933. An attractive feature of these buses was the luxurious maroon and beige moquette seating in place of the previous leather style. No. 179 was one of three diesel-engined buses to receive wartime blue and black livery. No. 177 is seen at Laird Street depot in November 1946. *T.H. Davies*

TD2 No.170 was the last survivor of the batch, being withdrawn in October 1948 and is seen in the parking area behind Laird Street depot in March 1946.   *T.G.Turner*

Five more Daimlers Nos.171-5 (BG746-50) completed the 1932 orders: they were similar to Nos.157-8 and, being non-standard vehicles in the fleet, were sold with them in 1938. No.171 is seen during the 1939-45 war after sale to Blair & Palmer of Carlisle.   *Omnibus Society*

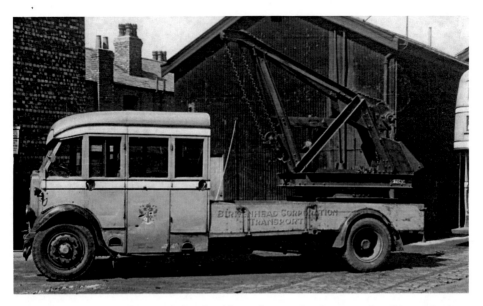

No. 183 is shown as a breakdown vehicle in Laird Street depot yard, with tram tracks still in position, in 1948. *J. Melbourne*

that of the petrol engine and there was a distinctive smell regarded by many as offensive. The engine noise was almost sufficient to drown the characteristic 'scream' of the TD1 and TD2 Titans as they laboured, fully loaded, up an incline in third. However, despite higher initial cost, the economic advantages were unarguable - cheaper fuel and more miles per gallon - and, with one exception, no more petrol engined buses were purchased.

A further nine diesel TD2s with Massey bodies of Leyland style (Nos.176-184) arrived in May 1933. They were the last to be delivered in the chocolate livery and the first to be fitted with moquette seats in place of the red leather cloth used for some years in Birkenhead buses and some refurbished trams. No.183 had a short life as a bus as its body was destroyed by fire in January 1936. It was rebuilt as a 5-ton breakdown crane in which form it lasted until 1953 when, ironically, it was damaged again.

The AEC Q

When No.185 arrived, it attracted attention wherever it appeared. It was the last petrol bus and the first to be painted in the new blue livery. It was also revolutionary in design being an AEC 'Q' with front entrance ahead of the front axle and the engine located under the stairs to the offside. The weight distribution enabled single wheels to be fitted to the rear axle. This remarkable bus had a 59-seat Metro-Cammell all metal body and was the only one of its type built to lowbridge standards with sunken gangway. An unusual feature was a light front bumper designed to trigger a tram-style lifeguard. Modern tubular-framed seats were covered with brightly patterned moquette.

The 'Q' type's transmission incorporated a fluid coupling and Wilson preselective epicyclic gearbox which called for much less physical effort from the driver compared with the contemporary crash box Leylands. The 7.4-litre engine was the same as fitted to the AEC Regent orthodox buses of the period. Many design features of the 'Q' were years ahead of their time and it was to be 25 years before the Leyland Atlantean revived the front entrance layout for double-deckers. The transport industry could not accept such a radical change and, although 348 'Q' type vehicles were manufactured, most were single-deckers, and only 23 two-axle double-deckers were built. However, four of these ran in Birkenhead as, in 1934, Wallasey Corporation bought two and in 1938 Crosville transferred their solitary example of this type from Liverpool to Rock Ferry depot.

By modern standards, the TD Titans were difficult to drive. Powerfully sprung clutch pedals tested the muscles of the left thigh and considerable judgement and practice were needed to change gear without making alarming grinding noises. One of management's contemporary problems was the conversion of tram drivers to bus driving. Many were elderly men who found it difficult to master the intricacies of 'listening for the revs' and steering the vehicle at the same time. The 'Q' showed that there were easier ways and its presence at Laird Street almost certainly influenced the Corporation to embrace the concept of the 'Gearless Bus'.

The revolutionary side-engined AEC 'Q' type was years ahead of its time and only 23 double-deckers were built. Birkenhead's sole example (No. 185, BG 1509) arrived in July 1933 and was the only Q to be fitted with a 'lowbridge' body which was built by the Metropolitan-Cammell Carriage & Wagon Co. of Birmingham. It was the last petrol-engined vehicle to enter the fleet and introduced a new livery of light blue and cream, replacing the previous dark maroon. It was sold for further service in 1940 to Worth's of Enstone, Oxfordshire, who collected several second-hand Qs.   *AEC*

These words were originally carried on the radiator grille of Leyland buses fitted with hydraulic torque converters, a form of fluid drive of Swedish origin, marketed as an aid to training tram drivers in conjunction with an advertising slogan "Bury a Tram and Plant a Titan in its Place".

The first experimental torque converter produced by Leyland in 1933 was fitted to TD1 No.87 so Birkenhead could claim to be the first user of the system. However, it proved unsuitable for the TD1 and was removed after a time. The transmission was controlled by a lever with four positions, neutral, converter, direct drive and reverse. The converter mode was used up to about 20 mph when the driver changed to direct drive. The system was easy to use though less fuel efficient, consumption increasing by about 1 mpg because of the inherent slip.

This form of transmission was fitted to all Birkenhead vehicles placed in service between 1934 and 1939, a total of 133 buses. No.184 was also fitted with one for about three years. Twelve vehicles were delivered in September 1934 in time for the Tranmere and Prenton tram conversions. They were all TD3c's (the 'c' denoting the torque converter) and the body order was divided into three parts. Nos.186-8 were the last lowbridge buses with side gangways upstairs and piano fronts, being built by Northern Counties who also built Nos.189-191. The latter were full height (14ft 6in) bodies with normal seating on the upper deck and had a distinctive upright

Six Massey-bodied Leyland TD3c buses (Nos. 192-7, BG 2657-62) arrived in October to complete the 1934 intake. The moquette seats were in the same maroon and beige colours as those in Nos. 176-84. Massey-bodied 192 is seen alongside Northern Counties-bodied 189 of similar appearance in March 1948.
T.G.Turner

front profile and domed roof. Nos.192-7 were outwardly indistinguishable but were built by Massey. All the Northern Counties bodies were metal framed. Nos.189-197 introduced a new feature as the route number indicator boxes were moved down to a new position just above the destination indicators. However, they were still of the small size and there was no number display to the rear.

But they certainly made a favourable impression on the public. One writer to the *Wallasey News* compared them favourably with contemporary Wallasey buses thus. 'I.....was astonished at the brightness of these fast moving vehicles. The lighting system is wonderful and the seats the last word in comfort.'

The TD3c differed from the TD2 only in the front end treatment, the bulkhead being brought forward by 6in. and a new deeper radiator of more modern appearance was fitted. The TD4c, which was launched in 1935, was outwardly similar but had Lockheed vacuum hydraulic brakes, larger clutch and an improved rear axle. Birkenhead took 10 in 1935 and 11 in 1936, the odd one being added to replace the burnt out No.183. The general lines of the bodies were similar to Nos.189-197 but the 1935 body order (which had originally been given to Leyland and cancelled) was again split between Massey (198-202) and Northern Counties (203-7). The small size route number boxes were now provided at both the front and rear. The 1936 batch (Nos.208-218) were all built by Massey and introduced the much larger route number indicators alongside

the destination indicators which were to remain standard for Birkenhead for the next 33 years. They were fitted with large rear bumpers, an unusual feature which was repeated on all buses up to No.318. However, these were all removed in 1954 when it became obligatory to fit reflectors.

The year 1937 saw the end of the trams and Birkenhead's largest bus order so far, 40 Leyland TD5c's (219-258), all with Massey bodywork with a new sloping front profile. The TD5 was identical to the TD4 except in chassis detail and half of the 1938 order for 20 chassis (259-268) received almost identical 54-seat bodies. The other half had extremely attractive, curvaceous all-metal bodies by Northern Counties, of five- instead of the usual six-bay design. The interior decor was lavish with buff leather cloth ceilings in the lower saloon, fading to blue at the sides and stainless steel window surrounds with polished wood edges. Nos.

Thirty-two Leyland TDI's were taken into stock in 1929-30, all fitted with standard 'towbridge' enclosed stairs bodies (Nos. 94-113, CM8721-40 and 114-125, CM9375-86). Most had been withdrawn by 1939 but Nos. 124-5 survived to carry wartime blue and black livery and were converted to run on producer gas from 1943 until withdrawn at the end of September 1944. No. 123 is shown receiving an engine overhaul at New Ferry depot in 1938.   *J. Melbourne*

Forty buses were ordered for 1937 delivery (Nos. 219-258, BG 5501-40) all bodied by Massey and fitted with blue leather cloth-covered seats for 54 passengers. By July 17 had been delivered, facilitating the withdrawal of the last of the trams on 17th of that month. No.224 was the third of the trio of diesel buses to be painted in wartime blue and black. The bodies of 226 and 235 were destroyed in the March 1941 air raid and replaced by new Massey bodies similar to No. 307 in 1942. No. 244 was destroyed by fire in September 1941 and not replaced. No. 233 is seen at the New Ferry terminus of route 64 in June 1948. *I. Kennedy*

259-268 had similar ceilings. All Northern Counties buses from 186 and others from No.198 upwards had blue interior trim and from No.219, all seats were upholstered in blue leather.

The final pre-war order was again a large one, for 40 TD5c chassis with a new style of five-bay body by Massey resembling, in some respects, the previous year's Northern Counties bodies without the heavy frontal treatment. The interior design was equally elaborate and, externally, the upper and lower cream bands had polished mouldings. Although the fleet was still expanding, the 1939 order also replaced 30 TD1s of 1929-30 vintage, several of which were not withdrawn until after war had been declared. Because of the great demand for buses to serve munition factories, the majority had second careers, many of them in Scotland.

The TD4c and TD5c buses were generally long-lived and many suffered grievous damage during the war, some being rebodied, but that is another story. As the older buses became due for a repaint, they emerged in the blue livery and the fleet was all blue by 1938.

Birkenhead entered the war with a fleet of 186 buses, all but one of Leyland manufacture. They were to give the town yeoman service during the next six gruelling years.

5 – The 1939-45 War

Much contingency planning had taken place in the year before the outbreak of war on 3rd September 1939. The visible signs to the man in the street were the erection of air raid shelters. Men were conscripted for military training and one of the camps was built in Arrowe Park. Behind the scenes much logistic work went on; the road passenger transport licensing system was to be suspended in favour of permits issued by Regional Traffic Commissioners with virtual absolute powers. Plans were drawn up for the rationing of petroleum products, all of which had to be imported, and many of the wartime difficulties of the bus operators centred around fuel supply and tyre shortages.

The 1938 order for 20 Leyland TD5c buses (Nos. 259-78, BG 6801-20) was divided equally between Massey Bros. and Northern Counties. The Massey-bodied vehicles (Nos. 259-68) were similar to the 1937 order but had a more streamlined cab. The lower saloon ceilings were covered in beige leathercloth fading into blue at each side, a very attractive feature also applied to the Northern Counties bodies and the 40 1939 deliveries. No. 261, in its first year, is seen on a test run at Port Rainbow.   *J. Melbourne*

The Blackout

A vital issue was the concealment of lights from enemy aircraft and during 1939 there were three practice blackouts on Merseyside. Conditions of almost complete darkness were simulated and aerial observations taken. When war came the real thing was very much worse. Blackout conditions were imposed on 1st September, two days before war was declared. It was a severe trial for the bus operators as, in the early days of the 'phoney war', everything tended to be overdone. Initially, the regulations were so stringent that virtually no light whatsoever was permissible and, apart from drivers' problems, conductors had difficulty in issuing tickets and giving change. At first operators used whatever was to hand to dim headlights such as cardboard

The body of No. 307 was destroyed in March 1941 and the chassis was fitted in 1942 with a replacement Massey body which was virtually indistinguishable from the original except that it lacked polished mouldings to the cream relief. It is seen at Woodside in October 1949.   *J.Manly*

or brown paper but eventually the Home Office developed a standard mask with slits directing the limited light allowed downwards.

Interior lights were reduced by fitting low powered bulbs, masking or removing some bulbs altogether. Mudguards, platform edges and handrails of buses were painted white as were kerbs and the bases of street lights, pillar boxes and other street furniture. Of course, there was little other traffic on the roads but working in these conditions can only be described as nerve-wracking and led to neuroses and other ailments. Extra running time had to be allowed for night driving.

Reduced Services

During July 1939, the Traffic Commissioners instructed all operators to prepare contingency plans on the basis of a 40% reduction in services, to be effected by operating wider headways during off-peak hours and on Sundays, cutting out late journeys and withdrawing non-essential services altogether. This 40% target was never reached. Fuel would be allocated on the basis of the timetables approved. Many of the operators' staffs were reservists or members of the Territorial Army and were mobilised immediately but the reduced services needed fewer staff to operate them and, in any case, there were plenty of unemployed men to draw upon. There were many special jobs to be done such as conveying evacuees to railway stations and moving hospital patients to supposed safe areas.

Operators were expected to have their contingency plans in operation within three weeks of the declaration of war and Birkenhead's and Crosville's emergency timetables were put into effect

No. 182 was one of several buses wrecked by a German bomb in Laird Street depot on the night of 13/14th March 1941. It was among several to receive replacement bodies by East Lancashire Coachworks. Alongside is No. 184, less extensively rebuilt by East Lancashire after war damage. The new body from 182 was transferred to the chassis of 217 in 1947. *T.G. Turner collection*

on 24th September. An early war casualty was the reduction of the all day 10-minute frequency on Woodside ferry sailings to quarter-hourly except at peak hours.

Services Modified or Withdrawn

12	Charing Cross – Seacombe : withdrawn on Sundays
38-40	Woodside – Bromborough (Manor Road)/Eastham : curtailed off-peak at Bromborough Cross (numbered 36)
42	New Ferry – Bromborough Pool Village : withdrawn
44	St. Paul's Road – Eastham Ferry : withdrawn
54	Rock Ferry – Port Sunlight : withdrawn
71	Woodside – Irby – Heswall : curtailed at Thurstaston (as 72)
79	Haymarket – Storeton Road (Birch Road) : withdrawn
85	Woodside – Greasby – Thurstaston : withdrawn

Surprisingly, the 16 service between Park Station and Arrowe Park was allowed to continue on Sundays only, running every 40-minutes until one hour after sunset, and continued to do so throughout the war, despite all the later cuts and economies. All other services had their frequencies drastically reduced. Cinemas and theatres were compulsorily closed for a time as it was feared that large assemblies should be discouraged to avoid large scale casualties in the event of a direct hit by a bomb. This and the blackout conditions reduced passenger demand and evening services were cut from 1st November.

The initial service cuts had resulted in some real hardship, the worst of which was the curtailment of the Bromborough service at the Cross. The Commissioner's thinking had been that Crosville buses would be able to pick up passengers up to Allport Road but, as they also had been severely reduced, they were frequently full before they reached Bromborough and occasionally at Eastham. As a compromise, the Commissioner allowed the Corporation service to be extended to Allport Road, traversing a loop via Allport Lane, Allport Road and Bromborough Village Road. This service took the number 37. However, Bebington Borough Council was dissatisfied with this arrangement and waged a persistent campaign for improvements throughout the war years. The Haymarket-Birch Road 'shopping bus' was reinstated on a reduced frequency on 9th December 1939 and a limited peak hour service to Heswall was reinstated from 10th January 1940.

As the 'phoney war' continued and nothing happened, some restrictions were relaxed. Cinemas reopened and new timetables which came into force on 1st February 1940 still provided late buses up to 11.0pm. In the summer of 1940 there was sufficient fuel available for some holiday services to be operated and extra buses were operated on the Arrowe Park, Moreton Shore, New Brighton and Thurstaston routes. In the same year, when an invasion by Germany was expected, all sorts of ludicrous precautions were taken, calculated to hinder the enemy should he land unexpectedly by sea or air. Signposts were removed and milestones painted over. Birkenhead's speciality was to make all bus steering wheels detachable and to insist that drivers remove them and carry them no matter how brief their absence from the vehicle was to be. The spectacle of 20 or so drivers at Woodside terminus, all carrying steering wheels, was highly diverting.

In January 1936 No. 183 was destroyed by fire and a breakdown crane was mounted on the salvaged chassis. Originally painted grey, it received blue and cream bus livery in 1946. The burnt remains of 183 are seen in Laird Street depot.   J.E. Marsh

The Air Raids

This period was brought to an end by the air raids, the first casualties and damage in Birkenhead occurring on 9th August 1940. Thereafter, night raids were frequent and considerable destruction was caused. On 7th September 1940 considerable damage was done to New Ferry depot, eight buses being damaged. The most concentrated attacks were on 20th-22nd December 1940, 12th-14th March and 1st-8th May 1941. In the March attack, the Cheshire side of the river sustained grievous damage, much of it to residential property. Laird Street depot, which was uncomfortably close to the docks, received its first bomb damage on 21st December 1940 when a specially constructed air raid shelter was totally destroyed, seven members of staff being killed. There was extensive damage to the garage and workshops and minor damage to the mess rooms and offices. The garage was devastated in another incident on 12-13th March 1941 damage being sustained also to the workshops, ticket room, uniform store, mess rooms and general offices. 136 of Birkenhead's 182 buses were damaged to some extent, eight bodies being totally destroyed and the chassis damaged and a further 22 needed stripping and rebuilding to some extent. Plant, tools and machinery were put out of action and stores and ticket stocks destroyed. One night cleaner was killed on the night of 13th March. Losses might have been greater but for a policy of dispersal whereby buses were kept overnight in Birkenhead Park and along Park Road West.

The final batch of utility Guys (Nos.339-42, BG 8649-52) were fitted with Park Royal bodies and entered service in April 1944. Unlike the previous utilities, they arrived in plain grey with no markings, the fleet numbers being chalked on! Within a month all four had been painted in blue and cream but without the fleet name on the lower cream band; it was located instead in smaller lettering above the manager's name on the front nearside lower panel. After 11 buses, of which 339 was one, the new style was abandoned and there was a reversion to the previous layout. No. 339 is seen parked up at Woodside with the lairages and the Mersey Railway power station chimney in the background. It carries the later style of Gill Sans lettering and numbers.
T.G. Turner collection

Despite the circumstances, some residents of Cavendish Road complained bitterly of this practice. Birkenhead was unlucky in having 11 buses damaged while parked on the upper drive of the Park on 18th October 1940 and in two further incidents a total of eight buses were damaged by anti-aircraft shells.

Other buses were caught by blast on the streets and many passenger shelters were destroyed. These included venerable cast iron and glass structures, some dating back to earlier tramway days, which were attached to buildings and covered the whole footway. Shelters at Market Place South, Park Entrance (attached to the Queens Hotel), Park Station and Claughton Village were victims of aerial attacks.

The provision of a very good service in the circumstances was a remarkable achievement. Not only were buses damaged but employees' homes were destroyed or damaged. In the face of the most appalling difficulties - diversions, staff shortages, damage to buses and bureaucratic demands - the standard of efficiency was unbelievably high, in general higher than in the 1960s when staff shortages and indifference to the needs of the public were at their worst. In the face of the bombing, many people voluntarily dispersed to what the less fortunate were prone to call 'funk holes' in the country. Some were lucky in that their places of employment were evacuated and they went with them but others commuted daily from Chester and North Wales. Those who sought refuge nearer home in the Wirral towns and villages added to the already serious peak hour problem on the buses. A peak hour service was run between Woodside and Upton on the suspended 85 route for a few days in 1941 to alleviate this problem. Interruption of rail services saw the bus operators called upon to provide vehicles to bridge the gaps and the destruction of Park Station and the adjoining carriage sheds disrupted not only the rail services but the buses which connected with them. Birkenhead Corporation shared in the provision of an emergency tunnel service between Birkenhead and Liverpool which ran for a few days in May 1941 when rail and ferry services were interrupted, the former following a direct hit on Park Station and the latter because of the presence of mines in the river.

Damaged buses were put back into service as quickly as possible, often with glass replaced by plywood. Some Wallasey Leyland Titan TD2 buses, nominally withdrawn but retained for emergencies, operated on the cross-docks services with Birkenhead crews after the Laird Street bombing and, in due course, 14 of the damaged buses were extensively rebuilt or rebodied as described elsewhere. As a stop-gap measure, six London Transport AEC Regent STs were hired from December 1941, the last returning in April 1944. Their archaic design with protruding cab and open staircase seemed strange to northern eyes. The four remaining single-deck buses were fitted with 'perimeter seating' for 31 or 32 seats, arranged around the sides of the saloon with room for about 30 standees.

The last bomb fell on Merseyside on 10th January 1942. Of an estimated 34,000 houses in Birkenhead, 25,000 (74%) were destroyed or damaged in some degree, some of them three times.

A Change of Management

Towards the end of 1941, Mr Cyril Clarke, the general manager, became eligible to retire but intimated his willingness to continue in service if requested. However, he wished to take his pension and be re-engaged at a reduced salary, a course of action which was approved by the

A rear view of No. 347, by this time with new style lettering, at Woodside in July 1956.   *T.G. Turner*

Transport and Finance Committees. However, the full Council refused to endorse this proposal, members saying publicly that it was wrong in principle, as if the pension payments would be a charge on the Corporation. It soon became clear that it would be impossible to obtain a new manager before Clarke's notice expired on 17th February 1942 and he was asked to continue until his successor could take over. In view of the Council's attitude, he felt unable to do so and, after his services ended, he made a public statement revealing that when, in September 1941, he had told the Transport Committee that there would be difficulty in meeting traffic demands if the air raid conditions of the previous winter were repeated, he experienced a stream of abuse followed by statements and charges reflecting on his competence. He asked for a Public Enquiry alleging that 'other sources of discontent are festering elsewhere in the body corporate'.

Clarke had been a loyal employee for 41 years and an efficient manager for 29 of them and it was most unfortunate that his career should have ended so acrimoniously. The pre-war undertaking was a model of efficiency and wartime needs were being met much more expeditiously than in many other towns. His successor was George A. Cherry, aged 42, who had been general manager at Rochdale since March 1936, with previous service at Hull and Rotherham and with the Yorkshire Traction Co. He was an engineer by training and took over at Birkenhead in May 1942.

Wartime Measures

By early 1941, fuel was in even shorter supply; last buses ran about 10.0pm from 20th January 1941 and there were further cuts in services in November and again during 1942-43, particularly on Sundays and during the evenings, with last buses as early as 9.0-9.30pm from 1st March 1943.

Not only was there a need to save fuel but manpower, tyres and wear and tear on buses needed to be conserved. The extent to which off-peak and weekend services were curtailed is demonstrated by the reduction in mileage operated from 6.36 million in 1938-39 to 4.68 million in 1942-43. In terms of miles per bus, the reduction was from 34,180 to 25,039 (27%).

Lack of spare parts and shortages of skilled labour made bus maintenance extremely difficult during the war years. Skilled men were directed to work elsewhere which was considered more important than looking after buses which were necessary to get workers to essential wartime employment. When George Cherry took over in May 1942 he found that 48 of the 186 buses in the fleet were off the road with serious defects. Following strong representations from the department, skilled men were directed from local garages but they were unwilling workers, transferred against their will, and they did not always give of their best; many had experience only of petrol engines and the majority of the buses were diesel-propelled. The Ministry of Labour, in conjunction with the trade unions concerned, drew up a scheme for the employment of female maintenance fitters and up to six of these were employed at any one time.

As a result of wartime conditions, new staff facilities of a type nowadays taken for granted were provided for the first time. In 1942 wash basins with hot water were installed in the workshops and Works Canteens were established in May of that year. At the time, canteens were valued as a means of supplementing the meagre food rations and they were established at Woodside, New Ferry and Laird Street though hot midday meals were available only at the latter. Cooked meals

The first new buses to arrive after the end of the 1939-45 war were eight 5LW Guys (Nos. 343-50, BG 8735-42) which joined the fleet in January 1946. They had Park Royal bodies of 'relaxed utility' specification with upholstered seats and rear destination boxes. All were painted in normal blue and cream but without the black lining which was added at Laird Street. No. 348 is seen at Woodside still with offset fleet name from new.   *J.Crutchley*

were originally prepared by a Communal Feeding Centre but eventually a kitchen was installed at Laird Street and, despite very low prices being charged, the canteens became self-supporting.

The Essential Works Order directed labour to certain employment and restricted the right to change jobs. The Ministry of Labour advised transport undertakings to form Works Committees with employer and employee members to deal with problems arising. The activities of this Committee undoubtedly cut down absenteeism among the traffic staff but it was necessary to recommend a few cases for prosecution *pour encourager les autres*. These Committees became a permanent feature of labour relations after the war ended.

Producer Gas Propulsion

The problems were exacerbated by the increasing age of the fleet as many buses which, under normal circumstances, would have been withdrawn, were kept in service. To these problems were added the tribulations of producer gas propulsion in 1943. All operators with more than 100 vehicles were directed to convert 10% of their fleet to this rather inefficient means of propulsion but it is doubtful if anyone ever reached this total. The fuel was generated in equipment mounted on a two-wheel trailer towed behind the bus and connected to the engine by a flexible pipe. Each conversion cost about £120; the units were notoriously temperamental, especially on hills. Birkenhead was ordered to convert 19 buses but, like most operators, dragged its feet and converted only nine elderly Leyland Titans, using them on the flattest possible routes such as 12, 21/22 and occasionally 26. After strong representations had been made, the Ministry of War Transport sanctioned the release of larger bore cylinder blocks to improve performance. Even so,

No. 352 is seen in Hoylake Road, Bidston on a journey from Cammell Laird's shipyard to Hurrell Road in April 1957.   *R.L. Wilson*

they had difficulty climbing Hamilton Street brow and in Park Road East, Exmouth Street and Bedford Road. With an improvement in the fortunes of war, they were all withdrawn on 30th September 1944.

One fuel-saving measure was the reduction of stopping places as this reduced low-gear work and cut wear and tear on tyres and brake linings. Eighty stops were eliminated and others repositioned in July 1942, following a directive from the Ministry of War Transport that stops should be about 440 yards apart. As a relic of tramway days, many stops were absurdly close together and no real hardship was caused by these measures.

Women were engaged as conductors and cleaners. There were eventually 260 conductors and auxiliary conductors were appointed in 1942 - regular passengers who travelled free while manning the platform to enable the conductor to collect the fares. Two female inspectors, appointed at the end of that year, were paid 90% of the male rate. In 1944 18 conductresses were trained as bus drivers as a precautionary measure but they were not subsequently used. A Female Welfare Officer was appointed to deal with special problems but the appointment was not renewed when the incumbent resigned in November 1945 as, by that time, the number of female employees had reduced considerably as men returned from the forces. Conductresses were phased out in June 1946.

The Formation of Queues Order which came into force on 12th April 1942, required six or more passengers to form a queue not more than two deep and made it an offence to jump a queue. This created a problem at Woodside and several other places in Birkenhead where different services had pulled up at a common loading point. At Hamilton Square station, 12 separate stopping places for

Eighteen more Guys arrived in 1944 fitted with very angular utility bodies by Massey Bros. (Nos. 321-38 BG 8554-8; BG 8628-32 and BG 8641-8). The arrival of these vehicles allowed the return to London Transport of the six AEC Tilling-type ST buses which had been on loan since December 1941 of which no photographs have been traced during their stay in Birkenhead. The upper deck coats of arms disappeared with the introduction of advertisements on the buses in 1946. No. 336 is seen at Woodside in March 1948.   *R.Marshall*

different services were fixed along Bridge Street and Hamilton Street, causing numerous services to be diverted via Chester Street and Bridge Street instead of following the direct route up Hamilton Street as hitherto. At Central Station, the stops were spread out along Borough Road towards the Haymarket. Numerous other places, such as Park Station, were also affected.

At Woodside, passengers and buses were mixed up; there was grave danger, particularly during the blackout and, in December 1942 the Corporation approved a plan for queue islands with crude shelters. One cannot help feeling that the contemporary quoted cost of £800 was somewhat understated. These islands, with some post-war improvement, continued in use until the reconstruction of the terminus in 1991-92.

Other measures were taken to discourage short-distance travel so that long distance passengers were not crowded out. Penny fares were abolished from Woodside terminus during the evening peak from 15th March 1941 and children's $^{1}/_{2}$d fares were withdrawn from 28th June 1943, never to return.

Special Services

Because of serious problems experienced by Crosville Motor Services Ltd. during the war, Birkenhead Corporation was called upon to provide several special services outside its normal operating area. These were worked on a contract basis, no fares being collected on the buses. Most of these have gone unrecorded but it is known that evening journeys from Ellesmere Port to Woodside were run and there were two shift services to Williams and Williams factory at Hooton Park which commenced at Laird Street depot and displayed route nos. 44 via Conway Street and New Chester Road and 88 via Park Road East and Old Chester Road. In addition, hundreds of members of HM Forces were conveyed, often at short notice and at all hours of the day and night.

From 1944, the Corporation ran some buses to and from Clatterbridge Hospital for employees and railway replacement services between Bidston and Birkenhead North, at Crosville's request. Clatterbridge was, of course, in the Corporation's agreed operating area but it did not publicly extend beyond Lower Bebington until after the war had ended. In May 1945, Bebington Corporation forwarded a petition signed by 815 people, demanding better transport facilities for Clatterbridge and Birkenhead agreed to extend the 50 service from Spital Cross Roads if the Commissioner consented and allocated additional fuel. More buses were required to carry workers to the Bromborough factories though their location enabled much of the demand to be catered for by buses running out to Eastham and Bromborough which would otherwise have been very lightly loaded. A special service was put on to Port Causeway for Fawcett Preston's staff, the number 35 being allocated by March 1943. Eventually, No. 33 was used for trips to Bromborough Dock and 31, whilst nominally denoting New Ferry-Bromborough Cross, was displayed for all inward workings to New Ferry depot, much as '4' was used when running into Laird Street. Birkenhead buses running short journeys on route 10 between Central Station and Liscard displayed the number 9 though Wallasey would have nothing to do with short working numbers.

Problems with Crosville Buses

There was dissatisfaction that Crosville buses were prohibited from carrying local traffic in Birkenhead and much of Bebington, even under wartime conditions, especially on inward journeys when there was no question of long distance passengers being excluded. At a series of meetings with the Councils during 1941, the company pointed out that at peak periods there were no empty seats anyway, this being demonstrated by a request to Birkenhead to issue contracts from Thingwall on the same terms as Crosville as the company's ticket holders, unable to board Crosville buses, were travelling on Corporation buses (as provided for in the 1930 Agreement) and creating extra clerical work. From 1st July 1942, Crosville contracts ceased to be available on Corporation buses. After a conference in December 1941, Birkenhead Council passed a resolution deploring 'the trivial nature of the modification [of the existing rules] offered by the company'. But Crosville knew that more stops meant extra running time, more buses and more staff which were simply not available and the Regional Transport Commissioner upheld their stand.

The worst affected area was Eastham. The Commissioner refused to allocate more fuel despite continuous lobbying by Bebington Corporation and eventually, Birkenhead Corporation found the fuel to run extra Eastham trips by cancelling journeys on other services. Another of Bebington's complaints was the exclusive use of elderly lowbridge buses on the Port Sunlight routes and the 64 between Woodside and New Ferry via Higher Bebington, both of which passed under Bebington Station bridge. At that time there were two spans, the original arch (since demolished) being hazardous to full height buses. The newest lowbridge buses dated from 1934

Northern Counties supplied the metal-framed bodies for the remaining four Guys new in 1946 (Nos. 351-4 (BG8743-46). For an unknown reason they arrived painted a deep royal blue which, though attractive, was in sharp contrast to BCT light blue; they were repainted into normal colours in May 1947. The rear of No. 354, still in dark blue, is seen in 1946.   *T.G. Turner*

and many were a good deal older so Bebington had a case. The problem was resolved by widening the footpath on the south side to force buses to keep to the centre of the road and, from early 1943, normal height buses were used on the 51/52 and 64 services.

The Forces Leave Service

Following the success of the Allied campaign in Europe, special leave trains were run between Dover and Liverpool and from 2nd January 1945, a special night bus service for service personnel was introduced leaving Lime Street station at 2.00, 3.15 and 4.30am, calling at a WVS hostel at 7 Hamilton Square and then on a circular route covering New Ferry, Port Sunlight, Prenton and Arrowe Park at a fare of 6d. It is not known on what basis this service was provided as in Liverpool, the Commissioner refused fuel for a similar service which was run with vans under Welfare auspices. It is interesting to record that in March 1945, the LMS Railway Co. demanded the payment of £2-2-0d (£2.10) per annum for the use of Lime Street station by buses and a request to waive this fee in view of the nature of the facility was refused. At that time, the service was losing money at the rate of £60 per year, but later in 1945, the general manager said that it was breaking even. It is believed to have continued until early 1947 when the special leave trains were withdrawn.

As the danger of air attack receded, operating conditions were relaxed. 'Starlight' street lighting, introduced on main roads in 1943, improved night driving conditions and the arrival of 24 Guy Arab buses with wooden-seated, utility bodies enabled some of the older Titans to be withdrawn and cannibalised to keep the others going a little longer. As early as December 1944, the Committee decided to replace the wooden seats with upholstered ones at £100 per bus and it is assumed that there was sufficient material in stock to do this. Many other operators were running wartime utility buses, unimproved, for some time after the war.

WARTIME STATISTICS

Year Ended 31 Mar	Revenue £000s	Index	Per Bus Mile d.	Passengers 000s	Index	Per Bus Mile d.	Mileage 000s	Index	Average Fare per Passgr. d.
1939	341	100	12.87	50,920	100	8.01	6,358	100	1.61
1940	338	99	14.53	49,442	97	8.86	5,584	88	1.65
1941	325	95	16.81	50,026	98	10.78	4,641	73	1.56
1942	352	103	17.78	51,221	101	10.79	4,750	75	1.65
1943	383	112	19.61	53,215	105	11.37	4,682	74	1.73
1944	405	119	20.62	55,143	108	11.69	4,720	74	1.77
1945	414	121	20.77	56,238	110	11.77	4,779	75	1.77
1946	429	126	20.39	57,749	113	11.44	5,051	79	1.79

6 – The Post-War Boom Years - 1945-52

The end of the war in Europe in May 1945 brought no respite from shortages and controls. Under the new Labour government, rationing continued and in some cases became stricter, bureaucratic interference being intensified as doctrinaire socialism was applied. Fuel rationing for buses was relaxed slowly and the retention of petrol rationing for private motoring brought public transport many additional passengers. There was a tremendous pent-up demand for pleasure travel and the limited facilities were taxed to the utmost in the immediate post-war years. There was full employment and peak hour demand was heavy throughout the year. In the year ending 31st March 1947, almost 67 million passengers were conveyed over 6.3 million miles compared with 51 million over 5.6 million miles in 1938-39. This increased each year until 1949-50 when 78 million passengers were carried and 7.6 million miles were run. Traffic then decreased slowly year by year as social habits changed, television keeping people at home in the evenings and private transport eating into both recreational and work journeys.

In pre-war days the life of a bus in the hands of a municipal operator was seven to eight years after which it was sold off, usually to be snapped up by some private operator who often doubled its lifespan. By these standards, enormous numbers of buses were time-expired when the war ended but many manufacturers needed to convert their assembly lines from some wartime activity. Birkenhead's main supplier, Leyland Motors, had been building military tanks and their post-war production was delayed.

In the autumn of 1945, plans were made for the restoration of suspended services and the implementation of improvements. Some of these involved the activation of some of the rights

Leyland Lion No.131 is seen outside the Laird Street offices, decorated for Victory celebrations in May and August 1945 after which it returned to service until May 1948.   *T.G. Turner collection*

A 1948 scene at Laird Street depot of buses of 1935, 1937 and 1938 origin in the bus wash area.

T.G.Turner collection

negotiated with Crosville in 1938. Late buses were restored only until 10.0pm at first because of both fuel and manpower shortages and the war had been over for almost a year before buses once more ran until 11.0pm or later. The delivery in the early part of 1946 of 12 Guy Arab buses of an improved utility standard enabled some plans to be put into effect.

From 7th January 1946, the Bromborough-Upton service (43) was extended along Saughall Massie Road to Overchurch Road, being renumbered 46, a supplementary peak hour service (14) being provided to and from Park Station. At the same time, the Crosville wartime service between Park Station and Overchurch Road was reinstated through to West Kirby. From the same date, hourly off-peak and half-hourly peak hour trips on the Woodside-Lower Bebington (50) service were extended to Clatterbridge hospital as No. 58, absorbing the special workers' journeys put into operation during the war. These buses traversed a clockwise loop formed by Clatterbridge Road, Mount Road and Brimstage Road; Clatterbridge Road was later stopped up during the construction of the M53 motorway.

From 1st May 1946, all the remaining suspended services were reinstated except the Rock Ferry-Port Sunlight (54) which had been relicensed as Tunnel Entrance-Port Sunlight, with peak hour journeys to and from Woodside, but it was never implemented. The route numbers of some services were changed, the Friday and Saturday New Ferry-Bromborough Pool Village (42) becoming 32 with some trips to and from Woodside as 34. The Woodside-Thurstaston via Greasby and Frankby service also returned with a 40-minute service and its number changed from 85 to 96, fitting in with other services in the 90s along Claughton Road and Tollemache Road.

The Circles

The Oxton and North Circles were, of course, long established and continued unchanged. However, new circular routes were devised in the post-war period, the first being the South Circle which commenced on 1st May 1946, though the name was not displayed on the buses for several years. It was not really a true circle, being a lengthy loop with a common section of route to and from Woodside. Its basis was the Woodside-Lever Causeway (84) service via Borough Road and Prenton Road West which was extended via Broadway, Kings Lane, Dacre Hill, Rock Lane West, Highfield Road, Rock Ferry Station, New Ferry, Bebington Road, Old Chester Road, Town Lane and Kings Road then by the reverse of the outward route to Woodside. The full journey occupied 58 minutes and buses ran every 40 minutes in each direction, showing the numbers 85 clockwise and 86 anti-clockwise. Bebington Corporation had pressed for improved internal links and this was a convenient way of supplying them. The Mount Road estate, west of Borough Road, was developed during 1948 and a peak hour service between Woodside and the top of Thornton Road (Lever Causeway) via Mount Road was provided by a new service 84 from January 1949.

In June 1947, the somewhat fanciful 'Prenton and Park Station Circle' commenced as an extension of the Haymarket-Birch Road 'shopping service' 79. From Woodside it ran via Grange Road, Oxton Road, Woodchurch Road, Storeton Road then broke new ground via Rose Mount, Christchurch Road, Slatey Road, Park Road South, Ashville Road (through Birkenhead Park), Park Station, Duke Street and Price Street to Woodside. It was the first ever service to cross Birkenhead Park and the first to use Price Street since horse trams stopped using it in 1881. It was also the first motor bus service to penetrate Oxton village since the short-lived Mersey Railway service of 1906. By a quirk of history, the district which had been a focal point of the horse-buses, had been unserved for over 40 years.

As all the route numbers in the seventies were in use, the choice of a number for the anti-clockwise direction presented some difficulty and eventually the physical reverse of 79 was

An early post-war view of the open parking area behind Laird Street depot showing the variety of buses then in service ranging from 184 of 1933 to 320 of 1943.   *T.G.Turner collection*

No. 216 was photographed in Town Lane on the South Circle No.85 service in May 1949, three months
before withdrawal. *T.G.Turner*

chosen - 97. A 20-minute frequency was given in each direction but as buses in both directions
departed from Woodside simultaneously, passengers for Oxton village still had only a 20-minute
service and, furthermore, the buses passed each other in the narrow streets of the village. After
five weeks' operation, the times of the 97 were advanced by 10-minutes to give alternate
departures in each direction.

This was the kind of service beloved by councillors determined to provide direct intersuburban
links where no sustained demand existed. It had no hope of being remunerative and, from
November 1947, it was redesignated the 'Prenton and Oxton Village Circle' and diverted at the
foot of Slatey Road to run via Park Roads South and East and Conway Street back to Woodside.
At the same time, it was rerouted along Borough Road and Whetstone Lane instead of Grange
Road in the clockwise direction from 5.10pm to the finish for the convenience of passengers
arriving at Central Station. This not only cut out the unremunerative Park section but shortened
the journey time so that three buses were needed instead of four. However, after a further four
months' trial, it was cut back to run between Woodside and Birch Road on weekdays only with
no service after about 7.0pm. Throughout these upheavals, the 79 had become a double-deck
route not because of the need for greater capacity but because of a shortage of single-deck buses.
Only three of the 1930 Lions survived the war and these were in such a precarious mechanical
condition that, on occasions, none was available for service. As the 44 service between St. Paul's
Road and Eastham Ferry needed a single-deck bus because of the low bridge at Trafalgar, there

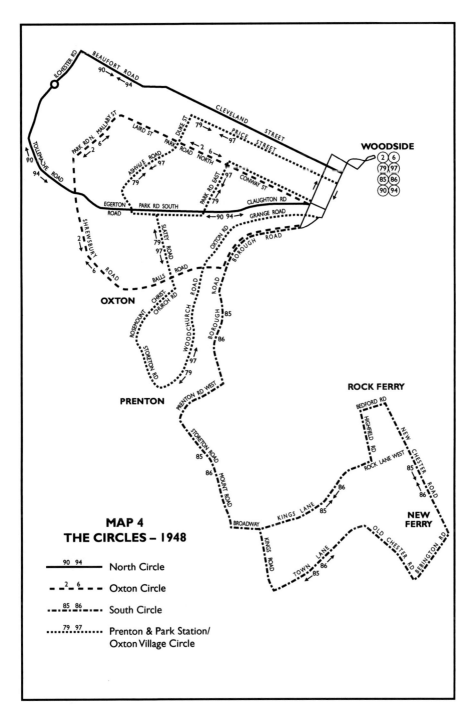

ILCHESTER RD
BEAUFORT ROAD
90
94
CLEVELAND STREET
PRICE STREET
LAIRD ST
DUKE ST
79
PARK RD N. MALLABY ST
2 6
PARK ROAD
2
97
TOLLEMACHE ROAD
90
94
ASHVILLE ROAD
97
79
PARK ROAD NORTH
2
6
97
CONWAY ST

WOODSIDE

(2)(6)
(79)(97)
(85)(86)
(90)(94)

PARK RD EAST
79
EGERTON ROAD
PARK RD SOUTH
CLAUGHTON RD
90 94
GRANGE ROAD
SHREWSBURY ROAD
2
6
SLATEY ROAD
79
97
OXTON RD
BOROUGH ROAD
BALLS ROAD

OXTON

ROSEMOUNT
CHRIST CHURCH RD
WOODCHURCH ROAD
BOROUGH ROAD
85
86
STONETON RD
97
79

PRENTON

PRENTON RD WEST
STONETON ROAD
85
86
MOUNT ROAD
BROADWAY
KINGS LANE
85
KINGS ROAD
TOWN LANE
86
85

ROCK FERRY

BEDFORD RD
HIGHFIELD RD
ROCK LANE WEST
NEW CHESTER ROAD
85
86
86

NEW FERRY

OLD CHESTER RD
BEBINGTON RD

MAP 4
THE CIRCLES – 1948

90 94 ———	North Circle
2 6 – – –	Oxton Circle
85 86 –·–·–	South Circle
79 97 ·········	Prenton & Park Station/ Oxton Village Circle

were occasions when it could not be run over the correct route, the double-deck bus running direct via New Chester Road between New Ferry and Bromborough. Spital Road, between Spital Cross Roads and Bromborough Road was not made suitable for buses until 1965.

Cross Docks Services

New Brighton was a popular venue for Birkenhead people and heavy duplication was required on the sole direct service, No. 10 from New Ferry via Old Chester Road, Chester Street, Bridge Street and Cleveland Street. The arrangement with Wallasey Corporation was that Birkenhead would provide the duplication required for traffic to New Brighton and Wallasey would take the people home. In practice, there was usually a mix of the two Corporations' buses, extra trips running to and from St. Paul's Road, Rock Ferry and Central Station. In 1946, there were talks with Wallasey about extending the scope of the cross-docks services to give direct facilities to and from New Brighton from a wider area of Birkenhead and Bebington. Wallasey wanted facilities to get its people into the Wirral countryside and a strategy was sought whereby both objectives could be achieved economically.

From 1st June 1947 two new services commenced daily operation for a three-month trial period. The first was an extension of the existing Charing Cross-Liscard joint service (11) at both ends to run between Higher Tranmere (The Wiend, Thornton Road) via Woodchurch Lane, Half Way House, Woodchurch Road, Oxton Road then over the existing route to Liscard. The extension to

Twenty Massey bodied Leyland PDIs, similar to those received in 1946-47, joined the fleet at the end of 1948 (Nos. 126-40, ACM 301-20); they were the last to be delivered with rear bumpers, these being removed from all buses in 1954 when the law required rear reflectors to be fitted. Nos. 126 and 133 await their next duties at Woodside in October 1961.   *T.G. Turner*

No. 119 stands at Thornton Road terminus on the joint route with Wallasey Corporation to New Brighton in May 1948. Note the rather ornate pre-war maroon and cream bus stop sign still in use.

T.H. Davies

New Brighton followed a different route from the No. 10 service. This service ran every 20 minutes and was augmented at busy times by an intermediate service between Charing Cross and Liscard. This new venture was an immediate success, providing not only for New Brighton traffic but giving new internal facilities within each town. Before the three-month experimental period was up, it was decided to run it until the end of October, a decision which was changed to daily operation to the same timetable throughout the year.

The second new service (No. 18) ran between New Brighton and Arrowe Park, following the Promenade, Sandcliffe Road, Belvidere Road, Poulton Bridge, St. James' Church, Tollemache Road, Ford Hill and Upton to Arrowe Park. The 40-minute frequency, requiring one bus of each Corporation, gave a direct service between the North End housing estates and New Brighton and enabled Wallasey people to reach the Wirral countryside without a change of bus. This, too, was a great success and it was decided to continue it until October and then on Saturdays and Sundays through the winter. This was the first regular service to use Poulton Bridge and it is of interest to note that Birkenhead declined to use the number 13, which was the obvious choice, being a vacant number in both operators' series and the number proposed for the abortive Central Station-Harrison Drive service planned in 1937. Several Birkenhead buses still had 'via Poulton Bridge 13' on their side destination blinds but Wallasey was put to the trouble of renumbering its existing route 18 to appease Birkenhead's superstitions. The extension of route 11 marked the end of the long-standing arrangement whereby 11 and 12 were worked by each operator on alternate weeks and thereafter buses of both Corporations appeared on each service daily.

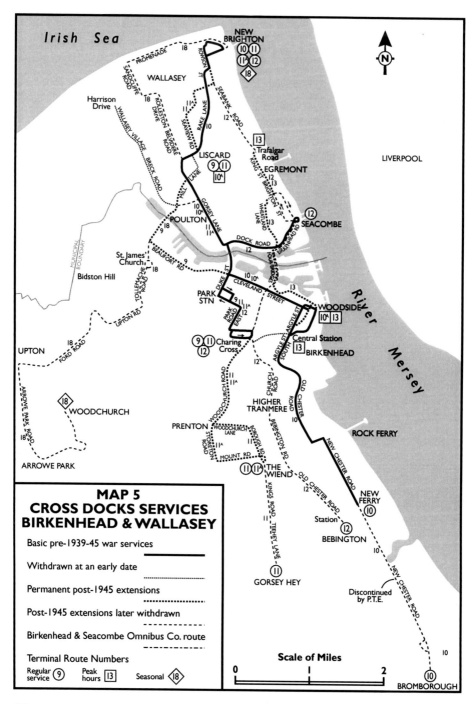

Irish Sea

NEW BRIGHTON
⑩ ⑪
⑪ ⑫
◈18◈

WALLASEY

PROMENADE 18
SANDCLIFFE ROAD
Harrison Drive 18
ROLLESTON BELMORE DRIVE ROAD
RONSON ST
WALLASEY VILLAGE
BRECK ROAD
WALLASEY BOUNDARY ROAD
SEAVIEW RD
MILL LANE
RAKE LANE 11
SEABANK ROAD
12
10

LIVERPOOL

LISCARD
⑨⑪
10ᴬ

⒔ Trafalgar Road
EGREMONT
KING ST BRIGHTON ST
WHEATLAND LANE
12
⒔

MUNICIPAL BOUNDARY

POULTON
18 9
11
GORSEY LANE
10 10ᴬ

St. James' Church
BEAUFORT RD
18

Bidston Hill

⑫ SEACOMBE
BIRKENHEAD RD
DOCK ROAD 12

River Mersey

TOLLEMACHE ROAD
UPTON RD

UPTON
18
FORD ROAD

ARROWE PARK ROAD
18

◈18◈ WOODCHURCH

PARK STN
9 11ᴬ
PARK ROAD EAST
DUKE ST
CLEVELAND STREET
10 10ᴬ
12
⒔
ARGYLE ST
SOUTH ARGYLE ST

WOODSIDE
10ᴬ ⒔

Central Station ⒔ BIRKENHEAD

⑨⑪ Charing Cross
⑫
12ᴬ

WOODCHURCH ROAD
11 11ᴬ

HIGH TRANCH ROAD
OLD CHESTER ROAD
10

ROCK FERRY

PRENTON
WOODCHURCH LANE
STORETON ROAD
11ᴬ
BOROUGH RD
MOUNT RD
11

HIGHER TRANMERE
BEBINGTON RD

⑪⑪ᴬ THE WIEND
12ᴬ
OLD CHESTER ROAD

NEW CHESTER ROAD

NEW FERRY ⑩

KINGS ROAD
TEEHEY LANE
11

Station
⑫ BEBINGTON
10

Discontinued by P.T.E.
NEW CHESTER ROAD

ARROWE PARK

⑪ GORSEY HEY

MAP 5
CROSS DOCKS SERVICES
BIRKENHEAD & WALLASEY

Basic pre-1939-45 war services ━━━━━

Withdrawn at an early date ·············

Permanent post-1945 extensions ▪▪▪▪▪▪▪

Post-1945 extensions later withdrawn ----

Birkenhead & Seacombe Omnibus Co. route ——

Terminal Route Numbers

Regular service ⑨   Peak hours ⒔   Seasonal ◈18◈

Scale of Miles
0   1   2

10
⑩ BROMBOROUGH

In April 1948 further developments to the joint services were proposed including the southward extension of No. 10 from New Ferry to Bromborough Cross and No. 11 from The Wiend to Gorsey Hey, Higher Bebington. It was also proposed to extend route 12, Seacombe - Charing Cross, at both ends to form a new through service between New Brighton and Bebington Station. Wallasey saw an opportunity to eliminate some loss-making mileage on their No.5, Seacombe-New Brighton Station service and proposed that the extension from Seacombe to New Brighton should be over this route, via Penkett Road, Mount Road and Albion Street. The territorial divisions on this route were as follows:-

	Miles	**%**
New Brighton - Seacombe via route 5	3.011	35.37
Seacombe - Charing Cross	2.653	31.16
Charing Cross - Bebington Station	2.850	33.47
Total	8.514	100.00

Revenue was shared equally on the Seacombe-Charing Cross route, the exact proportions being Birkenhead 49.05%, Wallasey 50.95% and it was proposed that this should continue.

Birkenhead saw the extension of the 12 to New Brighton as an extra means of getting trippers to the seaside and saw through the ruse to prop up Wallasey's ailing route 5. They refused to accept

Thirty new buses entered service in 1950, 15 Daimlers (Nos. 176-90, ABG 176-90) and 15 Guys (Nos. 191-205, ABG 291-305). They were identical to the 1949 deliveries but they introduced a change of livery style, the lower saloon window surrounds being painted cream and new style Gill Sans lettering was also used. Daimler 188 passes through the Haymarket on a route 10 short working on a rainy day in September 1962.   R.L. Wilson

the indirect route, insisting that the extension be made by the direct route along Seabank Road, Wallasey's route 1, and this was eventually conceded. These extensions came into force on 30th May 1949, alternate buses on route 10 also going through to Bromborough Cross. The extended 11 now commenced at 7.40am instead of 10.0am and was diverted slightly in Wallasey via Poulton Road and Mill Lane though the alternate short journeys between Liscard and Charing Cross continued to follow the old route via Oxton Road and Woodstock Road.

An amendment to the agreement governing the apportionment of revenue on route 10 was proposed to take effect from 1st April 1949 but was delayed until 1st September. The deduction of 10d per mile for operating costs was abolished and the revenue divided 59% to Birkenhead and 41% to Wallasey.

Bridge Delays

From their inception, the cross docks services had been disrupted by the raising of Duke Street Bridge to allow the passage of shipping. In the early days when there was no workmen's traffic and people were not always in a hurry, this was not particularly important, but during the war and just after, when thousands of workers were being conveyed from Wallasey into Birkenhead, these delays had serious consequences. Wallasey Corporation dealt with the morning peak hour traffic; in 1950, 23 buses were used, there being 20 peak hour trips to Central Station. A bridge delay on the first trip often meant that the second trip was not run at all. In the afternoon, Birkenhead supplied all but three of the extra buses needed.

These bridge closures were unpredictable and lengthy, delays of up to 40 minutes being common. The warning bells started ringing, the red stop lights came on and the gatemen closed the gates across the roadway. The bridge would then roll back on its bascules to allow shipping to pass. Further delays were caused by railway shunting. The main dock railway crossed Duke Street alongside Corporation Road, 200 yards on the Birkenhead side of the bridge and, even nearer to the bridge, wagons were moved on and off Rea's Jetty by rope and hydraulic capstan.

When the 11 and 12 were relatively short routes, their correction after a delay was a fairly simple matter, usually consisting of missing a complete round trip. On route 10, and ultimately on the extended 11 and 12, the delays were more disruptive and conflicting decisions made with the best intentions by regulators at different locations would often result in irregularities which took hours to sort out. At New Ferry when three buses arrived together it was common practice to load one to Liscard, one non-stop to the Tunnel Entrance via New Chester Road (thus making up about 10 minutes) and allow the third to follow the normal route. From 6th November 1950, Cammell Lairds' finishing time was changed from 5.0 to 4.30pm, spreading the afternoon peak for a time until other firms adopted earlier finishing times.

Following a series of meetings with the Dock Board and British Railways, it was agreed that the bridges would not be opened for barges only between 7.0 and 9.0am and that telephone advice would be given of delays whenever practicable. Wallasey Corporation agreed to station an inspector at the top of Gorsey Lane to divert buses via Poulton Bridge. This was the best arrangement that could be made. Much later, when motor traffic was greatly increased and the congestion created by waiting traffic itself became a problem, automatic warning boards were installed to warn drivers of the state of all three bridge crossings. By that time, use of the

Amongst the 1950 Guys was the prototype Massey metal-framed body, the most notable difference from the usual Massey design being the absence of curved end saloon windows. No. 201 is seen awaiting delivery in October 1950, five months after the rest of the batch.   *Massey Bros.*

Birkenhead docks by large ships had diminished and the bridge delays were less frequent and of shorter duration.

The first signs of retrenchment were apparent late in 1949 and from January 1950, the Bromborough and Gorsey Hey journeys on routes 10 and 11 were confined to weekday peak hours and summer Sundays. At the same time. route 12 reverted to Seacombe-Charing Cross, the Bebington Station journeys being run half-hourly only during the summer months, with an additional service between Bebington Station and Seacombe from approximately 2.30pm on Saturdays or 4.0pm on Mondays to Fridays until 6.0pm. After the 1950 summer season, the Sunday service to Gorsey Hey was curtailed at The Wiend. In June 1951 the short journeys on 11 between Liscard and Charing Cross were replaced by a new joint service 9 between the same points but running via Mill Lane, Poulton Bridge, Beaufort Road and Park Station. The Poulton Bridge suffered fewer delays from bridge closures and shunting so the route was popular on this account. The through journeys on 11 now reverted to the original route via Oxton Road and Woodstock Road.

With the passing of the post-war boom the New Brighton-Arrowe Park service was withdrawn altogether for the winter of 1951-52 and on its resumption for Easter 1952 it was extended a short distance beyond Arrowe Park to the entrance to the new Woodchurch housing estate at Ackers Road. The frequency now became every 45 minutes and a limited daily service in the afternoons

In 1951 the first 8ft. wide buses, permitted by new legislation, arrived (Leyland PD2/3 Nos.206-25, ABG 506-25). No. 212 poses in Birkenhead Park when new.   *T.G. Turner*

and evenings only was resumed in May. This service was extended through the estate to Orret's Meadow Road in July 1954. The Park Station-Arrowe Park weekend service (16) was extended to Landican Cemetery.

Disagreement with Wallasey

There was some disagreement between Birkenhead and Wallasey Corporations in 1947, when the latter wanted to extend its Moreton services along Pasture Road so that there would be a regular all day service to Moreton Shore, not only from Wallasey proper but also from Saughall Massie and points west of Moreton Cross. Pasture Road, which had been entirely within the County Borough of Wallasey since 1928, had been served by Birkenhead's buses since 1927 and Birkenhead's view was that a service of Wallasey buses along Pasture Road was unnecessary. In a letter to Wallasey's manager, W.R. Goodier, on 5th December 1947, Cherry said that Birkenhead ran up to 40 buses an hour to Moreton Shore at busy times though this argument was rather weak as, if such heavy duplication was necessary, it implied that there would be no room for local passengers in any case. Discussion dragged on and, in October 1948, Birkenhead suggested a restriction on the Wallasey buses, no passenger to be both picked up and set down between Moreton Schools and Leasowe Children's Hospital. A meeting between representatives of the two councils followed in which Wallasey agreed not to carry local passengers between Moreton Cross and the Shore and also allowed Birkenhead access to the housing estates at

Danger Lane and Town Meadow Lane for workmen's traffic. This was a rare, possibly unique, example of one municipal operator giving protection within its own boundary to another municipal operator.

Wallasey buses ran along Pasture Road from 30th May 1949. Birkenhead was granted a road service licence for a service (21B) between Market Place South and Bermuda Road (Town Meadow Lane) via Danger Lane, Pasture Avenue, Maryland Lane and Town Meadow Lane in June 1951. The route was listed in the time table and a fare list was published but, as far as can be ascertained, it was never run.

Thurstaston and Heswall

The Heswall via Irby (71) service was restored for the summer of 1946 with a frequency of 40 minutes, slightly better than pre-war. The pattern was generally a 20-minute frequency to Thurstaston with alternate buses extended to Heswall. However, as the relatively undeveloped and unremunerative section of the main road between Thurstaston and Heswall had had no evening buses during the war, it was given only a limited service in the evenings, provided by one bus shuttling between Arrowe Park and Heswall every 40 minutes, the main 20-minute service running between Woodside and Irby. From May 1949, a summer service (74) was inaugurated between Woodside and Thurstaston Shore on Saturdays and Sundays alternating every 40-minutes with the Heswall buses.

The five Ashcroft bodies supplied to Birkenhead Corporation are believed to have been the only bus bodies produced by the firm. They were very handsome with rounded end saloon windows and polished wood interior mouldings and served the town for 18 years. On a warm August day in 1957, No. 267 is seen fully loaded at Arrowe Park on the Heswall service. *R.L. Wilson*

When new the 1952 Guys continued the practice of carrying the rear registration number in a glazed panel on the lower cream band but these were later removed to the lower panel. Nos. 236 and 238 demonstrate the 'before' and 'after' styles in a busy scene at Charing Cross in April 1961.   *T.G. Turner*

The principal post-war residential development between Irby and Heswall was along Irby Road, the status of which had not been made clear in the Agreements between Birkenhead Corporation and Crosville. Its only bus route was a Crosville school service between Heswall and West Kirby. Consequently, when a regular bus service was needed, both operators claimed the right to run it. Eventually a compromise was reached, Birkenhead providing a service from Woodside to Heswall via Irby, Irby Road and Quarry Road while Crosville ran a local service between Heswall bus station and Somerset Road via Pensby Road and Irby Road. The new Corporation service was numbered 71A, the first example of the use of a letter suffix by the Corporation but there was no alternative as the available numbers were almost exhausted. From 4th June 1951, the Corporation ran a 20-minute service to Heswall, alternately via Thurstaston and via Irby Road, the evening service to Irby and the shuttle to Heswall being absorbed in the new timetable. Later the two operators were again to clash when a service was requested for Fishers Lane. At the same time the Corporation buses changed their inward route in the town centre to Hamilton Street, as used by Crosville, instead of Argyle Street.

Bebington and Bromborough

There was considerable housing development, both municipal and private, in Bebington and Bromborough in the post-war years. Municipal housing between New Chester Road and the railway was first penetrated from January 1948 by an extension of the trunk service 26 from Moreton, beyond Bromborough Cross to Acre Lane via The Rake and Ashfield Road.

Characteristically, the service was renumbered 28. As the housing extended northwards, there was a demand for further facilities which was met by diverting half of Acre Lane's 20-minute service along Palatine Road to Croft Avenue as 28A in 1954.

At the same time, the other trunk route 46 had been extended along the main road to Eastham Village, as route 42, alternate Sunday buses diverting at Upton to serve Arrowe Park instead of Overchurch Road as route 41. In January 1950 the 41/42 service was diverted via Allport Lane and Raeburn Avenue to Heygarth Road, augmenting the 38 service to Manor Road. The Arrowe Park service was withdrawn in January 1952 and, three months later, the whole service was curtailed at Bromborough Cross as 46 except at peak hours and after 12 noon on Saturdays. From the same day the 44 service was curtailed to run between New Ferry depot and Eastham Ferry enabling a regular hourly service to be given by one bus instead of an 80-minute frequency and this compensated to some extent for the withdrawal of the 42 off-peak. This service, which had traditionally started at 1.20pm from St. Paul's Road, had gained a morning service in 1947 with some short trips between Eastham Ferry and Bromborough Cross. The 44 did not run on Sundays but, in July 1948, the Corporation applied to the Licensing Authority to discontinue the summer Sunday service between Eastham Village and Eastham Ferry which was authorised on the Woodside and Eastham licence. This had never been advertised and it is not known to what extent it ran.

A works service to the Bromborough Power station site was commenced late in 1948. The industrial services in the Bromborough Port area became quite complex with special buses serving Fawcett Prestons and other works.

Two makes of chassis and three of bodywork made up the deliveries for 1955. Nos. 355-61 (DCM 975-81) were Guy Arab IV with Massey bodies; they introduced a slight livery change, the lower cream band being omitted and the name 'BIRKENHEAD TRANSPORT' being placed either side of the coat of arms. No. 355 is seen in Hamilton Square in March 1965.   *T.G. Turner*

There was a return to Guy for the 1952 order, the 59-seat bodies being supplied by East Lancashire, the first from this builder since the five wartime replacement bodies in 1942. The new buses (Nos. 226-40, BCM 926-40) were built to the now standard 8ft width; no offside route blinds were fitted, existing vehicles gradually having them panelled over. No. 239 is seen at Woodside.   *T. Lawson*

The Threat of Nationalisation

The Transport Act, 1947 authorised the nationalisation of all forms of transport and 'Area schemes' were envisaged for road passenger services. These were vigorously opposed even by Councils of a similar political hue to that of the government and certain restrictions were placed on the practice of making contributions to the Rate Fund as many undertakings proposed to transfer all their reserves to the Rate Fund rather than hand them over to some state board. In Birkenhead £16,560 was taken from the Reserves in 1946-47 in part funding of a record £68,600 contribution to the Rate Fund and the cost of new buses was partly met from revenue, the balance of the Reserve Fund being reduced to £27,461. A further £10,902 was taken in 1948-49 to help fund the final contribution to the rate fund of £15,000. Reserves were run down to nil in 1952-53 whereafter, with the threat of nationalisation gone following a change of government, they were built up in a responsible way. In bad times, undertakings might have to seek help from the Rate Fund. This never happened in Birkenhead but, in Wallasey, the ferries alone were costing the ratepayer 1/4d (6.6p) in the £ at one time. From 1937-38, in which year the trams ceased running, to 1949 when contributions ceased, the Rate Fund received £338,236 from profits made by the buses.

Interest on loans was a major item in the accounts of a municipal transport undertaking which would be carefully managed by the Borough Treasurer. The policy in immediate pre-war years was apparently to keep interest charges at about 30 per cent of the total outlay remaining in Capital Account. During the war, with plenty of cash being generated but nothing being paid out on renewals, this fell to a low of 9 per cent in 1944 and remained at 10 or 11 per cent until 1949-50 when the substantial intake of new buses took it up to 42 per cent, followed by a massive 48 per cent in 1950-51. By the late 'fifties, repayments were about 25 per cent, a level which was maintained consistently until 1967-68, though because of inflation, the actual amounts payable increased considerably. In the final full year, 1968-69, 20 per cent was paid.

The Birkenhead municipal transport department was a prosperous undertaking and even when in decline, was funded wholly from its own resources. Tables 1 and 2, following chapter 1, summarise the Appropriation and Capital accounts from 1937-38 (by which time the tramways influence was minimal) to 1968-69.

Higher Costs

During the war, although prices rose continually, shortage of materials, tyres and fuel kept total expenditure low. Basic wages remained the same but were augmented by 'war bonuses' which rose in accordance with increases in the cost of living. The theory was that when things returned

Birkenhead Central Station in the late 1950s with Borough Road running from left to right, Argyle Street in the foreground and Argyle Street South climbing up to Higher Tranmere in the background. Note the point duty policeman directing the traffic and the transport inspectors' hut on the small island. The buses on the left which are standing in Wilbraham Street are working short journeys, the one on the right showing No.67 being destined for Thornton Road, Higher Tranmere. Note the centre pillar in the rear platform windows, a feature of all Birkenhead buses of this era. The station buildings, dating from the opening of the Mersey Railway in 1886, are unaltered but this area is now dominated by a large roundabout and flyovers to the Mersey Tunnel and New Chester Road.. 		R.Tennant collection to normal after the war, these bonuses would be reduced or discontinued altogether. This reflected experience after the 1914-18 war when prices had fallen and wages were reduced. The trade unions, now much stronger, were determined to get these war bonuses consolidated before any reduction could be made. As events turned out, the post-1914-18 scenario was not repeated and prices continued to rise not fall. Wages for all grades rose virtually annually from 1949 as did the cost of everything used by a transport undertaking as the tables below demonstrate:-

Wages in the Post-1939-45 War Period
(converted to decimal coinage)

	31.3.39	31.3.47	31.3.50	31.3.51	31.3.52
Drivers	£3.40	£5.00	£5.38	£5.75	£6.30
Conductors	£3.20	£4.80	£5.18	£5.55	£6.05
Day Cleaners & Labourers	£2.80	£4.54	£4.92	£5.25	£5.63
Night Cleaners	£3.15	£4.98	£5.33	£5.65	£6.03
Mechanics	£3.92	£5.58	£6.23	£6.79	£7.02
Coach Builders & Painters etc	£4.11	£6.05	£6.23	£6.79	£7.02
Sheet Metal Workers	£4.02	£5.67	£6.23	£6.79	£7.02
Electricians	£4.06	£6.07	£6.23	£6.79	£7.02

Comparisons are affected by reductions in working hours from 47 or 48 to 44 in 1949-50

Overall Costs

	31.3.39	31.3.47	31.3.50	31.3.51	31.3.52
Traffic	£120,364	£205,049	£303,639	£298,249	£338,235
General Expenses	£18,556	£51,578	£40,678	£40,541	£39,812
Repairs and Maintenance	£35,873	£90,867	£99,652	£192,309	£106,565
Power Expenses	£46,974	£57,614	£69,660	£101,269	£123,753
TOTAL EXPENSES	£221,767	£405,108	£513,629	£632,368	£608,365
Capital cost of New Buses	£1,825		£3,655	£4,000	£4,000

To offset some of the additional costs, in 1946 a decision was made to allow advertising on bus exteriors, using the upper deck side panels and the lower rear. The 5-year contract was awarded to R Y Slaughter and Co., London. Shrewdly, the Transport department contracted to paint and maintain the initial advertisements at Slaughters' expense. In July 1946, No. 249 became the first bus to carry an advertisement. Revenue from advertising in 1946-47 was £6,439 including advertising on the backs of tickets.

Capital Projects

There were a number of capital projects which needed to be tackled without delay. Men were no longer prepared to work in dirty, cramped places and Laird Street depot was very much below current standards. Large numbers of buses were parked outside, creating late departure problems in the winter when they could not be started. In the 1947-48 financial year, work was completed on levelling and floodlighting the land behind the depot and 72 heating pipes were installed to keep radiators warm in the winter. Roof ventilators were fitted in the garages and numerous alterations made to the bodyshop and offices. These were interim measures pending the building of a garage extension but all kinds of bureaucratic obstruction hindered building work of any kind and it was not until 1956 that work started and 1959 before the garage extension was ready for occupation. It was 1962 before the new workshops were brought into use.

New Ferry depot's roof had been temporarily fixed following air raid damage and permanent repairs were effected during 1947-48; these, and some of the Laird Street costs, could be charged to the War Damage Commission. The head office exterior was painted in 1950 for the first time in 30 years!

New bus stop signs started to replace the old chocolate and cream boards in 1948. These were of a modern design with a BCT badge at the top of the pole and provision for the display of route numbers at the principal stopping places.

Good financial management made it possible for all these improvements to be paid for out of revenue.

A nostalgic view of vehicles of the 1-15 series entering New Ferry depot during the late night run in. The garage was built in 1932 on the site of the former tram depot and was closed as an economy measure in 1973. It was demolished and a post office and shops now occupy the New Chester Road site.

T.G. Turner collection

Higher Fares

Despite the enormous increases in costs, fares remained unchanged; the last adjustment had been a reduction in 1936. The withdrawal of unremunerative services during the war and the great increase in revenue on the other services had made this possible. The Labour government, losing popularity because of continued food and fuel rationing, shortages of almost everything and serious labour unrest, was determined to keep bus fares down, perhaps to gain support for its nationalisation plans. Fares, like all other aspects of bus services, could not be changed without the permission of the Traffic Commissioners (at that time known as the Licensing Authority for Public Service Vehicles) who would examine the financial position in the greatest detail and authorise only what was necessary to balance the books. Prudent operators who had historically created reserves for renewal of worn out fleets saw no reason for continuing the practice. Both Birkenhead and Wallasey Corporations formed sub-committees in 1950 to plan applications for increased fares and attempted to co-ordinate their policies. Details of these efforts are described in chapter 9.

7 – The Final Municipal Years

The 'fifties marked the start of the social changes which followed the spread of television and the growth of personal transport. The former kept people at home and deprived the buses of much of their evening traffic, leaving the Corporation with the need to continue running services until a late hour with greatly reduced patronage. Private transport was often, initially, a power-driven bicycle or motor-cycle which had a limited impact on bus travel. To the extent that it was used for work journeys, it relieved them of the provision of some very expensive facilities which under-utilised manpower and vehicles.

It was only when two wheels were exchanged for four that the inroads into bus patronage became serious as the effect on the off-peak operations was more apparent. In many cases, one member of a household would use the car for work trips but they all tended to use it for leisure pursuits. The peak requirement for the buses became sharper and a higher proportion of the manpower and assets was under-used. To these problems was added the increasing difficulty of attracting suitable labour to the buses in the face of competition from industries which offered a five-day week with regular hours, better pay and superior working conditions. This difficulty was to worsen with time and plagued the bus operators for almost thirty years.

The 'fifties and 'sixties were times of rising operating costs and falling receipts and the Transport Department was under constant pressure - from the Town Clerk and Borough Treasurer to effect economies, from militant trade unions who wanted higher wages and better working conditions

The Leyland PD2/12 body order was divided between East Lancashire (Nos.362-6, DCM 982-6) and Weymann (Nos. 367-71, DCM 987-91) whose rather austere Orion bodywork was fitted. East Lancashire bodied 365 is seen at Greasby on a short working of the 96 service in 1957. _R.L.Wilson_

No. 367 with Weymann Orion body was photographed at the since demolished Crosville Heswall bus station in March 1956. The Corporation paid £5 per year to use this terminus.   *R.L. Wilson*

and from pressure groups who wanted improved services and no fare increases. In late 1954, the forthcoming retirement of the Ferries manager presented an opportunity and the Council decided to combine the Ferries and Transport departments as 'Birkenhead Municipal Transport' under the control of the existing bus manager from 1st April 1955. The ferries undertaking was losing money but this was made good by the Mersey Tunnel Joint Committee. It was decided that some saving could be made by replacing the night ferry service by buses to be provided for alternate three-month periods by Birkenhead and Liverpool Corporations on hire to the Joint Committee. The fares of one shilling (5p) between midnight and 4.0am and 6d thereafter were to be collected at tunnel toll booths. The night ferry service operated for the last time on 13th May 1956 and at 12.10am on 14th, the first bus, provided by Birkenhead Corporation, left the Tunnel Entrance, Birkenhead for Liverpool, returning 10 minutes later. On the first night, 97 passengers were carried to Liverpool and 102 from Liverpool.

At the end of 1956, the fuel shortage caused by the Suez crisis led to some reductions in services. To some extent this was a blessing in disguise as it enabled the department to trim much unremunerative mileage, especially during the evenings and on Sundays and, in some instances, services were not fully restored when the fuel shortage ended in April 1957. Typical of the evening cuts were reductions in frequency from 10 or 15 minutes to 20 minutes; 20 minutes to 30 minutes and 40 minutes to an hour. But the 28/28A services were pruned back from Moreton to Hurrell Road in the evenings while the 46 service was cut back from Bromborough to New Ferry. The 51 (Claughton Village-Port Sunlight) service was cut back to Park Station except at peak hours and Saturday afternoons.

Time Recorders

The quality of some labour deteriorated as long-serving men left and there was a need to institute measures to control timekeeping. Time recording clocks were no new feature in Birkenhead; one, in Shrewsbury Road, had been sold by the Birkenhead Carriage Company to the Tramways Department in 1901. But they had not been used extensively as in Wallasey and many other towns. In the modern version, the conductor inserted his waybill and the time was stamped upon it. A system was devised whereby almost every route was covered though some were timed only in one direction. In most cases there were two clocks, one on each side of the road. The clocks were located at Durley Drive on Woodchurch Road (almost under the railway bridge), Kingsmead Road, Cemetery Gates (Tollemache Road), Tollemache Road (Shrewsbury Road), Park Station and Prenton Dell Shops. The only routes not controlled at all were those running direct along New Chester Road.

Housing Estates

Birkenhead's greatest post-war housing project was the Woodchurch estate, but its growth was phased in over several years, building work spreading gradually from south to north. The initial demand was absorbed by the main road services along Woodchurch Road but, in December 1952, when sufficient estate roads had been completed, a half-hourly all day service was provided to the eastern sector by extending the Prenton Dell Road (70) service to Grasswood Road via Ackers Road, Home Farm Road and New Hey Road; within six months it was extended to Orret's Meadow Road. A peak hour service had to be maintained to Prenton Dell Road which was now numbered 70A, the estate buses being restricted to passengers to Landican Lane and beyond on three trips during the main peak hours. One very early bus ran to Central Station via Storeton Road and Prenton Road West instead of Singleton Avenue.

No further extension of facilities was needed until May 1955 when another half-hourly service was run between Woodside and the western side of the estate, via Home Farm Road and Pemberton Road to Ferny Brow Road. No service was given on Monday to Friday mornings between 9.30 and 12.30pm or after 7.30pm. At peak hours and on Saturday afternoons the service along New Hey Road was augmented to give a combined 10-minute frequency. The Pemberton Road buses took the number 70A. No. 70B was allocated to occasional buses turning at Ackers Road and Prenton Dell Road became No. 75, the now less frequent Woodside-Arrowe Park buses thus numbered becoming 76. Departures from Woodside were not evenly spaced being at 5, 15, 35 and 45 minutes past each hour, the missing times being filled along Woodchurch Road by the Greasby buses (78). There were now nine restricted buses on Mondays to Fridays and four on Saturdays.

In March 1958, the 70A buses were extended a short distance to Hoole Road while in September 1959, the 70 service reached the corner of Houghton Road and Leeswood Road; these extensions marked the final development of the network under Birkenhead Corporation management. There were other developments on the south side of Woodchurch Road, some of the Prenton Dell (75) buses being diverted along Prenton Hall Road to Prenton Village Road, also in March 1958. It was June 1962 before this route got an all day service. This ran every 40 minutes, augmented at peak periods, taking the number 79. In the meantime certain of the 75 buses had been extended to Durley Drive and these continued to run at peak hours.

Fifteen Leyland PD2/40s with 59-seat Massey bodies (Nos. 1-15, FCM 991-8, FBG 909-15) entered service in 1957; No. 10 is preserved at the Birkenhead Bus and Tram Museum. No. 1 is seen when new at Central Station.   *R.L. Wilson*

Service 79 was an interim facility, pending the completion of roads in the area, and from 4th October 1965, the 79 and 80 (Prenton War Memorial) services were linked via Prenton Hall Road and Prenton Lane as the Prenton Circle, a 40-minute all day service (30-minutes Saturdays) being provided in each direction, with peak hour extras to and from Prenton Village Road via Woodchurch Road (79A) and Glenavon Road via Prenton Road West (80A). Most of the Durley Drive trips now ceased.

Other housing development was carried out by Bebington Corporation. Workmen's buses had been run, at first for building workers, into the new Mill Park estate at Eastham from about January 1954 as service 41 but no regular service was proposed until 1960 and this caused a major dispute between Birkenhead Corporation and Crosville. The latter maintained that as Mill Park was, technically, beyond Stanley Lane, it should be served by them. Furthermore, had Allport Lane been extended (which it later was as Bridle Road) they would be entitled to use it but the Corporation pointed to the clause in the 1930 Agreement which prevented Crosville running a service into Birkenhead which commenced in the Borough of Bebington. The Traffic Commissioners finally granted both applications and competitive services started on 17th October 1960. The 38 and 40 services were revised to give a service to Eastham Village via Allport Lane, Raeburn Avenue and Heygarth Road (39) and to Mill Park Estate via New Chester Road (41) with a combined off-peak frequency of 12-15 minutes. Crosville ran hourly as F7, giving a slightly faster service as they were restricted between Allport Road and Woodside. There was no means of co-ordinating a 24-minute Corporation service with an hourly Crosville service so there were times when two buses ran almost together. It was all very wasteful but continued until 1973.

East Lancashire supplied its final batch of bodies to the fleet in 1961, mounted on Leyland PD2/40 chassis (Nos.46-60, LCM 446-60). The attractive design was very similar to that provided for Guys 382-6 built in 1956. No. 55 is seen at the Thurstaston Church terminus of route 96 in October 1961. *R.L. Wilson*

From November 1964, the peak hour 42 service to Heygarth Road was diverted to the Brookhurst Estate via Allport Road, some of the supplementary 38 journeys to Manor Road being extended to Heygarth Road in replacement.

Economies

The afternoon peak hour extension of the Port Sunlight-Claughton Village service to Boundary Road (57) was abandoned in November 1953 when the service was diverted via Laird Street and Mallaby Street to facilitate crew reliefs being done outside the depot; the Upton-Bromborough service was similarly rerouted in May 1954. In 1953 the former 'shopping bus' (79) between Woodside and Birch Road was cut short at the Haymarket off peak, running as it had done in pre-war days. In 1962, when its number was appropriated for the Prenton Circle, it was renumbered 97.

Despite falling traffic, there were still some innovations. A new peak hour joint cross-docks service (13) between Central Station and Trafalgar Road, Egremont via the Four Bridges started in January 1955 and was soon established as a permanent feature of the network. This was the first municipal service to use the Four Bridges route on a permanent basis. On the other side of the coin, the peak hour extension of route 11 to Gorsey Hey, Higher Bebington was withdrawn in 1956. A new summer service (87) between New Ferry and Moreton Shore combined some of the features of the pre-war extended 16 and the Crosville New Ferry-Moreton Shore service which was never resumed after the war. It ran for three seasons, 1960-62, and in its last year gained some traffic in connection with an experimental hovercraft service between Moreton and

Rhyl. Crosville had agreed not to restore the New Ferry-Moreton Shore service in return for Birkenhead Corporation not objecting to local fares being charged between Moreton and Arrowe Park on a new Liscard-Parkgate service.

During the 'sixties, changes were made as much to save staff as to reflect the fall in passengers and some of the summer services such as 18 and 74 eventually faded out as staff could not be spared to man them. The extended summer service on 12 between Bebington Station and New Brighton was truncated at Higher Tranmere (top of Bebington Road) and run only at weekends from 1963 and abandoned altogether after the following season. Summer 1964 saw the extension of the 51 route beyond Claughton Village to Upton and Saughall Massie. It was a complicated arrangement with buses running to Park Station, Laird Street, Claughton Village, Upton or Overchurch Road at different times and almost all the local journeys to and from Park Station and the Upton direction were absorbed by the new arrangement. Initially there was an off peak service (56) between Park Station and Bebington Station but this was soon replaced by a modified timetable through to Port Sunlight.

The general manager, George Cherry, retired on 30th April 1964 after 22 years' service with the undertaking. His successor was Mr Frank S Brimelow who had started his career at Warrington and had held managerial positions at Middlesbrough, Stalybridge and Stockport.

Service frequencies were cut from 17th January 1966 in an exercise calculated to bring the supply more in line with the demand and to reduce the chronic staff shortage. By 1968, manpower resources were such as to make it impossible for new services to be introduced except

The new vehicles for 1962-63 were Leyland PD2/40s with a reversion to Massey for bodywork. Nos. 61-75, (MCM 961-75) entered service in 1962 and Nos. 76-90 (OCM 976-90) in 1963. No. 62 passes through the Haymarket in July 1962. *T.G. Turner*

at the expense of some existing facility. However, political pressure led to the commencement of a service between Park Station and Ford Estate (Sixth Avenue) via Upton Road from 1st July 1968. One bus ran four morning peak hour trips at 40-minute intervals with three afternoon trips, all on Mondays to Fridays only. The service was labelled as 'experimental' and carried the number 15A.

The residents of these estates so far from the town centre were to a large extent displaced from poor housing in the inner areas. While dispersal of this kind was most desirable socially, the economics of bus operation were not helped. The Transport Department thrived on high residential density as, although passengers in the inner areas paid a lower fare, the rate per mile was higher. The fare scales were tapered as part of municipal policy to make living in the new estates more affordable. Thus on the 15A service a passenger travelling from Park Station to Claughton Village travelled at the rate of 4.27d per mile, Noctorum Lane 3.20d, Warren Drive 2.87d and Sixth Avenue 2.51d. A combination of falling traffic and dispersal of the population caused the average passengers per mile figure to fall from 10.39 in 1951 to 8.72 in 1961 and 7.02 in 1969.

Unfortunately, the peak hour requirements were such that the fleet could not be reduced commensurately with the traffic, making operations more expensive all-round as the fixed costs had to be spread over a smaller number of miles. The reduction in efficiency caused by the concentration of lost traffic at off-peak times is indicated by the average miles run by each bus. In the peak post-war year, 1948-49, 220 buses averaged 34,758 miles; in 1966-67, 225 buses averaged 26,041 miles, a fall of 25 per cent.

Daimler Fleetline No. 105, in normal livery, is seen in Argyle Street in April 1969, followed by one of the first batch of Leyland Atlanteans.   *T.G. Turner*

Traffic Congestion Problems

The growth of road traffic caused serious congestion and delays to buses, particularly in the town centre where Mersey tunnel traffic tended to create massive traffic jams. The first one-way traffic scheme came into force on 1st September 1961 and some alterations were made to bus services a few days beforehand. Routes 71-74 could no longer run inward via Hamilton Street and they reverted to their former route via Argyle Street. Three years later they were again diverted via Grange Road in the morning peak in an effort to avoid the tunnel queues in Borough Road. To keep buses away from the tunnel entrance in the 1961 scheme, route 10 was diverted northbound via Argyle Street, Hamilton Square Station, Canning Street and Taylor Street and southbound via Canning Street and Hamilton Street. A peak hour service (10A) between Liscard and King's Square, Chester Street provided for industrial traffic and the 13 from Egremont was similarly rerouted. There were several other minor alterations.

Whilst these had some beneficial effects, the traffic problem continued to grow and the long term solution was to segregate the tunnel traffic so that its effect on town traffic was minimal. This involved the building of two flyovers, one from Conway Street and another from Borough Road and the creation of a huge reservoir to absorb vehicles waiting to pay tolls. In this exercise, the Haymarket, Market Place South and several other streets disappeared entirely. A further flyover connected Central Station and Chester Street.

The first rear-engined buses, Daimler Fleetlines fitted with Weymann Orion style 77-seat bodies (Nos.101-9, RCM 501-9) arrived in 1964. They appeared in a non-standard almost all-blue livery, believed to have been applied to speed up deliveries following factory delays. They were repainted into normal livery in 1968, considerably improving their appearance. The first to arrive, No. 103, is being inspected by drivers at Laird Street depot in August 1964.   *T.G. Turner*

Because of the need to demolish many buildings and realign roads, traffic in the town was disrupted during the two years needed to carry out these works. From about July 1967, the 10A and 13 services were curtailed at Bridge Street because St. Mary's Gate and adjoining side streets used for turning, were engulfed by road works. Then, at about 10.0am on 1st May 1968, all buses running from Woodside outward via Hamilton Street were diverted via Hinson Street into Argyle Street, the Haymarket, Grange Street and the eastern ends of both Borough Road and Conway Street being closed to all traffic. The flyovers were opened on 14th July 1969; none was immediately used by scheduled bus traffic though the relief to traffic congestion was beneficial to timekeeping on all services

Concessionary Fares

For many years, transport operators had been arguing that it was unjust that they should be expected to carry the burden of social cost involved in the provision of concessionary travel to elderly and blind people. When the facilities offered to these people had been very limited and the operators had been prosperous, there was no serious problem but the numbers of concessionary ticket holders was steadily increasing and the facilities were more widespread. Legislation was eventually passed by which the financial burden was borne by the general rate fund and the first contributions to transport department revenue were received in the 1964-65 financial year. Contributions for this part year totalled £4,571 and were paid not only by Birkenhead but also by Bebington, Hoylake and Wirral councils all of whose residents benefited from facilities on Birkenhead Corporation buses. In the full year 1967-68 the amount received was £45,949, 3.9% of total revenue.

One Man Operation

The elimination of conductors on lightly-trafficked routes was seen as a means of achieving a meaningful economy provided the premium rate paid to the drivers was kept under control. In Birkenhead, it was felt desirable to eliminate reversing of one-man buses, though this was not a legal requirement and it was practised extensively elsewhere. The prospect of one-man operated double-deck buses was unimaginable in those days, even though it was legalised in 1966.

The most obvious first choice in Birkenhead was the former 'shopping bus' (97) between Woodside and Storeton Road (Birch Road). To overcome the reversing problem, it was extended over a long loop via Rose Mount, Fairclough Lane, Village Road, Claughton Firs and Bennetts Hill, rejoining the outward route in Woodchurch Road. This brought buses back into Oxton Village after an interval of almost 17 years when it was put into effect on 12th April 1965, using Leyland Leopard single-deck buses (91-4) placed in service in 1964. The service ran to and from Woodside at peak hours, terminating at the Haymarket at other times until the road closures in May 1968 after which it ran from Woodside all day.

From 29th March 1967, the 44 route between New Ferry and Eastham Ferry no longer needed single-deck buses as, following the strengthening of Spital Road, it was diverted via Church Road and Spital Cross Roads, no longer passing under the low bridge in Bromborough Road. The extra running time was found by curtailing it on all but a few early morning trips, at Mayfield Drive where there was a reversal, thus disqualifying it as a candidate for one-man operation.

No. 93 is seen in Town Lane on the South Circle, carrying Merseyside PTE logo after removal of the rear route boxes.

J.Manly

There were, in fact, no further one-man routes for two years, when joint route 12 between Seacombe and Charing Cross was converted on 13th March 1967. With it went the last vestige of the extended route - the 7.6am trip from Bebington Station to Seacombe. As Wallasey Corporation had no suitable buses, the whole service was worked by Birkenhead, additional mileage being run by Wallasey on other joint routes to compensate. The service remained at every 40 minutes, doubled in peak hours and the running time from increased from 13 to 17 minutes. However, as in the case of the 97, the extra time was taken out of the layover.

Labour Problems

The undertaking had always enjoyed good labour relations having adopted the Agreement reached in 1919 between the Municipal Tramways Association, Tramways and Light Railways Association and the National Transport Workers' Federation which reduced working hours to 48 and introduced other improvements. There was a Whitley Council which dealt with disputes and changes in conditions. Except for the General Strike of 1926 there had been no strikes but the post-war years were notable for stormy industrial relations in many industries, and full employment and labour shortages created fertile grounds for indiscipline. Early in 1951, when the first signs of staff shortages were seen, the management began protracted negotiations with the Transport & General Workers' Union locally about the re-employment of women as conductors. The union was obdurate but the Corporation engaged nine women resulting in a strike which took most of the buses off the road for $3^1/_2$ days. The dispute was wholly unnecessary as by August 1952, there were 160 women working in the transport department.

In November 1965, in two separate awards, one for craft workers and another for drivers and conductors, the staff were granted a reduction of working hours from 44 to 40 per week, the cost to the department being £67,000 per annum. The road staff believed that they should have a five day week and went on strike on 20th/21st December 1965 while the claim was being negotiated. The negotiations continued after resumption of work and the net result was a great deal of inconvenience to the public and a loss of wages to the employees. In the past, services had been covered by overtime payments but in 1964-65, for the first time, scheduled mileage was not operated because of staff shortages.

The later months of 1967 were beset by very serious labour problems. There was unrest in all the municipal transport undertakings throughout the country but Birkenhead was one of the worst affected. Talks on wages, hours of work and holidays reached deadlock and in October, bans on overtime and standing passengers were applied. The undertaking was already so understaffed that the effects were immediate and services became erratic and completely unreliable. A strike of drivers and conductors broke out about midday on 10th November, crews taking their buses back to the depots as word spread. Despite local, regional and national talks, it dragged on and any public sympathy which there may have been for the men soon evaporated as one offer after another was rejected. Eight other widely spread undertakings - Caerphilly, Cardiff, Colchester, Luton, Middlesbrough, Nottingham, Southend and West Bridgford - were affected simultaneously and others, including Wallasey, for shorter periods. Public anger mounted when, first, Wallasey men went back to work on 16th December and the dispute was declared over on 23rd but the Birkenhead drivers and conductors decided to take Christmas off and return on 28th, the last to go back in the whole country. Engineering staff worked normally during the strike, ensuring that the fleet was better maintained than usual.

The Leopards had standard route displays at the rear but these were removed by Merseyside PTE in 1971. No. 94 is seen inside Laird Street depot in 1969. *T.G. Turner*

Traders were understandably alarmed that the absence of buses would have a devastating effect on Christmas shopping and eventually hired coaches and provided free services on Wednesdays and Fridays commencing on 6th December. The seven routes listed below employed 11 vehicles on half-hourly services to and from Charing Cross. All were luxury coaches hired from outside the town.

1	Woodchurch Estate
2	Prenton Dell
3	Higher Tranmere (The Wiend), calling at St. Catherine's Hospital.
4	Brackenwood (Gorsey Hey) via Kings Road & Borough Road
5	Bebington Station (calling at Dacre Hill)
6	St. James' Church via Tollemache Road
7	Moreton Road (Royde Road) (calling at Upton & Pool Lane, Woodchurch)

According to press reports, 14,000 passengers were carried on the first two days.

During the strike, Crosville crews refused to carry standing passengers and imposed extra restrictions on local passengers, arbitrarily fixing a first setting down point at Sparks Lane, Thingwall instead of Landican Cemetery and similarly on other routes.

When the buses started to run again after six weeks, the staff situation was worse than ever as large numbers of men, unable to stand the financial consequences, had left the department to take up jobs elsewhere. Passenger loss earlier in the year had been at the much reduced rate of 2.6%

In sharp contrast to the curvaceous design of their double-deck bodies, those supplied for Leyland Leopard L1 single-deck chassis in 1964 were box-like and angular in appearance. The arrival of these buses (Nos. 91-94, RCM 491-4) allowed the four 1948 Leyland PS1s to be withdrawn. No. 93 is preserved at the Birkenhead Bus and Tram Museum. No. 92 is seen passing road works at Central Station in July 1969.   T.G. Turner

but on resumption of services the level was 17% though this had reduced to 10.2% by March 1968 by which time the staff shortage was 17.5%. Skilled fitters were impossible to recruit. The strike was a major factor in the permanent loss of passengers, 212,022 fewer passengers (15%) being carried in 1967-68 than in 1966-67.

The agreements which followed the end of the municipal bus strikes cleared the way for further one-man operation including double-deck buses though there was serious doubts about the practicability of this at the time. With only four single-deck buses in the fleet, Birkenhead's options were severely limited.

The South Circle (85-86) became one-man operated on Sundays from 20th January 1969 to enable the rosters to be simplified as the 97 did not run on Sundays. This was the only day when there was a full service on the South Circle as it had been reduced to a peak hour service on weekdays since 26th June 1967. This had provoked some complaints from residents of the Mount Road estate, resulting in alternate journeys on the 11 being run from The Wiend via Mount Road and Storeton Road instead of Borough Road and Woodchurch Lane from 2nd October 1967. These buses showed 11A; no Wallasey buses ran on these times.

Finally, in the last month of Birkenhead Municipal Transport's existence, the first one-man double-deck buses took over the Oxton Circle (2 & 6) using fare-boxes and a flat fare of 6d for any distance, no tickets being issued. Dual entrance Leyland Atlanteans were employed, passengers alighting by the centre door.

Further batches of Massey-bodied Leyland PD2/40s followed in 1959 (Nos. 16-30, HCM 516-30) and 1960 (Nos. 31-45 JBG 531-45). No. 20 was the first bus in the fleet to be painted in the Merseyside Passenger Transport Executive blue-cream-blue livery in April 1970 and is seen soon afterwards at Woodside.

T.G. Turner

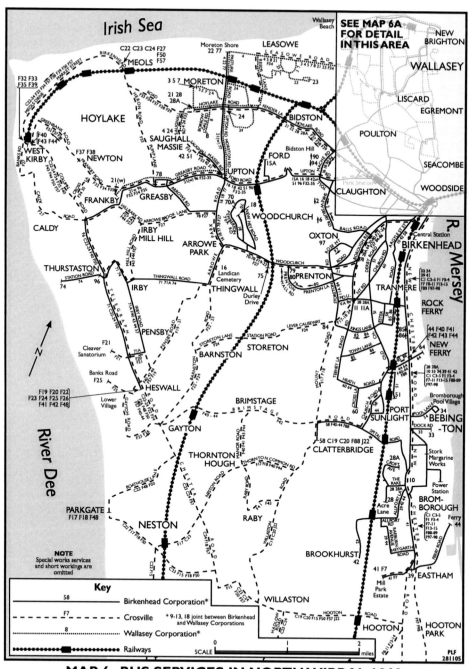

MAP 6 : BUS SERVICES IN NORTH WIRRAL 1969

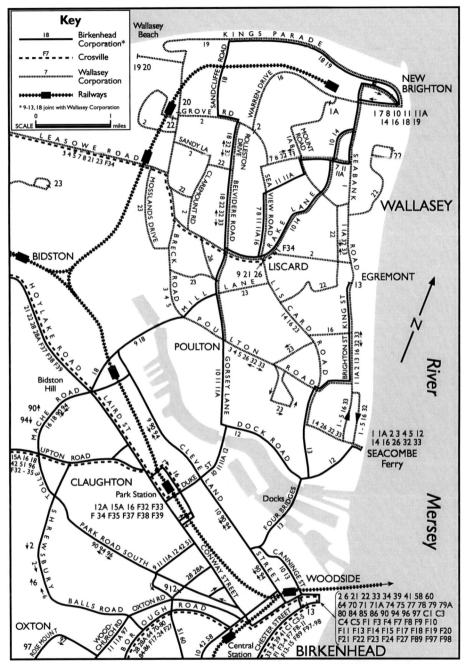

MAP 6A : BUS SERVICES IN NORTH WIRRAL 1969

8 – Wartime & Post-War Buses

At the outbreak of war, there were about 40 double-deck and six single-deck buses, dating from 1930-32, which would normally have been withdrawn within the next year or so. Initially, the vehicle requirement was greatly reduced and several of the older buses were delicensed and put into mothballs. However, in June 1940, Crosville was crying out for buses to meet new demands as many new industries had been moved into North Wales which was considered to be safe from enemy attack. Nine 1930 TD1s and the AEC 'Q' were licensed and went on loan until October when Birkenhead found that it needed them to cover the increased demands of industry. On its return, the 'Q' was sold and went on to have a second life with an Oxfordshire operator, T. Worth of Enstone, who collected second-hand Qs, and ran it for nine years, two years longer than in Birkenhead.

Of the six single-deck Leyland Lions, four (127, 129-31) were converted to 'perimeter seating' whereby the seats were rearranged around the sides of the bus and extra handrails were installed down the centre. Thirty passengers were allowed to stand but the extra weight did the bodies no good at all. No. 126 was converted to an emergency ambulance and 128 was badly damaged in

No photographs are known of London Transport vehicles running in Birkenhead during the war but one of the six, ST866 (GJ 2042), a 1930 AEC Regent, new to Thomas Tilling Ltd., was pictured on a Derby Day special after the end of the war. When running in Birkenhead the windows were covered with anti-blast netting and the headlamps were masked but otherwise the bus was unchanged.

an air raid in 1941, the remains being sold to the Fire Service. No. 127 broke down irrevocably in 1944 and remained parked in the depot until sold for scrap in 1946. Titan No. 168 was burnt out on 12th March 1940 and never ran again. This reduced the fleet to 181. Birkenhead's worst air raids were on 12-14th March 1941. A direct hit on Laird Street depot damaged 140 buses, many of them seriously. Broken windows were replaced by plywood to get buses back on the road quickly and a number of Wallasey Corporation Leyland Titan TD2s which had been officially withdrawn in July 1940 but had been kept for emergency use, were used on the cross-docks services with Birkenhead crews for a few days. Another bus (244) was destroyed by fire in September 1941.

The destruction caused by the air raids reduced demand for a few months but the air raids ended in January 1942 and the shortage of buses was hampering the provision of essential services. A number of London Transport AEC Regents were available for hire to provincial operators and six were loaned to Birkenhead Corporation from December 1941, being returned between November 1943 and April 1944. These were petrol-engined vehicles, dating from 1930-31, with open staircases and protruding cabs, having been taken over from Thomas Tilling Ltd. when the London Passenger Transport Board was formed in 1933. To local eyes, the design was most antiquated, reflecting the ultra-conservatism of the Metropolitan Police in matters of bus design. The destination equipment consisted of a box for a roller-blind front and rear, designed to be used with a board displaying the intermediate points served. In Birkenhead, side route blinds were fitted in these boxes. They were used mainly on the North Circle and Woodside-Moreton services displaying 'via Claughton Rd 90', 'via Cleveland St 94' or 'via Park Station 21 (or 22)'.

As mentioned earlier, in an effort to reduce the consumption of petrol, all of which had to be imported in those days, the government ordered all bus operators with fleets of 100 or more buses to convert 10 per cent of their fleets to producer gas propulsion. The gas was produced from anthracite in equipment mounted on a two-wheel trailer towed behind the bus and the power output was such that buses had to be confined to routes with as few gradients as possible. A switch enabled a small quantity of petrol to be used for starting up. Most operators managed to find excuses for dragging their feet and Birkenhead was no exception. Of the 18 vehicles due to be converted, only nine were done, the first entering service in February 1943. As torque-converter vehicles had been found unsuitable, all the vehicles converted were old. In September 1944, with a change in the fortunes of war, the government cancelled the scheme and all were withdrawn on 30th September 1944, only two (164 and 167), which ran until May 1947, being converted back to run on petrol. The power output was low; it was a struggle to get up the hill from Woodside and climbing Whetstone Lane would have been impossible. For this reason, they were used on the flattest routes, mainly routes 12, Seacombe-Charing Cross, 21-22, Woodside-Moreton and, occasionally, 26 Bromborough-Moreton, though the climb up Bedford Road was a severe trial.

The Ministry of Supply issued licences for the Corporation to have the badly damaged buses repaired. The bodies of seven were extensively rebuilt by Massey and the other seven had completely new bodies fitted, five by East Lancashire Coachbuilders of Blackburn and two by Massey. These new bodies were to a high standard, not of utility specification, and one wonders how this was done at a time of such strict controls. All this work was carried out in 1942.

The Utility Guys

During the 1939-45 war, the Ministry of Supply strictly controlled the manufacture of new buses and allocation was made on the recommendation of the Regional Transport Commissioner who based his decisions on the wartime needs of each particular undertaking. Leyland Motors production line was turning out tanks and only Guy and Daimler double-deck buses were obtainable. Most were powered by the well-tried Gardner diesel engine, though there was no experience of this in Birkenhead. For normal conditions, the 5-cylinder 5LW engine, with a capacity of just under 7 litres, was fitted; only operators with hilly routes qualified for the 6-cylinder 6LW engine.

Bodies were built to the Ministry's 'utility' specification by various bodybuilders, Birkenhead's main supplier, Massey Bros., being one of these, but the operator had no say in what would be allocated. Features of the specification were single skin construction, wooden slatted seats, only one opening window on each side of each deck, no side or rear destination equipment and angles instead of domes for the roof to enable unskilled labour to be employed. Many had unglazed rear emergency 'windows' but Birkenhead managed to avoid this feature.

Birkenhead was allocated 24 utility Guy Arab 5LW buses which arrived piecemeal during 1943-44. All seated 56, 30 upstairs and 26 inside, which was the wartime standard for highbridge

September 1943 saw the arrival of the first utility buses, Weymann-bodied 5LW Guy Arabs (Nos. 319-320 BG 8552-3). They were basic wartime buses with wooden slatted seats and finished in all over grey, though with the usual lettering and including, for the first time, the town coat of arms on the upper deck panels. Normal Birkenhead destination equipment was fitted at the front only. Painting in normal blue and cream livery began in April 1944 and from 1945, upholstered seats were fitted. No. 319 is seen at Woodside after repainting.   *T.G. Turner collection*

During accident damage repairs in 1947, the opportunity was taken to fit No. 341 with rear destination boxes taken from the body of 217 which was being scrapped. The attractive moquette seats from the same source were also fitted. The improved 341 is seen at Woodside in April 1948. *T.G. Turner*

vehicles. There were detail differences as three bodybuilders were involved and each interpreted the specification slightly differently. Nos. 319-20 were by Weymann, 321-38 by Massey and 339-42 by Park Royal. Although the specification provided for one large front destination indicator, Birkenhead's vehicles had the normal display, but to the front only. It is possible that they were modified at Birkenhead before entering service, using equipment salvaged from scrapped vehicles. Furthermore, in 1945, the Transport department managed to find the resources to fit upholstered seats at a cost of £100 per bus, 338 being the first bus so treated. All the wartime Guys were delivered in battleship grey and the Weymann and Massey-bodied buses were complete with the usual transfers; Birkenhead somehow managed to find the paint to apply the normal livery after a few months.

A further batch of 12 Guy Arab 5LWs were delivered in January and February 1946, the body order being divided between Park Royal (343-50) and Northern Counties (351-4), the latter being of all-metal construction. The war was now over and the bodies were finished to a 'relaxed' specification with rounded domes, upholstered seats and full destination equipment, though the Park Royals lacked an offside route indicator. They arrived painted blue though Northern Counties used the wrong shade, producing a darker finish not unlike that of Rochdale; they were repainted in the correct colour in May 1947. No. 351 had straight lower panels but those of 352-4 were outswept. Later, 343-50 had their half-drop windows replaced by sliders.

The Gardner engine was rugged and reliable and demonstrated in Birkenhead a viable alternative to the hitherto all-conquering Leyland. This wartime experience was to have a significant effect on future vehicle policy.

The Post-War Leylands

In the immediate post-war years, there was a desperate shortage of new buses as all fleets were in arrears with replacements. Birkenhead did better than most, having placed orders long before the war ended and, despite their love affair with the Gardner engine, the transport department reverted to Leylands. The first batch of Leyland PD1s outwardly resembled the last pre-war buses, having Massey bodies of very similar appearance, though the interior decor was less extravagant. The main differences were the large radiator, sliding instead of half-drop windows and the fitting of saloon heaters, the first in Birkenhead, and a feature which received very favourable comment in the local press at the time. They were fitted with the Leyland 7.4 litre E181 engine and constant-mesh gearboxes which produced a distinctive whine; they entered service between October and December 1946.

It had been intended to number them 355-66 but, at the last minute, it was decided to go back to 101, perhaps to signify the start of a new era, so they came as 101-12. This was an unfortunate decision as later there was a muddle when numbers 'caught up' with those of buses still in service. Perhaps numbers from 401 up would have been a wiser choice. Rear bumpers were fitted, as in pre-war days to buses 208-318. They were followed, between May and August 1947, by a further batch of 13 identical buses (113-25) though, for an unknown reason, the registration numbers were not in sequence. A third similar batch of 20 (126-45) came late in 1948 and were the last to have rear bumpers; these were removed from the fleet in 1954 when regulations governing rear reflectors came into force.

The first post-war buses built to full peacetime specification were 12 Leyland Titan PD1s (Nos. 101-12, BG 9221-32) with Massey bodies of similar outline to the TD5s of 1939. They were the first to be equipped with saloon heaters and began entering service towards the end of 1946. No. 105 is preserved at the Birkenhead Bus and Tram Museum. Further identical vehicles followed in summer 1947 (Nos. 113-25, BG 9531-36 & BG 9672-78, not in sequence). No. 117 is seen passing Central Station in 1960. The practice of moving the front registration number plate from the radiator to the cab dash commenced in 1957.
T.G. Turner

Only the 44 route between St.Paul's Road and Eastham Ferry, which passed beneath the low bridge in Bromborough Road, Lower Bebington required single-deck buses and the last remaining Leyland Lions, which were also the last petrol-engined buses in the fleet, were withdrawn in June 1948 with the arrival of four Leyland Tiger PS1s (Nos.97-100, ACM 106-9) with Massey 33-seat rear entrance bodies. They were the first single-deck buses in Birkenhead to be fitted with rear destination equipment. Due to an error in the motor taxation office ACM 106 was also issued to a motor cycle so No. 97 was reregistered ACM 194 before entering service. It is seen in Birkenhead Park when new in this posed photograph, still showing its original registration number.

Outstanding orders were completed by the delivery, in June 1948, of four Leyland PS1 33-seat single-deck buses with rear-entrance Massey bodies. They had a full destination and route number display to the rear, a feature never carried by previous single-deck buses. They were numbered 97-100, commencing a tradition that single-deck buses should be numbered in the nineties which was to last for over 20 years. No. 97 had to be re-registered after a short time as the number (ACM 106) had accidentally been allocated to a motor-cycle, also. At last the unreliable, worn out, 18-year old Lions could be withdrawn.

The Rebuilding Programme

Wartime conditions had demonstrated that the pre-war accepted life of seven or eight years for a bus (based on the seven-year loan period) could be exceeded and, with proper maintenance, which had not been available during the war, could be doubled. The existing fleet was appraised and a rehabilitation programme was started. Spares for torque converters had not been available during the war and, furthermore, the complexity of the equipment and higher fuel consumption (about one mile per gallon less) was no longer acceptable at a time when fuel costs had risen, largely because of heavy taxation. The torque converters of the 1939 TD5c's were replaced by

133

Daimler demonstrator GHP 259 came to Birkenhead on loan in 1948 and an order for 15 Daimler CVG6 chassis with Gardner engines and Massey bodies (Nos. 161-75, ACM 619-33) was placed for 1949 delivery. No. 173 is seen at Woodside, showing the attractive chromium-plated radiator fitted to these buses.　　　*T.Lawson*

There was a reversion to Guys for the next new buses (Nos. 146-60, ACM 604-18) which were delivered in summer 1949. Fitted with the usual Massey bodywork, these vehicles had 6LW Gardner engines and featured the new lower bonnet line. No. 148 is seen at the bodybuilders, ready for delivery in May 1949.
Massey Bros.

gearboxes between November 1947 and 1950, 315 being the first to be done; a pool of spares to keep the others on the road was thus created. In 1951, 33 of this batch had extensive body overhauls, 13 by the Corporation and 20 by Massey, the latter being painted in the post-war livery with cream round the lower saloon windows. Interestingly, one of the Massey batch was 307 which had had a new Massey body in 1942. Surprisingly, one of the seven unrebuilt buses (314) was one of the last to be withdrawn, in November 1957. Refurbishment cost an average of £600 per bus but without this treatment they would not have been passed by the Ministry of Transport examiner

No. 301 was the first of the 1939 batch of TD5s to be withdrawn, in January 1951, believed to be due to a chassis defect. It became an illuminated tableau for the 1951 Festival of Britain and again in 1953 for the Queen's coronation. For these duties it was converted back to its original 'Gearless' state, its gearbox going into No. 278.   *T.G. Turner collection*

when the wartime Defence Permit system finally gave way to a resumption of certificates of fitness in September 1951.

Because of a cracked chassis, 301 was withdrawn in 1951 and converted to an illuminated bus in connection with the Festival of Britain, a National Savings Week in 1952 and the Coronation in 1953. It was refitted with a torque-converter, its gearbox going into 278 and was withdrawn in 1953.

Individual vehicles of earlier batches received attention, 1937 TD5c 228 being rebuilt in 1948 and gearboxes were fitted to three more 1938 buses in 1952. In 1947, all the wartime rebodied buses except 307 were renumbered 355-61, the body from 182 (a 1933 chassis) being transferred to 217, the old body of which was scrapped.

In 1951 20 vehicles had their bodies rebuilt by Massey Bros. at Wigan and 13 were treated in the Corporation's bodyshop. Those done by Massey were repainted into the livery introduced the previous year with cream lower deck window surrounds and plain Gill Sans lettering. No. 299 is seen in its new guise in Borough Road in March 1956.   *T.G.Turner*

In January 1948, a Daimler demonstration bus came on loan and as, by 1949, the supply situation for new buses had eased and the Corporation was able to indulge its enthusiasm for the Gardner engine, ordering 15 Guy Arabs and 15 Daimler CVG6, all fitted with the more-powerful six-cylinder 8.4-litre 6LW engine and sporting the lower bonnet line which had become fashionable. The Guys (146-60) went into service between May and July 1949, followed by the Daimlers (161-75) in August and September. All carried Massey bodies virtually identical to those of the earlier Leylands. There were repeat deliveries in 1950, this time the 15 Daimlers (176-90) coming first, in January to March and the 15 Guys (191-205) following on. One Guy (201) did not arrive until October, having been fitted with a prototype metal-framed body; it was externally distinguishable by not having the usual curved end saloon windows and outswept lower panels. The 1950 buses were the last 7ft 6in wide buses to enter the fleet and also introduced a livery variation. The area between the lower and centre cream bands was also finished in cream and the shaded lettering of the title was replaced by modern Gill Sans letters and figures.

During this period, there was a massive clear-out of old buses, many of which were in a battered state. The last 1930-31 double-deckers went in 1947, TD2s by 1948, TD3s by 1949, unrebuilt TD4s by 1950 and TD5s up to 268 (including two rebodied ones) in 1951. The fleet then numbered 225 and was to remain close to that number for the rest of the undertaking's existence, reaching a maximum of 229 in 1963 and falling to 217 in 1969.

There was a return to Leyland in 1951 when, during January, 20 Titan PD2/3 buses (206-25) were received with 8ft wide Leyland bodies seating 57. These had deep sliding windows and

In 1953, 15 Guy buses (Nos.323-37) had their five-cylinder Gardner 5LW engines replaced by the smoother and more powerful six-cylinder 6LW version and were sent to Massey Bros. to have new 7ft 9in wide metal-framed bodies fitted. They were renumbered 241-55. No. 242 (ex-324) is seen at the Haymarket in May 1959. In 2007 this bus is being restored at the Birkenhead Bus and Tram Museum.

R.L. Wilson

sliding cab doors, their roomy interiors being appreciated by passengers and crews alike. These were the first Leyland bodies to be purchased for 19 years and were the last as Leyland gave up body-building shortly afterwards. They were the last buses to have offside destination indicators. The PD2 was powered by the new O.600 8.4-litre Leyland engine. Birkenhead was never tempted to enclose radiators despite the trend towards 'tin-fronts'.

The Committee was ordering on the basis of lowest tender and, in 1952, Guy Motors won the order for 15 Guy Arab Mk III buses with 6LW engines, the body order going to East Lancashire Coachbuilders who had been patronised only once before, for wartime replacement bodies. They repeated the deeper sliding windows of the Leylands and this became a feature of Birkenhead buses for many years. They lacked offside route indicators and these gradually fell into disuse on the rest of the fleet, being painted or panelled over.

The Gardner 6LW engines proved to be very economical and required a minimum of maintenance and it was decided to rehabilitate 15 of the wartime Guys. Nos. 323-37 had new Gardner 6LW engines and 7ft 9in wide all-metal Massey bodies fitted and re-entered service in 1953, renumbered 241-55. The bodies, which seated 59, were similar to that fitted to 201 but wider. The remaining utility buses were withdrawn in 1954, except 319 which became a breakdown vehicle in 1951 and survived as such until 1968 when it was 25 years old.

Following withdrawal from passenger service in 1953, No. 319 was converted into a breakdown crane, replacing No. 183. The upper deck was later removed and it ran in this form until 1968.

T.G. Turner collection

The department continued to alternate between Leyland and Guy orders and patronised several bodybuilders. The 1954 order went to Leyland who supplied 15 PD2/12 models (256-70), 10 fitted with Weymann bodies of the lightweight Aurora type and five bodied by a local firm, Ashcroft, who are believed to have used Metal Sections framework. The result was quite pleasing with Massey-like rounded saloon windows but these were the only buses built by Ashcroft.

The seven Guy Arab Mk IV buses delivered in May 1955 carried Massey 59-seat bodies similar to those fitted to the refurbished wartime Guys but to the full 8-ft width. The fleet numbers were catching up and they were numbered 355-61. They introduced a variation to the livery, the lower cream band being eliminated and the title, shortened to 'Birkenhead Corporation', was moved down to appear either side of the municipal crest. From No. 362 onwards, this was changed to 'Birkenhead Transport'. No. 359 was destined to be the last Guy to run in Birkenhead in October 1972. The following month five Leyland PD2/12 (362-6) entered service with East Lancashire Coachbuilders bodies followed in August by a further five (367-71) with Weymann Orion bodies. Thus the 1955 order for 17 buses was divided between two chassis manufacturers and three bodybuilders.

The 1954 deliveries comprised 15 Leyland PD2/12 Titans, ten (Nos. 256-65, CBG 556-65) bodied by Weymann and five (266-70, CBG 566-70) by the Birkenhead firm of Ashcroft Brothers. Weymann No. 260 was photographed when new at Woodside.   *T.Lawson*

The last Guy buses were purchased in 1956. Ten (372-81) had Massey bodies of similar type to the previous batch and five (382-6) had East Lancs. bodies, similar to 362-6. No. 378 was exhibited at the 1956 Commercial Motor Show and had a different interior finish from the other Massey bodies. They were the first buses in Birkenhead to be fitted with flashing direction indicators.

The fleet now comprised 100 Leyland and 124 Gardner-engined buses. Apart from the single-deck Leylands, New Ferry depot, which ran the New Chester Road services and routes 10, 28 and 51, had only Guys but this was not a fixed allocation, buses being changed over in service for maintenance as necessary. In 1951, New Ferry exchanged the 51 for the 85/86 and Guys were run from Laird Street depot, mainly on routes 51 and 60/66. Daimlers usually worked routes 42/46 and 70 but could turn up elsewhere. From the late 'fifties, it became the practice to put new buses on route 11 for a few days and then on to route 42.

Ten more Massey-bodied Guy Arab IVs added to the fleet in 1956 (Nos. 372-81, EBG 53-64, 750-3) were identical to those delivered the previous year, although No. 378 was exhibited at the 1956 Commercial Motor Show and had detail differences from the remainder of the batch. A further five Guy Arab IVs with East Lancashire bodies (Nos. 382-6, EBG 754-8) completed the 1956 intake and these were the last Guys to be purchased by Birkenhead Corporation. 381 with Massey body is seen at Woodside station in December 1964.   *T.G. Turner*

Leyland Atlantean demonstrator 398 JTB, painted in the dark green and cream livery of Maidstone & District Motor Services, was given a trial in 1960 but the management was obviously not impressed as no rear-engined buses were bought for another four years and they were Daimler Fleetlines. The Atlantean was photographed in Conway Street working on the Woodside-Moreton services in July 1960.   *T.G. Turner*

Another rear-engined bus came to Birkenhead on trial in 1962, this time a Daimler Fleetline. Presumably the trial was successful and an order for nine such vehicles followed. The demonstrator was painted cream with a blue relief band and is seen on the Woodchurch service in December 1962.   *R.L. Wilson*

Leyland Standardisation

From 1957, most of the orders went to Leyland, the PD2/40, an updated version of the PD2/12 with the same vacuum braking system, becoming the standard until 1966. Although the maximum permitted length of double-deck buses on two axles had been increased from 27ft to 30ft in 1956, Birkenhead did not immediately take advantage of the concession. Massey bodywork was fitted except in 1961 when East Lancashire gained the order. However, bodywork design did not stand still and seating capacity increased from the standard 59 in 1958 to 61 in 1959, 63 in 1960 and 65 in 1963, the extra capacity being obtained by a judicious rearrangement of the seating, such as the use of a seat for three at the rear of the upper deck and a rearward facing seat at the front of the lower saloon. Fleet numbers reverted to 1, a number not used since the first Corporation bus was scrapped in 1927, and a policy of replacing 15 buses per year put in place. Deliveries were as follows:-

July 1957 - February 1958	Nos. 1-15
April 1959 - January 1960	Nos. 16-30
April 1960 - February 1961	Nos. 31-45
July - November 1961	Nos. 46-60 (East Lancs. bodies)
July - December 1962	Nos. 61-75
June - December 1963	Nos. 76-90

There was a return to Massey-bodied Leyland Titan PD2/40s in 1965 in the form of Nos. 110-24 (BBG 110-24C). No. 118 is seen at Woodside station in August 1965.   *T.G. Turner*

During 1960-63, the Corporation experimented with rear-engined high capacity buses, a demonstration Daimler Fleetline and two Leyland Atlanteans running on service in the town. This resulted in an order being placed for nine Daimler Fleetlines fitted with Weymann 77-seat bodies (101-9), powered by Gardner 6LX 10.45 litre engines, which entered service in August and September 1964 on Woodchurch Road routes. The four ageing PS1 single-deckers were also replaced by four underfloor-engined Leyland Leopard L1 buses (91-4). They had the same Leyland O.600 engine but with air instead of vacuum brakes. The 42-seat Massey bodies were fitted for one-man operation and had a front entrance and centre exit. Like their predecessors, they were stationed at New Ferry. All the 1964 buses and subsequent deliveries were fitted with fluorescent lighting.

Throughout these years, new deliveries were matched by withdrawals. The last pre-war buses were withdrawn in 1957; the actual last to run has not been recorded but 293, 299, 303, 305, 310 and 314, all 1939 TD5s, survived longest. The 1947 PD1s were withdrawn in 1959-61, the 1948 PD1s in 1961-63 and the first post-war Guys and Daimlers in 1962-65. The transport department were not convinced of the superiority of the large-capacity double-deck bus which had enabled Wallasey to reduce mileage, preferring to maintain headways with orthodox vehicles.

In 1965, there was a reversion to the usual 15 PD2/40s with Massey bodywork (110-24), though 66 seats were squeezed into that year's deliveries; another batch of 15 (125-39) which arrived in 1966 having a noticeably more upright profile and straight instead of curved side panels enabling them to be interchanged with underfloor-engined types. In 1967, it was the mixture as before (140-54) except that there was a change to the PD2/37 variant which had air instead of vacuum

A further 15 further Leyland PD2/40s were delivered in 1966 (Nos. 125-39, DBG 125-39D). The Massey bodies had an upright frontal design quite different from the curves previously associated with the bodybuilder. The object was to increase the capacity and 66 seats were fitted. The lower body sides were straight to facilitate standardisation of body parts with Atlanteans. No. 125 is seen when new followed by a vehicle in the previous Massey style. *T.G. Turner*

brakes. However, economics and the advent of the bus grant, dictated a change to rear-engined high-capacity buses and 13 PDR1/1 Atlanteans (155-67), seating 77, were commissioned between September and November 1968. Massey had been taken over by Northern Coachbuilders whose bodies were fitted, though they had been built in the former Massey works. Eight of them were equipped for one-man operation in 1969. They were followed, in 1969, by 15 somewhat similar buses (168-82) but with dual entrance bodies seating 71, current wisdom being that a separate exit was needed for successful one-man double-deck operation. These were of model PDR1/2, incorporating a Daimler gearbox instead of the Leyland Pneumocyclic gearbox. Five of this batch arrived in February and March 1970 and thus were delivered to Merseyside PTE.

There were two Birkenhead Corporation orders still outstanding, one for 13 more dual-entrance Atlanteans with Northern Counties bodywork (183-95) and the other for two single-deck Atlanteans (95-6) with dual-entrance 40-seat bodies from the same builder. Single-deck Atlanteans were very rare and they were chosen in the interests of standardisation; they were of type PDR2/1, 32ft 6in long with O.680 engines. All these were delivered to the PTE during 1970; they came in Merseyside PTE blue and cream livery which combined Birkenhead blue with Wallasey cream.

Northern Counties provided the bodywork for the first Leyland PDR1/1 Atlanteans to join the fleet. Nos. 155-67 (LCM 155-67G) entered service in autumn 1968 and the following year they were used on the first route to be converted to double-deck one-man operation, the Oxton Circle, using a flat fare system. No. 157 is seen with Fleetline 103 at Woodside in September 1968.   *T.G. Turner*

Preserved Leyland PD2 No. 10, passing through Bidston village on a re-creation of the Woodside-Moreton route.   *T.G. Turner collection*

Birkenhead Buses in the PTE

A total of 224 buses was transferred to the PTE comprising:-

161	Leyland Titan PD2
28	Leyland Atlantean
4	Leyland Leopard L1
22	Guy Arab Mk IV
9	Daimler Fleetline
TOTAL 224	(including 5 arriving late)

Nine PD2s were transferred to Wallasey to replace 1951 buses. Subsequently, other ex-Birkenhead vehicles were also based at Seaview Road depot, Wallasey. Large numbers of PD2s were transferred to Liverpool and St. Helens in 1973-76 and the single-deckers went to Southport. Some of the Atlanteans also went to Liverpool towards the end of their lives. Five Birkenhead buses have been preserved, Leyland PD1 No. 105, Leopard L1 93, Leyland PD2s 10 and 152 and Guy Arab 242. Two more PD2s (131 and 147), which were converted to service vehicles, lasted long enough to be transferred to Merseybus in October 1986.

Eighteen further Northern Counties-bodied Atlanteans arrived in 1969-70 (Nos. 168-82, MBG 368-82H). The bodies were of quite a different style to their predecessors, having front entrance and centre exit and centre staircase. Upper deck window surrounds were finished in cream, there being no mouldings for the usual cream band. A further batch ordered by Birkenhead Corporation (Nos. 183-95, OBG 383-95J) were delivered after the formation of Merseyside PTE and never carried Corporation livery, being finished in the blue-cream-blue scheme. No. 182 stands at Woodside with a bus of the earlier style behind in November 1969.   T.G. Turner

9 – Fares & Tickets

Birkenhead's motor bus undertaking started operations at a time when post-war inflation had brought about steeply rising costs but, unlike the conditions which prevailed after 1945, the trend was reversed and costs stabilised by 1921-22 and thereafter started to decline.

While Birkenhead's first buses did not encroach on tram routes to any great extent, a policy of tramway protection was adopted so that, wherever there was a choice, it was cheaper to travel by tram than by bus. Fares on the early bus routes were expensive by later standards when technical improvements and greater activity resulted in reduced costs despite higher fuel prices in the 1930s. Between 1924 and 1936, the trend in fare levels was consistently down whereafter they remained stable for 15 years. In 1919, it cost 10d to travel 6.44 miles from Rock Ferry pier to Moreton Cross at a rate of 1.55d per mile. The minimum, and the most popular fare was 2d; 30% of bus riders paid 2d and 25% paid 3d. The fares on the other pioneer bus services were equally expensive: Charing Cross to Seacombe was 5d and to Liscard 6d; Rock Ferry pier to Port Sunlight cost 4d.

The fall in the level of fares over the next few years was facilitated by a mix of lower costs, social policies and competitive pressures. Fares to Moreton were reduced on 5th April 1924, less than a month after Crosville started their Park Station - West Kirby service for, even though the Corporation services were protected, it became cheaper to ride to Moreton Schools on a company bus than to the Cross on a Corporation bus. 7d day return tickets between both Upton and Moreton and Park Station were introduced on 1st January 1925; the Upton fare subsequently fell to 5d when the single came down from 4d to 3d.

When the Claughton Road trams were replaced, the minimum bus fare was $1^{1}/_{2}$d over the tram track and 2d beyond and in all subsequent tramway conversions, the bus fare scale was marginally higher.

Fares came down on 30th November 1925 on all bus routes except the cross-docks services which fell into line in March 1926. There were now 1d fares on buses. By 1929, when fares were again reduced, the fare from Charing Cross to Liscard had almost halved from 6d to $3^{1}/_{2}$d and the Rock Ferry-Moreton fare had fallen from 10d to 6d for a greater distance to Bermuda Road; it subsequently fell to 5d. Several intermediate fares were reduced from 16th June 1930, examples of the new fares being Charing Cross-Hurrell Road 2d, Woodside to St. James Church 2d, to Cavendish Drive 2d, to Kings Lane (Dacre Hill) 2d, Charing Cross-Reeds Lane 3d, Market Place South-Kingsland Road (via Oxton Road) $1^{1}/_{2}$d, Charing Cross-Storeton Road $1^{1}/_{2}$d. For a time, a $^{1}/_{2}$d adult ticket was issued on the Haymarket-Storeton Road 'shopping bus' for short journeys along Grange Road, to encourage riding between one shop and another. They were used by 73,216 passengers in 1931-32 but were withdrawn soon after as uneconomic.

Through Tickets to Liverpool

Through tickets by tram and ferry to Liverpool had been suggested as long ago as 1860 when the original street railway opened but the proposal was haughtily rejected by the Ferry Committee. However, there is some evidence of an agreement with the Wirral Tramway Co. for through tickets from the New Ferry line in 1887. The ferries were to receive two-thirds of a penny per passenger and this would have been acceptable as the New Ferry trams could equally well have fed the rival Tranmere ferry. However, no further details have come to light. Limited through tickets had been introduced on the tramways from 1st July 1905 and weekly booklets of 12 tickets were issued for a time. After suspension during the 1914-18 war to discourage travel, the through tickets were reintroduced but issued only to Upton Road to encourage people to visit Bidston Hill for recreation.

Before 1928, through tickets to Liverpool were controversial as shopkeepers opposed any measure which might encourage Birkenhead people to shop in Liverpool. The first through tickets on buses were, surprisingly enough, bus and rail tickets between Moreton and Liverpool via Park Station, introduced on 18th August 1923 on a seasonal basis at 1/- from Moreton, 11d from Reeds Lane and 9d from Bidston. There was no daily service from Moreton to Woodside until September 1923 and the facility was aimed at attracting traffic away from the Wirral line. The Mersey Railway, still an independent line, was not interested in how its passengers got to and from its trains and one can speculate that there was acrimonious correspondence between the Mersey and the newly-formed LMS Railway Co. which had absorbed the LNW and the Wirral in the grouping of 1923. As the railway competed with the ferry, there were also misgivings in municipal circles, and bus and ferry tickets at the same rates were also issued from 8th October 1923. The rail tickets were discontinued in October 1925. When the Charing Cross-Port Sunlight route opened on 23rd March 1925, fares came down on the Rock Ferry-Port Sunlight route and a 9d bus and ferry ticket was introduced between Port Sunlight and Liverpool Landing Stage.

The general scheme introduced on 1st April 1928 was in response to great reductions in Mersey Railway excursion fares, in particular a 6d day return from Birkenhead to Liverpool. Through tickets were issued on all tram and bus routes to and from Woodside and Rock Ferry. The ticket prices were generally based as follows:-

On 1d, 1^1/$_2$d & 2d stages - the return bus fare (minimum 3d) plus single boat fare of 2d.
On higher fares - the return bus fare (minimum 6d)

There were some variations at first, but there was soon a fixed scale of 5d for 1d and 1^1/$_2$d stages, 6d for 2d, 2^1/$_2$d and the shorter 3d stages; 8d for the longer 3d and first 4d stages and 10d for the longer 4d and all 5d stages. The ferries received 2^1/$_2$d from each ticket so the issue of a 5d ticket from a 1d stage was good business for the buses as their share was also 2^1/$_2$d! Under this scale, the Liverpool-Rock Ferry-Port Sunlight fare came down from 9d to 6d. All these tickets were available for return on day of issue or the following day; later, Saturday's tickets were valid for return on Mondays. Following the agreement with Crosville in 1930, through tickets were extended to Allport Road, Bromborough (10d), Eastham Village (1/-), Eastham Ferry - (1930-31 only 1/2d), Thingwall (1/-), Thurstaston (1/2d) and Heswall (1/4d). These tickets were interavailable with Crosville between common points. When the 85 service to Thurstaston via Frankby started in 1932, issue of through tickets was limited to the Corporation area at Upton Cricket Ground (10d). This was amended in 1939 and Crosville 1/4d tickets were offered from West Kirby via Irby Mill Hill though it is doubtful if there were many takers and they were limited to Lower Caldy Cross Roads after the war. Crosville wanted to extend the area of availability to Ellesmere Port and Parkgate but the Ferries Committee objected as they were

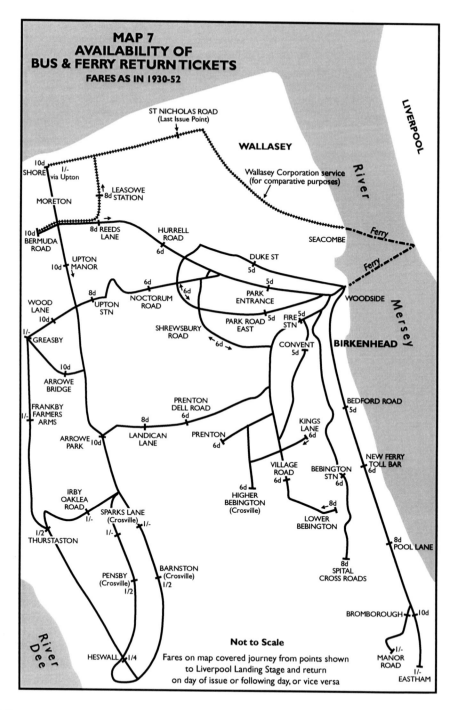

MAP 7
AVAILABILITY OF
BUS & FERRY RETURN TICKETS
FARES AS IN 1930-52

LIVERPOOL

River

Mersey

River Dee

ST NICHOLAS ROAD
(Last Issue Point)

WALLASEY

Wallasey Corporation service
(for comparative purposes)

10d SHORE
1/- via Upton

LEASOWE
8d STATION

MORETON

10d BERMUDA ROAD

8d REEDS LANE

HURRELL ROAD

6d

SEACOMBE

Ferry

Ferry

UPTON MANOR 10d

DUKE ST
5d

5d

WOODSIDE

8d UPTON STN

6d

NOCTORUM ROAD

6d

PARK ENTRANCE

WOOD LANE 10d

SHREWSBURY ROAD

PARK ROAD EAST 5d

FIRE STN 5d

6d

BIRKENHEAD

1/- GREASBY

CONVENT 5d

10d

ARROWE BRIDGE

BEDFORD ROAD 5d

FRANKBY FARMERS ARMS 1/-

PRENTON DELL ROAD 6d

8d LANDICAN LANE

PRENTON 6d

KINGS LANE 6d

ARROWE PARK 10d

NEW FERRY TOLL BAR 6d

IRBY OAKLEA ROAD

VILLAGE ROAD 6d

BEBINGTON STN 6d

SPARKS LANE
(Crosville) 1/-

1/-

HIGHER BEBINGTON
(Crosville) 6d

8d

LOWER BEBINGTON

1/2 THURSTASTON

PENSBY
(Crosville) 1/2

BARNSTON
(Crosville) 1/2

8d POOL LANE

8d SPITAL CROSS ROADS

BROMBOROUGH 10d

Not to Scale

HESWALL 1/4

Fares on map covered journey from points shown
to Liverpool Landing Stage and return
on day of issue or following day, or vice versa

MANOR ROAD 1/-

1/- EASTHAM

never too happy with their share. The Corporation also inherited a series of contracts between Thurstaston or Irby and Woodside. Crosville contracts from Heswall and Thingwall were also accepted on Corporation buses.

Through tickets were available in both directions being sold on trams and buses and at the ferry turnstiles, the ferry version being an Edmondson card ticket of the type used by the railways. Thousands of day trippers from Liverpool were attracted by the low fares and, in the 1930s, the extent of the facilities was illustrated by a large diagram on a board at Liverpool Landing Stage headed by the slogan "Twixt Mersey and Dee". The revenue brought in by this traffic far outweighed any loss of patronage to local shops caused by traffic to Liverpool.

Most railway passengers left the tram or bus at Park, Central or Hamilton Square stations but ferry passengers travelled all the way to Woodside. The cheap bus or tram ticket was thus offset by the longer ride and also the traffic generation factor.

In 1946-47 2,727,782 passengers (4.1%) bought bus and ferry tickets. From a revenue point of view they were more important to the Ferries than to the buses. In 1947-48, bus and ferry ticket holders made up 32% of ferry passengers producing 26% of the revenue but these proportions declined over the next few years. The cost of ferry contracts influenced the equation and passengers would carefully calculate the cost of concessionary tickets on both modes and choose the cheapest combination.

Workmen's Returns

Unlike the tramways, the buses had no statutory duty to provide cheap fares for 'artisans, mechanics and daily labourers' but a limited range of workmen's return fares was offered in 1925. From May 1927, 6-day weekly tickets for one return journey each weekday were issued between Moreton and Park Station for 3/- (15p) or Woodside for 4/-(20p) and similarly priced tickets were made available from Upton from 19th October 1927, the Woodside ticket involving a change of buses at Park Station. The Moreton ticket was reduced to 3/6d when the through fare came down to 5d. These were originally measures calculated to curb competition from Crosville. As routes were extended, tickets were issued from Greasby (3/6d) and Arrowe Bridge (3/-) and an Upton-Central Station ticket was available on the Upton-Bromborough route. These tickets were sold at transport offices and certain tobacconists in the villages. Whilst the original workmen's fares were issued only up to 7.40am, the weekly tickets were not restricted as to time. A general scheme of workmen's returns, based approximately on single fare for the return journey (minimum 3d) was brought in on 16th June 1930 on all except the cross-docks services which had no early buses in those days. A 2d ticket over certain stages was introduced from 28th December 1931, when buses replaced trams on the New Ferry route, to compensate for the loss of 1d and $1^{1}/_{2}$d work singles and $1^{1}/_{2}$d meal-time returns on the trams. A $2^{1}/_{2}$d single ticket was introduced at the same time but was not universally applied, some routes having no $2^{1}/_{2}$d stages. When the Prenton and Tranmere tram routes were converted to bus operation on 1st October 1934, 2d WRs again had to be conceded and, as one of the stages was Singleton Avenue to Woodside, the facility had to be extended to all the other routes which covered this section. Previously, a $1^{1}/_{2}$d workmen's single had been issued between Bebington Road (Mount Road) and Woodside when the Tranmere trams had been curtailed at Whitfield Street in October 1928.

149

It was rare for single-deck bodywork to be placed on Atlantean chassis but, for the sake of standardisation, Birkenhead ordered two such vehicles with Northern Counties 40-seat dual-door bodies (Nos. 95-6, OBG 495-96J) which arrived in January 1971 painted in Merseyside PTE livery. No. 96 is seen turning at Woodside and the rear view of No. 95 was photographed on the bus park there in 1971.

T.G. Turner collection/A. Murray Rust

In the early years of the buses, as with the trams, fares were under the full control of the Corporation and often came into local politics. A would-be councillor would try to win a few votes by promising to have a stage lengthened or a fare reduced. After February 1931, fares were authorised by the Traffic Commissioners who initiated moves to bring Birkenhead, Wallasey and Crosville conditions into line as far as possible. The Traffic Commissioners placed a duty on the bus operator to prove a need for increased fares but for 20 years this was irrelevant as the trend was downwards.

Crosville had issued cheap tickets between New Ferry and Bromborough, particularly after 5.0pm and these were not initially made available by the Corporation when they took over responsibility for this section. The exception was a 3d schoolchildren's return between Eastham village and New Ferry. There was a 1d fare between Bromborough Cross and Pool Lane which was issued up to 8.30am, between 12.0noon and 2.0pm on Saturdays and from 5.0pm on Mondays to Fridays. This is shown in the February 1932 fare list but not in that dated November 1930. However, with the downward trend of fares during the 1930s, these fares were absorbed into the ordinary fare list, 1d becoming the ordinary fare between Pool Lane and Bromborough Cross and $1^1/_2$d single, the half fare (applicable to children up to 16 when travelling to and from school) between Eastham and New Ferry.

In 1934, the Traffic Commissioners queried the conditions under which workmen's tickets were issued in Birkenhead which did not comply with their standing rules. Whereas most operators' tickets were valid for return on day of issue only and for one journey in each direction, Birkenhead's terms were generous to the extent that tickets could be used for return on any route, at any time over any corresponding stage. The Council resisted any change stating the the conditions were based on the practice of casual dock labourers buying a ticket to seek work. If no work was available, the man walked home and used the return half the following day. It was felt that great hardship would be caused if the Commissioners' rules were applied. Tickets were issued up to 8.0am on weekdays and were widely used.

The Commissioners did not press the point but proposed that a common formula for all fares be agreed by Birkenhead and Wallasey Corporations and Crosville in North Wirral. After some discussion, this was agreed and brought into operation on 19th April 1936 when 2d workmen's returns were extended to all routes. Crosville accepted municipal conditions which were usually more generous than their own. One of the results was the co-ordination of children's fares with free travel below age 5 and half fare up to 16th birthday. The LMS Railway unsuccessfully objected to free travel up to the child's fifth birthday as their limit was age three. Halfpenny children's tickets, which had been issued on trams and on route 79, were introduced for all 1d stages but Crosville would not adopt this in its own area. The facility was not, therefore, available on Corporation buses beyond the borough boundary on the Heswall and Thurstaston via Frankby routes.

Use of workmen's returns on the cross docks routes was approved from 1st August 1935 and tickets were accepted for return on buses of either Corporation. Wallasey tickets were accepted in Birkenhead only on cross docks services or sections of those services and the same applied to Birkenhead tickets in Wallasey. Implications were that a Birkenhead 2d return issued say, from New Ferry to Central Station on a Bromborough-Upton bus, could be used for the second journey from Liscard to New Brighton on an independent Wallasey bus running from Moreton to New Brighton! It is doubtful if such generous conditions were available anywhere else.

In the year-ended 31st March 1947, 9,311,374 workmen's return tickets were issued of which 60% were of the lowest value - 2d. The workmen's returns represented 13.92% of all tickets issued, this apparently low figure being clarified when it is realised that 32,762,410 passengers of the 53,953,509 ordinary single ticket holders (60.72%) travelled over 1d or $1^1/_2$d stages for which no workmen's returns were available.

Cheap Day Return Tickets

The social policy of making it easy to get to Arrowe Park led to the issue of cheap 6d day return tickets from Woodside and 4d tickets from the Fire Station, Whetstone Lane, from the inception of the service in September 1928. The November 1930 fare list shows these fares as being available only on Saturday afternoons and evenings. They were issued on the outward journey only after 12.0 noon and were extended to other parts of the town as new routes were started. On the 16 route, the 6d fare was applied from Park Station and Woodward Road and the 4d fare from Mallaby Street and Bedford Road. A 4d day return from Gautby Road to Moreton Shore was introduced in July 1936 and was subsequently available from June to September each year. There were half fare tickets for children on all these stages. A resolution by the Tramways and Motors Committee on 13th July 1932 authorising special low children's return tickets to Arrowe Park from Central Station and Park Station for 2d after 1.0pm on Mondays to Fridays during the school summer holidays 'and that such fares be put into operation without delay' seems not to have been implemented. It would have had to be submitted to the Traffic Commissioners so there would have been no prospect of its introduction that year. The Arrowe Park tickets were popular, (the Moreton ones less so), 527,438 being issued in 1946-47.

Competition from the Mersey Railway and Crosville were powerful factors which influenced fare-fixing policies in Birkenhead and the large numbers of passengers attracted to the buses brought prosperity not only to the transport undertaking but to the town in general.

Wartime Measures

Wartime conditions improved the pure economics of bus operation in Birkenhead as loss-making facilities were withdrawn to save fuel and passengers increased as war industries expanded. Costs rose inexorably but the extra traffic was more than sufficient to cover them and bus fares were therefore not increased as the operators could not prove need as the law required. This was fine during the war and for a few years afterwards but the eventual need to catch up with other cost rises had serious effects, as will be seen.

As there was a need to discourage travel, 1d fares were withdrawn on outward journeys from Woodside during the evening peak hours from 15th March 1941, to prevent longer distance passengers being crowded out by short riders. From 28th June 1943 the $^1/_2$d children's and schoolchildren's fare was 'temporarily' withdrawn for the same reason. In this case the facility was never restored.

One of the arrangements made between the Corporation and Crosville in 1930 was for the interavailability of contracts between Heswall or Thingwall and Woodside. These tickets were issued only by Crosville while contracts between Thurstaston or Irby and Woodside were issued by the Corporation. Because of wartime pressures, it was found in 1942 that many Thingwall passengers were being carried on Corporation buses so, at Crosville's request, the Corporation also issued Thingwall contracts on the same terms, interavailability being abolished from 1st July. This saved time and labour as the acceptance of a Crosville contract for travel on a Corporation bus involved the issue of a ticket and the payment by the company of 5d for a Heswall trip or $3^3/_4$d for a Thingwall trip.

Post-War Fare Increases

The post-war traffic boom kept fares at their 1936 level until costs overtook the additional revenue. A £15,800 increase in receipts in 1948-49 was accompanied by expenses higher by £60,879 compared with the previous year and by the following year there was no alternative but to seek authority for a general fares increase. The fare table was 'a condition attached to a road service licence' and therefore could not be altered without the permission of the Traffic Commissioners (at that time called the 'Licensing Authority for Public Service Vehicles'). The procedure was cumbersome and slow and very often, by the time an operator was able to put into effect higher fares necessitated by increased wages or other costs, a further round of increases necessitated another application for a second rise in fares. The operator had to prove a need for the increase and this required the laying bare of its finances at the public hearing. Following the publication of the details in *'Notices and Proceedings'*, local authorities and other bodies with a *locus standi* were entitled to object and to be heard. Increases in bus fares became an emotive issue. Whilst higher rates and the cost of almost every other commodity were accepted philosophically, bus fare increases were fought tooth and nail as if the unfortunate operators were somehow immune from the inflationary cost increases of the time. Among the worst were non-operating local authorities such as Bebington Corporation and Hoylake UDC who would have been incensed if Birkenhead had objected to them raising their rates - if that had been possible.

A Co-ordinated Approach Fails

An increase of 2d in bus and ferry returns from 1st April 1949 went wholly to the Ferries undertaking, though it still had to be approved by the Commissioners. A joint sub-committee was formed by Birkenhead and Wallasey to produce, if possible, co-ordinated applications. It was proposed to increase fares by $^1/_2$d but Wallasey wanted an additional 1d on fares of 4d and above. However, because of its heavy industrial traffic, Birkenhead calculated that a 1d increase on the higher fares would bring in more revenue than needed and proposed increases of $^1/_2$d on all single fares. This resulted in all fares over 4d having an odd $^1/_2$d, a source of considerable difficulty for conductors. However, in line with the government's policy limiting fares increases, the Licensing Authority, unimpressed by the large transfers of surpluses to the Rate Fund in earlier years, mentioned in chapter 6, authorised only the raising of the 1d minimum fare to $1^1/_2$d to come into effect in February 1951. However, in the meantime, Crosville had been granted a $^1/_2$d increase which was applied on 8th January 1951 to the outer ends of routes 71, 72, 73, 78 and 96. Following a rise of $4^1/_2$d per gallon in the fuel tax, a further increase was applied from 1st August 1951, the higher fares being raised by $^1/_2$d as planned. The minimum workmen's day return ticket became 3d for a 2d or $2^1/_2$d stage, 4d for a 3d stage then single fare plus $^1/_2$d for the higher values. The maximum single fare was $8^1/_2$d for a journey between Eastham and Overchurch Road or Bromborough and New Brighton or Moreton.

Operators everywhere were campaigning against anachronistic workmen's return tickets which were issued for cheap travel at a time when the highest costs were incurred. From 31st March 1952 workmen's tickets were issued as concessionary single tickets in the morning only, passengers paying the full fare on the return journey. When a third general increase came into effect on 18th May 1953, the higher single fares were increased, eliminating at least some of the odd halfpennies. A mileage scale was adopted which reduced the work involved in managing future increases as new fares were applied to the same structure each time.

The Corporation managed to hold the 1953 fares unchanged until the Suez crisis when a temporary surcharge was imposed between 7th January and 14th April 1957 to meet the cost of an additional fuel tax and higher cost of the fuel itself. However, costs were rising steadily and a further permanent increase took effect from 18th November 1957. Single fares up to $3^1/_2$d were increased by $^1/_2$d and higher fares by 1d. Bus and ferry tickets were increased proportionately and workmen's single tickets were abolished. Fare increases now became regular occurrences during the 1960s. The first, on 9th June 1962, introduced a $2^1/_2$d minimum and $^1/_2$d and 1d increases on higher fares. The minimum children's fare became 2d. On 4th September 1963 1d was added to all fares except $3^1/_2$d which increased to 5d, the minimum fare being 3d. The next increase, on 25th April 1965 eliminated the last fraction ($3^1/_2$d). Children's fares became - up to two children below 5 free, up to 14 (16 for schoolchildren) half fare, minimum 2d, to nearest 1d above. From 7th July 1966 the department introduced its last independent fares increase. The various distances covered by individual fares are shown in the table below.

The last deliveries of front-engined, rear platform buses came in 1967. They were Leyland Titan PD2/37s (Nos. 140-54, GCM 140-54E) with air brakes and Massey bodywork similar to their predecessors. No. 152 is preserved at the Birkenhead Bus & Tram Museum. No. 142 is seen in the snow at Port Sunlight in February 1969.
P. Anderson

Birkenhead and Wallasey increased their fares on different dates so Birkenhead conductors often had to deal with two increases within a short time. Wallasey fixed the fares in Moreton as well as on the Wallasey section of the cross-docks services. Eventually, Birkenhead printed separate fare lists for cross-docks services to avoid the necessity of reprinting the whole fare list when Wallasey fares changed. There were also Crosville increases at the outer ends of the Heswall, Thurstaston and Greasby routes. Bus and ferry tickets were available for adults only and based on a scale related to the single fare.

There was interavailability of all bus and ferry return tickets with Crosville to and from Allport Road, Eastham; Clatterbridge; common points beyond Landican Cemetery up to Heswall; Arrowe House Farm (the junction of Arrowe Park Road and Arrowe Brook Road) or Brookdale Avenue, Greasby and points between Farmers' Arms, Frankby and Lower Caldy Cross Roads, the fares being within the range 2/3 to 2/11d. This scale was in force at the time the undertaking was handed over to the Merseyside PTE.

COMPARISON OF FARES AND DISTANCES (miles)

Ord. Fare	Before 1.4.51	1 Apr 1951	18 May 1953	18 Nov 1957	9 Jun 1962	4 Sep 1963	25 Apr 1965	7 Jul 1966
1d	.997	-	-	-	-	-	-	-
1½d	1.482	.997	.75	-	-	-	-	-
2d	2.399	1.482	1.0	.75	-	-	-	-
2½d	2.693	2.399	1.75	1.0	.75	-	-	-
3d	3.788	2.693	2.5	1.75	1.0	.75	.5	.5
3½d	-	3.788	2.75	2.5	1.75	1.0	-	-
4d	5.221	-	3.75	2.75	2.5	1.75	1.0	1.0
4½d	-	5.221	-	-	-	-	-	-
5d	6.615	-	4.75	3.75	3.25	2.5	1.75	1.4
5½d	-	6.615	-	-	-	-	-	-
6d	8.622	-	5.75	4.75	4.0	3.25	2.5	1.75
6½d	-	8.622	-	-	-	-	-	-
7d	9.730	-	7.0	5.75	4.75	4.0	3.25	2.5
7½d	-	9.720	-	-	-	-	-	-
8d	-	-	8.25	7.0	5.75	4.75	4.0	3.0
8½d	-	11.122	-	-	-	-	-	-
9d	-	-	9.5	8.25	7.0	5.75	4.75	3.5
10d	-	-	11.0	9.5	8.25	7.0	5.75	4.0
11d	-	-	-	11.0	9.5	8.25	7.0	4.75
1/-	-	-	-	-	11.0	9.5	8.25	5.75
1/1	-	-	-	-	-	11.0	9.5	7.0
1/2	-	-	-	-	-	-	11.0	8.25
1/3	-	-	-	-	-	-	-	9.5
1/4	-	-	-	-	-	-	-	11.0

The distances in the first two columns, before the mileage scale was adopted, are averages.

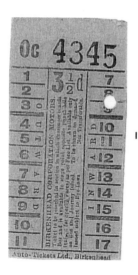

1

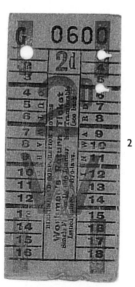

2

3

6

5

7

8

156

Ticket showing:

		C 00439		Mon.
3/-				
	Outward from Birkenhead	BIRKENHEAD CORP. TRANSPORT. (FOR CONDITIONS SEE BACK.) Weekly Ticket. Available for ONE RETURN JOURNEY EACH WEEK DAY as per fare list.	Inward to Birkenhead	

DURING :-

Week Ending **1 MAR 1947**

C 00439   **3/-**

Sat.   BIRKENHEAD CORP. TRANSPORT. (SEE BACK)

4

1. This 3¹/₂d ordinary single ticket with 'Birkenhead Corporation Motors' title dates from 1st April 1928 and was applicable to only one stage - from Charing Cross to Liscard, jointly with Wallasey Corporation. From that date there were no other odd ¹/₂d tickets above 2¹/₂d until 1951. It was punched in the stage number where the passenger boarded.

2. Workmen's return tickets were issued at single fare before 8.0 am and followed the same layout as the ordinary single tickets of the same value. It was punched in the boarding stage (5) and cancelled with nippers in stage 1.

3. Special 6d adult day return tickets were issued to Arrowe Park from Woodside (routes 71, 77, 78), Park Station and Woodward Road (both route 16) in the summer season. The aim was to encourage the use of the park. The significance of the Woodward Road fare was that it was the last stop in Birkenhead on a route which extended to New Ferry in Bebington. The residents of that borough were not to be offered any concessions.

4. Weekly tickets were issued only between Upton or Moreton and Park Station and from Upton or Arrowe Bridge being a relic of competition with Crosville before the Agreement of 1930.

5. The 5¹/₂d ordinary single dates fom the fares increase from 1st April 1951 which introduced odd halfpennies from 3¹/₂d to 8¹/₂d. All except the 3¹/₂d value disappeared in the next fares increase on 18th May 1953.

6. The 1d 'package ticket' was issued for parcels which were not passengers' luggage or for the latter if exceeding 28lb in weight.

7. The 11d ferry and bus return is an Edmondson card as issued by the Ferries Department at Woodside and dates from the 1957 'Suez Crisis' when 1d was added to the cost of all bus and ferry tickets. Many were adapted by a rubber stamp overprint but the volume of 11d tickets sold justified a special print.

8. This 5d child bus and ferry ticket was of the style issued on the buses and was issued for a 10d adult fare such as Moreton to Liverpool.

Fleet No.	Reg. No.	Chassis Make and Type	Body Make	Type and Capacity	Year in Service	Year Withdrawn	Notes
1-10	CM 1701-10	Leyland 'O'	Leyland	B32R	1919-20	1927	
11-2	CM 1711-2	AEC 'B'	LGOC	O16/18R	1921	1925-6	A
13-5	CO 3398-400	Straker Squire 'A'	Straker Squire	B32R	1922	1927	B
16	CM 4006	Straker Squire 'A'	Straker Squire	B32R	1922	1927	C
17	CM 4686	Thornycroft BT	Strachan & Brown	B20F	1923	1928	
18-23	CM 4836-41	Leyland G7	Leyland	B32R	1923	1928-9	
24-9	CM 5339-44	Leyland SGH7	Leyland	FB40R	1924	1930	
30-2	CM 5345-7	Leyland LG1	Leyland	H28/24RO	1925	1930	
33-7	CM 6040-4	Leyland LG1	Leyland	H28/24RO	1925	1930	
38	CM 6045	Guy 'J'	Buckingham	B20F	1925	1930	
39-41	CM 6046-8	Leyland SG11	Leyland	B36R	1925	1931	
42-3	CM 6049-50	Leyland LG1	Leyland	H26/26RO	1926	1931	
44-51	CM 6600-7	Leyland LG1	Leyland	H26/26RO	1926	1931	
52-4	CM 6608-10	Guy 'BB'	Guy	B27D	1926	1930	
55-64	CM 6611-20	Leyland LSP2	Leyland	H28/27R	1927	1933	
65-74	CM 7384-93	Leyland PLSC3	Leyland	B36R	1927-8	1935	
75-8	CM 8060-3	Leyland PLSC3	Leyland	B36R	1928	1935	
79-93	CM 8064-78	Leyland TD1	Leyland	L27/24RO	1928	1938	D
94-113	CM 8721-40	Leyland TD1	Leyland	L24/24R	1929-30	1939	
114-25	CM 9375-86	Leyland TD1	Leyland	L24/24R	1930	1939-44	
126-31	CM 9387-92	Leyland LT2	Leyland	B35R	1930	1939-48	
132-51	CM 9756-75	Leyland TD1	Leyland	L27/24R	1930-31	1944-7	
152-6	BG 200-4	Leyland TD1	Leyland	L27/24R	1931	1944-6	
157-8	BG 205-6	Daimler CH6	Massey	L27/26R	1931	1938	
159-63	BG 472-6	Leyland TD1	Massey	L27/24R	1931	1944-7	
164-70	BG 739-45	Leyland TD2	Leyland	L27/24R	1932	1940-8	
171-5	BG 746-50	Daimler CH6	Massey	L26/26R	1932	1938	
176-84	BG 1500-8	Leyland TD2	Leyland	L27/24R	1933	1947-8	E
185	BG 1509	AEC 'Q'	MCCW	L31/28F	1933	1940	
186-8	BG 2651-3	Leyland TD3c	NCME	L26/24R	1934	1948-9	
189-91	BG 2654-6	Leyland TD3c	NCME	H28/24R	1934	1948-9	
192-7	BG 2657-62	Leyland TD3c	Massey	H28/24R	1934	1949	
198-202	BG 3423-7	Leyland TD4c	Massey	H30/24R	1935	1949-52	F
203-7	BG 3428-32	Leyland TD4c	NCME	H30/24R	1935	1949-52	F
208-18	BG 4381-91	Leyland TD4c	Massey	H30/24R	1936	1949-52	G
219-58	BG 5501-40	Leyland TD5c	Massey	H30/24R	1937	1950-1	H
259-68	BG 6801-10	Leyland TD5c	Massey	H30/24R	1938	1950-1	
269-78	BG 6811-20	Leyland TD5c	NCME	H30/24R	1938	1953-5	
279-318	BG 7701-40	Leyland TD5c	Massey	H30/24R	1939	1951-7	
319-20	BG 8552-3	Guy Arab 5LW	Weymann	H30/26R	1943	1951-4	
321-5	BG 8554-8	Guy Arab 5LW	Massey	H30/26R	1943-4	1954-69	J
326-30	BG 8628-32	Guy Arab 5LW	Massey	H30/26R	1943-4	1954-69	J
331-8	BG 8641-8	Guy Arab 5LW	Massey	H30/26R	1943-4	1954-69	J
339-42	BG 8649-52	Guy Arab 5LW	Park Royal	H30/26R	1944	1954	
343-50	BG 8735-42	Guy Arab 5LW	Park Royal	H30/26R	1946	1957-9	
351-4	BG 8743-6	Guy Arab 5LW	NCME	H30/26R	1946	1957-9	
101-12	BG 9221-32	Leyland PD1	Massey	H30/26R	1946	1959-60	
113-25	BG 9531-78	Leyland PD1	Massey	H30/26R	1947	1959-61	K
97-100	ACM 194,107-9	Leyland PS1	Massey	B33R	1948	1964	L
126-45	ACM 301-20	Leyland PD1	Massey	H30/26R	1948	1961-3	
146-60	ACM 604-18	Guy Arab 6LW	Massey	H30/26R	1949	1962-3	
161-75	ACM 619-33	Daimler CVG6	Massey	H30/26R	1949	1963-5	
176-90	ABG 176-90	Daimler CVG6	Massey	H30/26R	1950	1964-6	
191-205	ABG 291-305	Guy Arab 6LW	Massey	H30/26R	1950	1965-6	
206-25	ABG 806-25	Leyland PD2/3	Leyland	H31/26R	1951	1966-7	M
226-40	BCM 926-40	Guy Arab 6LW	East Lancs	H33/26R	1952	1968-9	
256-65	CBG 556-65	Leyland PD2/12	Weymann	H33/26R	1954	1969-73	
266-70	CBG 566-70	Leyland PD2/12	Ashcroft	H33/26R	1954	1972-3	
355-61	DCM 975-81	Guy Arab IV 6LW	Massey	H31/28R	1955	1972	
362-6	DCM 982-6	Leyland PD2/12	East Lancs	H31/28R	1955	1973	
367-71	DCM 987-91	Leyland PD2/12	Weymann	H33/26R	1955	1972-3	
372-81	{ EBG 59-64 EBG 750-3 }	Guy Arab IV 6LW	Massey	H31/28R	1956	1970-2	

Fleet No.	Reg. No.	Chassis Make and Type	Body Make	Type and Capacity	Year in Service	Year Withdrawn	Notes
382-6	EBG 754-8	Guy Arab IV 6LW	East Lancs	H31/28R	1956	1971-2	
1-8	FCM 991-8	Leyland PD2/40	Massey	H31/28R	1957-8	1972-4	
9-15	FBG 909-15	Leyland PD2/40	Massey	H31/28R	1957-8	1972-4	
16-30	HCM 516-30	Leyland PD2/40	Massey	H33/28R	1959-60	1974-5	N
31-45	JBG 531-45	Leyland PD2/40	Massey	H35/28R	1960-61	1973-4	
46-60	LCM 446-60	Leyland PD2/40	East Lancs	H37/28R	1961	1973-4	
61-75	MCM 961-75	Leyland PD2/40	Massey	H35/30R	1962	1973-5	
76-90	OCM 976-90	Leyland PD2/40	Massey	H35/30R	1963	1972-5	
91-4	RCM 491-4	Leyland L1	Massey	B42D	1964	1974-7	
101-9	RCM 501-9	Daimler CRG6LX	Weymann	H44/33F	1964	1977-8	
110-24	BBG 110-24C	Leyland PD2/40	Massey	H36/30R	1965	1973-4	
125-39	DBG 125-39D	Leyland PD2/40	Massey	H36/30R	1966	1973-4	
140-54	GCM 140-54E	Leyland PD2/37	Massey	H36/30R	1967	1975-7	
155-67	LCM 155-67G	Leyland PDR1/1	NCME	H44/33F	1968	1980-1	
168-82	MBG 368-82H	Leyland PDR1/2	NCME	H44/27D	1969-70	1981	Some P
183-95	OBG 383-95J	Leyland PDR1A/1	NCME	H44/27D	1970	1981	P
95-6	OBG 495-6J	Leyland PDR2/1	NCME	B40D	1970	1981	P

Key to Body Type Code

B = Saloon Bus FB = Fully fronted saloon bus H = Highbridge type double deck L - Lowbridge type double deck
O = Open top double deck.   Figures denote seating capacity - upper deck first.
Final letter denotes door position. F = Front R = Rear D = Dual RO = Rear, open staircase.

Notes

A	Second hand from London General Omnibus Co.Ltd.
B	Second hand from Plymouth Corporartion
C	Second hand from W.B.Horn, Birkenhead
D	Rebuilt with enclosed stairs 1933.
E	182 damaged in air raid 1941; given new East Lancs H30/26R body in 1942; body transferred to 217 (356) in 1947.
	183 destroyed by fire in 1936; chassis used for a breakdown crane, in service until 1953.
F	198, 204 and 206 damaged in air raids 1941 and fitted with new East Lancs H30/26R bodies in 1942;
	renumbered 355, 357 and 358 in 1947-8.
G	214 fitted with new East Lancs H30/26R body in 1942; renumbered 359 in 1947.
	217 renumbered 356 in 1947 on receiving new body from 182.
H	226, 235 rebodied by Massey in 1942; renumbered 360-1 in 1947.
J	319 rebuilt as breakdown crane in 1951 and ran until 1968. 323-37 rebodied with new Massey 7ft9in bodies and
	fitted with 6LW engines 1953. Renumbered 241-55 and ran until 1969.
K	Registration and fleet numbers not in sequence.
L	97 was for a short time registered ACM106 in error.
M	First 8ft wide buses.
N	21-3, 25-30 transferred to Wallasey by PTE 1970 and renumbered 21-3B, 25-30B; renumbered 321-3, 325-30 in 1971.
P	Ordered by Birkenhead Corporation but delivered to Merseyside PTE.

All buses from 1919 to 1932 up to 168, 171-5 and 185 had petrol engines; all others had diesel engines.

APPENDIX 2
LIST OF SERVICES

The principal services are listed, followed by the supplementary services applicable to the same route.

OCTOBER 1930

1	Woodside-Moreton (Bermuda Road or Shore)
2	Woodside-St. James' Church via Claughton Road
3	Rock Ferry Pier-Moreton (Bermuda Road) via Derby Road
4	Rock Ferry Pier-Port Sunlight via Dacre Hill
5	Bromborough-Upton or Eastham-Woodside
6	Woodside-Kings Road (Kings Lane) via Whetstone Lane
7	Park Station-Port Sunlight via Derby Road
8*	Charing Cross-Liscard
9*	Charing Cross-Seacombe
10	Market Place South-Storeton Road (Birch Road)
11	Woodside-Prenton Dell Road via Singleton Avenue
12	Woodside-Lower Bebington (Spital Cross Roads) via Old Chester Road
13*	New Ferry-New Brighton via Old Chester Road, Argyle Street & Liscard
14	Woodside-Arrowe Park-Upton-Park Station-Woodside and vice versa
15	New Ferry-Eastham Ferry
16	Upton-Moreton Shore
17	Woodside-Heswall via Irby and Thurstaston

JANUARY 1931

10*	New Ferry-New Brighton via Old Chester Road & Cleveland Street		
11*	Charing Cross-Liscard via Park Station & Duke Street Bridge		
12*	Charing Cross-Seacombe via Park Station & Duke Street Bridge		
21	Woodside-Moreton (Bermuda Road) via Park Station & Bidston		
22	Woodside-Moreton Shore via Park Station & Bidston		
		20	Woodside-Moreton Cross
		23	Woodside-Hurrell Road
		24	Market Place South-Hurrell Road
26	Rock Ferry Pier-Moreton (Bermuda Road) via Derby Road & Park Station		
		25	Charing Cross-Hurrell Road
40	Woodside-Eastham Village via New Chester Road		
		00	Special Buses to Planters
		41	Woodside-Eastham Ferry
		42	New Ferry-Eastham Ferry
		--	New Ferry-Bromborough Pool Village (Fridays & Saturdays only)
43	Bromborough-Upton via Old Chester Road & Park Station		
		15	Charing Cross or Park Station-Upton
		45	Central Station-St.Paul's Road
		47	Bromborough-Charing Cross
		48	New Ferry-Charing Cross
44#	St.Paul's Road-Eastham Ferry via New Chester Road		
46	New Ferry-Bromborough Cross via Lower Bebington and Trafalgar		
50	Woodside-Lower Bebington (Spital Cross Roads) via Old Chester Road		
		55	Central Station-Town Lane or Bebington Station

160

51	Claughton Village-Port Sunlight	
	52	Park Station-Port Sunlight
	53	Charing Cross-Port Sunlight
	56	Charing Cross-Port Sunlight Recreation Ground
54	Rock Ferry Pier-Port Sunlight via Dacre Hill	
60	Woodside-Kings Road (Kings Lane) via Whetstone Lane & Church Road	
	61	Woodside-Bebington Road
	62	Central Station-Kings Road
	63	Central Station-Bebington Road
71	Woodside-Heswall via Irby & Thurstaston	
	72	Woodside-Thurstaston
	73	Woodside-Irby
	74	Central Station-Irby
77	Woodside-Moreton Shore via Arrowe Park & Upton	
	70	Woodside-Prenton Dell Road
	75	Woodside-Arrowe Park
	76	Central Station-Arrowe Park
	78	Woodside-Arrowe Park-Upton-Park Station-Woodside (not in operation)
79	Market Place South-Storeton Road (Birch Road) via Oxton Road (Not Sundays)	
90	Woodside-St.James' Church via Claughton Road	
	91	Market Place South & St. James' Church

AUGUST 1939

2	Oxton Circle via Conway Street, Shrewsbury Road & Borough Road	
	3	Woodside-Upton Road
	4	Woodside-Laird Street
6	Oxton Circle via Borough Road, Shrewsbury Road & Conway Street	
	7	Woodside-Laird Street via Shrewsbury Road
10*	New Ferry-New Brighton via Old Chester Road & Cleveland Street	
11*	Charing Cross-Liscard via Park Station & Duke Street Bridge	
12*	Charing Cross-Seacombe via Park Station & Duke Street Bridge	
16+	Park Station-New Ferry via Upton, Arrowe Park & Woodchurch Lane	
21	Woodside-Moreton (Bermuda Road) via Park Station & Bidston	
22	Woodside-Moreton Shore via Park Station & Bidston	
	20	Woodside-Moreton Cross
	23	Woodside-Hurrell Road
	24	Market Place South-Hurrell Road
	25	Market Place South-St.James' Church
26	Bromborough-Moreton (Bermuda Road) via Borough Road & Park Station	
	27	New Ferry-Hurrell Road
38	Woodside-Bromborough (Manor Road) via New Chester Road	
40	Woodside-Eastham Village via New Chester Road	
	42	New Ferry-Bromborough Pool Village (Fridays & Saturdays only)
	49	Woodside-New Ferry
	00	Buses to Planters (Bromborough Port)
43	Bromborough-Upton via Old Chester Road & Park Station	
	15	Park Station-Upton
	45	Central Station-St.Paul's Road
	47	Bromborough-Charing Cross
	48	New Ferry-Charing Cross

44#	St.Paul's Road-Eastham Ferry via Lower Bebington & Raeburn Avenue
50	Woodside-Lower Bebington (Spital Cross Roads) via Old Chester Road
55	Central Station-Town Lane or Bebington Station
51	Claughton Village-Port Sunlight
52	Park Station-Port Sunlight
53	Charing Cross-Port Sunlight
56	Charing Cross-Port Sunlight Recreation Ground
57	Bidston Road (Ashburton Road)-Port Sunlight
54	Rock Ferry Pier-Port Sunlight via Bedford Avenue
60	Woodside-Heath Road via Whetstone Lane, Church Road & Kings Road
65	Central Station-Bebington Road
66	Woodside-Thornton Road
67	Central Station-Thornton Road
64	Woodside-New Ferry (Gt.Eastern Hotel) via Borough Road & Kings Road
63	Woodside-Village Road
71	Woodside-Heswall via Irby & Thurstaston
72	Woodside-Thurstaston
73	Woodside-Irby
74	Central Station-Irby
77	Woodside-Moreton Shore via Arrowe Park & Upton
70	Woodside-Prenton Dell Road
75	Woodside-Arrowe Park
76	Central Station-Arrowe Park
78	Woodside-Greasby via Arrowe Park & Arrowe Bridge
79	Haymarket-Storeton Road (Birch Road) via Oxton Road (Not Sundays.)
80	Woodside-Prenton (War Memorial) via Prenton Road West
84	Woodside-Thornton Road (Mount Road) via Prenton Road West
81	Central Station-Storeton Road (Prenton Lane)
82	Woodside-Singleton Avenue
83	Woodside-Storeton Road (Prenton Lane)
85	Woodside-Thurstaston via Claughton Road, Greasby & Frankby
90	North Circle via Claughton Road & Cleveland Street
91	Market Place South & Cemetery Gates
92	Woodside-St.James' Church via Claughton Road
94	North Circle via Cleveland Street & Claughton Road
95	Woodside-Station Road via Cleveland Street

AUGUST 1949

2	Oxton Circle via Conway Street, Shrewsbury Road & Borough Road
3	Woodside-Upton Road
4	Woodside-Laird Street
5	Upton Road-Woodside via Chester Street
6	Oxton Circle via Borough Road, Shrewsbury Road & Conway Street
7	Woodside-Laird Street via Shrewsbury Road
10*	Bromborough or New Ferry-New Brighton via Old Chester Road & Cleveland Street
9*	Central Station-Liscard (number not used by Wallasey)
11*	Gorsey Hey (Higher Bebington)-New Brighton via Charing Cross & Liscard
12*	Bebington Station-New Brighton via Charing Cross, Seacombe & Seabank Road
16+	Park Station-Arrowe Park via St. James' Church & Upton
18*	Arrowe Park-New Brighton via Upton, Poulton Bridge & Belvidere Road

21	Woodside-Moreton (Bermuda Road) via Park Station & Bidston	
22	Woodside-Moreton Shore via Park Station & Bidston	
	20	Woodside-Moreton Cross
	23	Woodside-Hurrell Road
	24	Market Place South-Hurrell Road
28	Bromborough (Acre Lane)-Moreton (Bermuda Road) via Borough Road & Park Station	
	26	Bromborough Cross-Moreton (Bermuda Road)
	27	New Ferry-Hurrell Road
	29	New Ferry-Charing Cross or Park Station via Borough Road
34	Woodside-Bromborough Pool Village (Saturdays only)	
	32	New Ferry-Bromborough Pool Village (Fridays & Saturdays only)
38	Woodside-Bromborough (Manor Road) via New Chester Road & Allport Lane	
40	Woodside-Eastham Village via New Chester Road	
	30	Inward buses to Ivy Street
	31	New Ferry-Bromborough Cross
	33	Woodside or Ivy Street-Bromborough Dock
	35	Woodside-Port Causeway
	36	Woodside-Bromborough Cross via New Chester Road
	37	Woodside-Allport Road
	49	Woodside-New Ferry
	88	Woodside-Bromborough Power Station
	00	Buses to Stork Margarine Works
42	Eastham Village-Overchurch Road via Old Chester Road & Park Station	
	14	Park Station-Overchurch Road
	15	Park Station-Upton
	41	Eastham Village-Arrowe Park via Upton (Sundays)
	43	Bromborough Cross-Upton
	46	Bromborough Cross-Overchurch Road
	47	Bromborough or New Ferry-Charing Cross
	48	Bromborough or New Ferry-Park Station
44#	St. Paul's Road-Eastham Ferry via Lower Bebington, Trafalgar & Raeburn Avenue	
58	Woodside-Clatterbridge via Old Chester Road & Lower Bebington	
	50	Woodside-Spital Cross Roads via Old Chester Road
	55	Woodside or Central Station-Bebington Station
51	Claughton Village-Port Sunlight via Derby Road	
	52	Park Station-Port Sunlight
	53	Charing Cross-Port Sunlight
	56	Charing Cross-Bebington Station
	57	Port Sunlight-Boundary Road (Ashburton Road) (pm peak hours)
60	Woodside-Cross Lane (Stanton Road) via Whetstone Lane & Kings Road	
	66	Woodside-Thornton Road via Whetstone Lane
	67	Central Station-Thornton Road via Whetstone Lane
	68	Woodside-Village Road via Whetstone Lane
	69	Woodside or Central Station-Bebington Road
64	Woodside-New Ferry (Great Eastern Hotel) via Borough Road & Kings Road	
	63	Woodside-Village Road via Borough Road
	65	Central Station-Village Road via Borough Road
71	Woodside-Heswall via Irby & Thurstaston	
	72	Woodside-Thurstaston
	73	Woodside-Irby
	74	Woodside or Central Station-Thurstaston Shore

77	Woodside-Moreton Shore via Arrowe Park & Upton
	70	Woodside-Prenton Dell Road
	75	Woodside-Arrowe Park
	76	Central Station-Arrowe Park
78	Woodside-Greasby via Arrowe Park & Arrowe Bridge
79	Woodside-Storeton Road (Birch Road) via Oxton Road (not Sundays.)
80	Woodside-Prenton (War Memorial) via Prenton Road West
	81	Central Station-Storeton Road (Prenton Lane)
	82	Woodside-Singleton Avenue
	83	Woodside-Storeton Road (Prenton Lane)
84	Woodside-Lever Causeway via Borough Road and Mount Road (not Sundays)
85	Woodside-South Circle via Storeton Road, Kings Lane & New Ferry
86	Woodside-South Circle via Storeton Road, Town Lane & New Ferry
90	North Circle via Claughton Road & Cleveland Street
	91	Market Place South-Cemetery Gates
	92	Woodside-St.James' Church via Claughton Road
94	North Circle via Cleveland Street & Claughton Road
	95	Woodside-Station Road via Cleveland Street
96	Woodside-Thurstaston via Claughton Road, Greasby & Frankby
99	Buses from any point to Cammell Laird's (Green Lane)

JUNE 1967

2	Oxton Circle via Conway Street, Shrewsbury Road & Borough Road
	3	Woodside-Upton Road
	4	Woodside-Laird Street
	5	Upton Road-Woodside via Chester Street
6	Oxton Circle via Borough Road, Shrewsbury Road & Conway Street
	7	Woodside-Laird Street via Shrewsbury Road
9*	Charing Cross-Liscard via Poulton Bridge (not Sundays)
10*	Bromborough or New Ferry-New Brighton via Old Chester Road & Cleveland Street
	10A*	New Brighton or Liscard-King's Square (peak hours)
11*	Higher Tranmere (Wiend)-New Brighton via Charing Cross & Liscard
12*	Charing Cross-Seacombe via Park Station & Duke Street Bridge
13*	King's Square-Egremont (Trafalgar Road) via Four Bridges (Peak hours)
16	Park Station-Landican Cemetery via St. James' Church, Upton & Arrowe Park (Sat & Sun)
18*	Woodchurch Estate.-New Brighton via Arrowe Park, Upton & Poulton Bridge (summer)
21	Woodside-Moreton (Bermuda Road) via Park Station & Bidston
22	Woodside-Moreton Shore via Park Station & Bidston
	20	Woodside-Moreton Cross
	23	Woodside-Hurrell Road
	24	Market Place South-Hurrell Road
28	Bromborough (Acre Lane)-Moreton (Bermuda Road) via Borough Road & Park Station
28A	Bromborough (Croft Avenue)-Moreton (Bermuda Road) via Borough Road & Park Station
	26	Bromborough Cross-Moreton (Bermuda Road)
	26B	Buses to Bromborough via Port Causeway & Old Hall Road
	27	New Ferry-Hurrell Road
	29	New Ferry-Charing Cross or Park Station via Borough Road
	37	Buses to Bromborough Dock via Borough Road
34	Woodside-Bromborough Pool Village (Saturdays only)
	32	New Ferry-Bromborough Pool Village (Fridays only)

39	Woodside-Eastham Village via Raeburn Avenue & Heygarth Road	
41	Woodside-Mill Park Estate via New Chester Road	
	30	Inward buses to King's Square
	31	New Ferry-Bromborough Cross
	33	Woodside or Kings Square-Bromborough Dock
	35	Woodside-Port Causeway
	36	Woodside-Bromborough Cross via New Chester Road
	36B	Woodside-Bromborough Cross via Port Causeway & Old Hall Road
	38	Woodside-Bromborough (Manor Road) via New Chester Road
	40	Woodside-Eastham Village via New Chester Road
	40B	Buses to Eastham via Port Causeway & Old Hall Road
	41B	Buses to Mill Park via Port Causeway & Old Hall Road
	49	Woodside-New Ferry
	88	Woodside-Bromborough Power Station
	89	Woodside-Eastham Dock
	89B	Woodside-Eastham Dock via Port Causeway and Old Hall Road
	00	Buses to Stork Margarine Works
42	Bromborough (Brookhurst Estate)-Overchurch Road via Old Chester Road & Park Station	
	14	Park Station-Overchurch Road
	15	Park Station-Upton
	43	Bromborough Cross-Upton
	46	Bromborough Cross-Overchurch Road
	47	Bromborough or New Ferry-Charing Cross
	48	Bromborough or New Ferry-Park Station
	59	Buses to Bromborough Dock via Old Chester Road
44	New Ferry-Eastham Ferry via Lower Bebington, Spital Station & Raeburn Avenue	
58	Woodside-Clatterbridge via Old Chester Road & Lower Bebington	
	50	Woodside-Spital Cross Roads via Old Chester Road
	55	Woodside or Central Station-Bebington Station
51	Overchurch Road-Port Sunlight via Charing Cross & Derby Road	
	51A	Upton-Port Sunlight via Park Station, Charing Cross & Derby Road
	51B	Claughton Village-Port Sunlight
	52	Park Station-Port Sunlight
	53	Charing Cross-Port Sunlight
	56	Charing Cross-Bebington Station
60	Woodside-Cross Lane (Stanton Road) via Whetstone Lane & Kings Road	
	60A	Woodside-Cross Lane (Heath Road)
	66	Woodside-Thornton Road via Whetstone Lane
	67	Central Station-Thornton Road via Whetstone Lane
	68	Woodside-Village Road via Whetstone Lane
	69	Woodside or Central Station-Bebington Road
64	Woodside-New Ferry (Great Eastern Hotel) via Borough Road & Kings Road	
	61	Bromborough-Wirral Grammar School
	63	Woodside-Village Road via Borough Road
	65	Woodside-New Ferry (Toll Bar) via Borough Road & Kings Road
70	Woodside-Woodchurch Estate via Singleton Avenue & New Hey Road	
70A	Woodside-Woodchurch Estate via Singleton Avenue & Pemberton Road	
	70B	Woodside-Ackers Road or Orrets Meadow Road
71	Woodside-Heswall via Irby & Thurstaston	

71A	Woodside-Heswall via Irby, Irby Road and Quarry Road	
	71B	Woodside-Somerset Road
	72	Woodside-Thurstaston Cross
	73	Woodside-Irby
	74	Woodside-Thurstaston Shore (Summer Sundays)
77	Woodside-Moreton Shore via Arrowe Park & Upton	
	75	Woodside-Durley Drive
	76	Woodside-Arrowe Park
	76A	Woodside-Upton Village via Arrowe Park
	76B	Woodside-Upton (Warwick Road) via Arrowe Park
	77A	Woodside-Moreton Cross via Arrowe Park
78	Woodside-Greasby via Arrowe Park & Arrowe Bridge	
79	Woodside-Prenton Circle via Singleton Avenue,Prenton Hall Road & Prenton Road West	
80	Woodside-Prenton Circle via Prenton Road West, Prenton Hall Road & Singleton Avenue	
	79A	Woodside-Prenton Dell via Singleton Avenue
	80A	Woodside-Glenavon Road via Prenton Road West
	81	Central Station-Storeton Road (Waterpark Road)
	82	Woodside-Singleton Avenue
	83	Woodside-Storeton Road (Waterpark Road)
84	Woodside-Thornton Road (Lever Causeway) via Borough Road & Mount Road	
85	Woodside-South Circle via Storeton Road, Kings Lane & New Ferry	
86	Woodside-South Circle via Storeton Road, Town Lane & New Ferry	
90	North Circle via Claughton Road & Cleveland Street	
	92	Woodside-St.James' Church via Claughton Road
94	North Circle via Cleveland Street & Claughton Road	
	93	Woodside-Station Road or St. James' Church via Stanley Road
	95	Woodside-Station Road or St. James' Church via Ilchester Road
96	Woodside-Thurstaston via Claughton Road, Upton, Greasby & Frankby	
97	Woodside or Haymarket-Oxton Village loop via Oxton Road	
99	Special buses from any point to Cammell Laird's (Green Lane)	

NOTES

* Joint service with Wallasey Corporation
+ Summer service. Winter Sunday service between Park Station & Arrowe Park
# Afternoons & evenings on weekdays only.
 Additional suffix letters were used for occasional short workings and diversions.

APPENDIX 3
DESTINATION EQUIPMENT

The earliest Birkenhead buses displayed destinations in the form of paper labels in the top light above the nearside windscreen. These were replaced by roller blinds mounted in the same position at an early date. The 'B' type ex-London buses are believed to have carried destination boards on the front of the upper deck, as used in London. Side roller blinds were added soon; these were of a crude design without proper frames, worked by a handle on each roller, tension being retained by spring washers. No destination equipment was carried at the rear.

Some destinations were arranged in two lines e.g. MORETON, BERMUDA ROAD; MORETON EMBANKMENT; ROCK FERRY VIA PARK STATION; WOODSIDE VIA CLAUGHTON ROAD. On some Lions and Titans these displays were arched. No destination was displayed to the rear.

In 1926, a system of route numbers was announced in the timetables, illuminated numbers being displayed to the rear. No clear picture of this equipment has survived but it is thought that stencils were used, the lights of the saloon shining through. It is said that these numbers originated as a system to denote in which lane the bus should be parked but it was developed into a system which reached No. 17 before being scrapped in favour of a more sophisticated system in 1931. Although it was used in timetables up to 1930, it seems to have fallen into disuse on the buses long before then.

The second batch of Titans were equipped with two roller blinds front and rear and equipment either side mounted in proper wooden frames worked by a handle and gears. At the time, there were about 40 displays in use and about half were included on each roll, thus minimising the amount of turning necessary. In addition, the lower roll had a few intermediate points e.g. VIA CLAUGHTON ROAD, VIA DERBY ROAD, VIA OLD CHESTER ROAD. On most routes, the destination was shown in the appropriate aperture, the other one being turned to a blank. However, MORETON appeared on top with BERMUDA ROAD below and on the cross town routes, VIA DERBY ROAD or VIA OLD CHESTER ROAD distinguished the New Ferry-Upton from the Rock Ferry-Moreton buses. The side blinds had some composite displays such as KINGS ROAD VIA HIGHER TRANMERE and ST. JAMES' CHURCH VIA CLAUGHTON ROAD.

Following the introduction of route numbers on 1st January 1931, it was decided that, in most cases, the two terminal points should be shown simultaneously with the route number. Blinds were recast so that all the appropriate names were on the top or bottom. One or two names were on both e.g. WOODSIDE but CENTRAL STATION was always on the bottom only. However, there were some routes for which the blind had to be changed at each terminus viz. LISCARD or SEACOMBE to CHARING CROSS as, originally, all the names were on the top blind.

There were inconsistencies. VIA IRBY & THURSTASTON on two lines appeared on early blinds for use with WOODSIDE and HESWALL, both on the top but later buses had HESWALL on the bottom roll with IRBY AND on the top roll for use with WOODSIDE, CENTRAL STATION, HESWALL or THURSTASTON. The 77 route displayed MORETON ARROWE PARK or WOODSIDE ARROWE PARK and, when a double deck bus was used, the 85 showed WOODSIDE or THURSTASTON VIA FRANKBY. As THURSTASTON was normally on the bottom roll, it suggests that a few buses were reserved for use on this service. It was also the practice to show GREASBY on the nearside indicator and FRANKBY on the offside. There was a similar convention on the 77 route, buses showing ARROWE PARK on the nearside and UPTON on the offside.

The 40 buses delivered for the final tram replacement programme in 1937 retained the system though the names on the rolls were reallocated, resulting in some displays being reversed e.g. UPTON

BROMBOROUGH instead of BROMBOROUGH UPTON. For the Oxton Circle, VIA BOROUGH ROAD and VIA CONWAY STREET were added. However, the 1938 deliveries had all the destinations on the top roll, arranged more or less alphabetically, and only 'vias' on the lower roll. The upper blind also included a number of new names e.g. BROMBOROUGH POOL VILLAGE, POOL LANE, HEYGARTH ROAD. These buses also introduced a new side blind comprising via's with route numbers thus VIA ARROWE PARK 71. Many road or place names appeared several times with different numbers. Thus VIA OLD CHESTER ROAD appeared five times with 10, 00, 43, 50 and without a number; VIA PARK STATION appeared ten times with 11, 12, 20, 21, 22, 23, 24, 26, 27 and 43. On the end of the roll there were five displays to indicate passenger restrictions, previously displayed on cards. These read 'PASSENGERS FOR BEYOND.......ONLY' with PRENTON ROAD EAST (for 64), LANDICAN LANE (for 71, 72), LAIRD STREET (for limited stop 21), SINGLETON AVENUE (for 77) and TOLLEMACHE ROAD (for 85).

The old EXPRESS (on the top) was replaced by LIMITED STOP (usually on the bottom) but ENGAGED was retained for out of service display. The older buses continued to use the old system though some were fitted with blinds for the new system after the war. The practice of never changing the blinds was to die hard, however, and lazy habits were assisted by the inclusion on the lower roll of names which could be used as destinations, the presence of the VIA prefix being conveniently ignored. Thus WOODSIDE VIA NEW FERRY and SEACOMBE VIA CHARING CROSS were used for thirty years or more by crews intent on never turning an indicator blind!

One of the features of the pre-war and, to some extent, the first post-war blinds was the imprecision of the displays. Thus NEW FERRY could denote the depot, Great Eastern Hotel, Bolton Road, Pool Lane or even Lever Causeway, the theory being that the route number provided the detail. PRENTON was used for Prenton Dell Road, the War Memorial, Storeton Road (Waterpark Road), Lever Causeway (which was in Higher Bebington) and Birch Road (which was in Oxton). KINGS ROAD, too, continued to be used as a destination on the 60 route for many years after it was extended successively to Gorsey Hey, Pulford Road and Cross Lane. It was only in the later years of the Corporation transport department that separate displays were provided.

Extraordinarily, no firm instructions were ever issued as to the correct 'via' to be displayed on the lower roll and the conductors could choose from a wide range. Thus on route 80 there was VIA BOROUGH ROAD, VIA PRENTON ROAD WEST or VIA PRENTON LANE to choose from. Route 78 had VIA BOROUGH ROAD, VIA SINGLETON AVENUE, VIA ARROWE PARK or VIA ARROWE BRIDGE. Even the clockwise Oxton Circle could choose VIA BOROUGH ROAD or VIA SHREWSBURY ROAD.

The pre-war side rolls were retained on the first batches of Leyland PD1s but the route numbers were eliminated from No. 126 onwards. Subsequent issues made good the deficiencies and much more detail was added as time went on. The 1948 destination blind was recast with WOODSIDE three times (instead of two, and better spaced) and intermediate blanks but a number of places were probably accidentally omitted e.g. VILLAGE ROAD, TRANMERE and BEBINGTON ROAD. TOWN LANE was used for the former but there was no alternative for the latter. 'POOL' was erroneously printed as 'PORT' in BROMBOROUGH POOL VILLAGE. The lower roll inexplicably included VIA BARNSTON which was on a Crosville route and VIA POULTON BRIDGE was wrongly shown as VIA POULTON VILLAGE. The 1950 blind was profligate with superfluous detail, to the extent that it included IVY STREET, KINGS SQUARE and TUNNEL ENTRANCE which were to all intents and purposes the same place! Later blinds included BEBINGTON ROAD and MOUNT ROAD (BEBINGTON ROAD), again the same place

No blind originating before 1938 has survived complete but examples of the contents of specimen blinds from 1938 to 1969 are given in the following pages.

Route Numbers

When the all-embracing route number system was introduced in 1931, all buses were fitted with two square boxes each containing a roll of numbers from 0 to 9. These were mounted above the single destination indicator on single-deck buses and Leviathans and in the front upper-deck windows on Titan double-deckers. No numbers were displayed to the rear.

In 1934, new buses 189-97 had the route number mounted below the upper deck windows and above the destination and on the subsequent delivery, (Nos. 198-207) numbers were also shown in a comparable position at the rear. The side indicators were also moved up into the bodywork above the rear window on each side. From bus No. 208, delivered in 1936, larger numbers were positioned alongside the destination display on the nearside front and rear and this layout was retained for the rest of the undertaking's life.

By the late 'forties, almost every route number between 00 and 99 was in use and it was decided that future needs would have to be met by the use of suffix letters. From Guy No. 146 the 'units' roll was made slightly wider and this roll ran from 0 to 9, 0A to 9A and 0B to 9B. The first suffixed number to be used was 71A in 1951 and all buses from TD5 269 to Guy 354 and PDIs and PSIs were equipped with an extension to the units blind containing the following:-

A
16
B
18
A
70
B
71
A
28
B

The last number was almost certainly added later as 28A was not introduced until 1954. The blind was designed so that one number and one letter would fill the aperture; thus A followed by 70 = 70A and 70 followed by B = 70B.

Some blinds issued in the 'sixties also included 0C to 9C but there is no evidence that any C-suffixed numbers were ever used.

After 1951 (buses numbered 206-25), offside indicators were not fitted and those on other buses tended to fall into disuse.

APPENDIX 4
BUS DESTINATION BLINDS

Where two lines are bracketed, they form one display, with lettering approximately half the usual height.

1938-48

TOP BLIND	BOTTOM BLIND	SIDE BLIND
WOODSIDE	VIA ARROWE PARK	VIA ARROWE PARK 71
ARROWE PARK	VIA ARROWE BRIDGE	VIA ARROWE PARK 72
BEBINGTON STATION	VIA BEBINGTON ROAD	VIA ARROWE PARK 73
BROMBOROUGH POOL VILLAGE	VIA BOROUGH ROAD	VIA ARROWE PARK 77
BROMBOROUGH	VIA CHARING CROSS	VIA ARROWE PARK
CENTRAL STATION	VIA CENTRAL STATION	VIA BOROUGH RD 63
CHARING CROSS	VIA CLAUGHTON ROAD	VIA BOROUGH RD 64
CLAUGHTON VILLAGE	VIA CLEVELAND STREET	VIA BOROUGH RD 80
EASTHAM	VIA CONWAY STREET	VIA BOROUGH RD 26
ENGAGED	VIA CLAUGHTON VILLAGE	VIA BOROUGH RD 27
FRANKBY	VIA DERBY ROAD	VIA BOROUGH RD
FOOTBALL MATCH	VIA FRANKBY	VIA BEBINGTON RD 54
GREEN LANE	VIA GREASBY	VIA CLEVELAND ST 94
GREASBY	VIA IRBY	VIA CLEVELAND ST 95
HESWALL	VIA KINGS ROAD	VIA CLAUGHTON RD 90
HIGHER BEBINGTON	LIMITED STOP	VIA CLAUGHTON RD 91
HAYMARKET	VIA LISCARD	VIA CONWAY ST 2
HURRELL ROAD	VIA NEW CHESTER ROAD	VIA CONWAY ST 25
HEYGARTH ROAD	VIA NEW FERRY	VIA DERBY ROAD 51
HARRISON DRIVE	VIA OXTON ROAD	VIA DERBY ROAD 52
IRBY	VIA OLD CHESTER ROAD	VIA DERBY ROAD 53
KINGS ROAD	VIA PARK STATION	VIA DERBY ROAD
LAIRD STREET	VIA PRENTON ROAD WEST	ENGAGED
LOWER BEBINGTON	VIA PRENTON LANE	VIA FRANKBY 85
LISCARD	VIA POULTON BRIDGE	VIA GREASBY 85
LANDICAN LANE	VIA ROCK FERRY	VIA KINGS ROAD 64
MORETON CROSS	VIA SHREWSBURY ROAD	VIA NEW CHESTER RD 38
MORETON SHORE	VIA SINGLETON AVENUE	VIA NEW CHESTER RD 00
MORETON BERMUDA ROAD	VIA UPTON ROAD	VIA NEW CHESTER RD 40
NORTH CIRCLE	VIA UPTON	VIA NEW CHESTER RD 42
NEW BRIGHTON	VIA WHETSTONE LANE	VIA NEW CHESTER RD 49
NEW FERRY		VIA OLD CHESTER RD 00
OXTON CIRCLE		VIA OLD CHESTER RD 10
POOL LANE		VIA OLD CHESTER RD 43
PLANTERS		VIA OLD CHESTER RD 50
PARK STATION		VIA OLD CHESTER RD
PORT SUNLIGHT		VIA POULTON BGE 13
PRENTON		VIA PARK STATION 11
ROCK FERRY		VIA PARK STATION 12
ST.JAMES CHURCH		VIA PARK STATION 20
SINGLETON AVENUE		VIA PARK STATION 21
STORETON ROAD		VIA PARK STATION 22
STATION ROAD		VIA PARK STATION 23
ST. PAULS ROAD		VIA PARK STATION 24
SEACOMBE		VIA PARK STATION 26
TUNNEL ENTRANCE		VIA PARK STATION 27
THURSTASTON		VIA PARK STATION 43
UPTON		VIA SINGLETON AV 70
UPTON ROAD		VIA SINGLETON AV
VILLAGE ROAD		VIA SHREWSBURY RD 6
WOODSIDE		VIA ST.JAMES CHURCH
		VIA WHETSTONE LA 60
		VIA WHETSTONE LA 65
		VIA WHETSTONE LA 66
		VIA WHETSTONE LA 67

{ PASSENGERS FOR BEYOND
{ PRENTON RD EAST ONLY

{ PASSENGERS FOR BEYOND
{ LANDICAN LANE ONLY

{ PASSENGERS FOR BEYOND
{ LAIRD ST ONLY

{ PASSENGERS FOR BEYOND
{ SINGLETON AV ONLY

{ PASSENGERS FOR BEYOND
{ TOLLEMACHE RD ONLY

1948 DESTINATION BLIND
* denotes 'ROAD' later painted out

ARROWE PARK
BEBINGTON STATION
BOUNDARY ROAD
BROMBOROUGH CROSS
BROMBOROUGH PORT VILLAGE
CENTRAL STATION
CHARING CROSS
CLATTERBRIDGE
CLAUGHTON VILLAGE
CROSS LANE
EASTHAM
EASTHAM FERRY
WOODSIDE
FOOTBALL MATCH
FORD ESTATE
FRANKBY
GREASBY
HAYMARKET
Blank
HESWALL
HURRELL ROAD
IRBY
LAIRD STREET
LISCARD
MANOR ROAD
MILL PARK ESTATE
MORETON-BERMUDA ROAD
WOODSIDE
(continued in second column)

MORETON CROSS
MORETON SHORE
NEW BRIGHTON
NEW FERRY
NORTH CIRCLE
OSMASTON ROAD
OXTON CIRCLE
PARK STATION
PORT SUNLIGHT
TRANMERE
PRENTON DELL ROAD*
ST. JAMES CHURCH
WOODSIDE
ST. PAULS ROAD
SAUGHALL MASSIE
SEACOMBE
SPITAL CROSS ROADS
STATION ROAD
STORETON ROAD
STORK MARGARINE WORKS
THORNTON ROAD
THURSTASTON
TOWN LANE
UPTON
Black blank
WOODCHURCH ESTATE
{ TOWN MEADOW LANE
{ BERMUDA ROAD
{ GORSEY HEY
{ HR BEBINGTON

Rear view of Guy No. 148 showing the absence of a bumper and the relocation of the registration number in a glazed panel on the lower cream band.
Massey Bros.

171

TOP BLIND	BOTTOM BLIND	SIDE BLIND
Blank	Blank	
ARROWE PARK	VIA ARROWE PARK	VIA ARROWE PARK
BEBINGTON STATION	VIA BOROUGH ROAD	VIA BOROUGH ROAD
BOUNDARY ROAD	VIA CONWAY STREET	VIA CONWAY STREET
BROMBOROUGH	VIA CLAUGHTON ROAD	VIA CLAUGHTON ROAD
BROMBOROUGH POOL VILLAGE	VIA CLEVELAND STREET	VIA CLEVELAND STREET
CENTRAL STATION	VIA CENTRAL STATION	VIA CENTRAL STATION
CHARING CROSS	VIA CHARING CROSS	VIA CHARING CROSS
CLATTERBRIDGE	VIA CLAUGHTON VILLAGE	VIA CLAUGHTON VILLAGE
CLAUGHTON VILLAGE	VIA DERBY ROAD	VIA DERBY ROAD
CROSS LANE	VIA FOUR BRIDGES	VIA FOUR BRIDGES
EASTHAM FERRY	VIA HEYGARTH ROAD	VIA HEYGARTH ROAD
EASTHAM VILLAGE	VIA HGR TRANMERE	VIA HGR TRANMERE
WOODSIDE	VIA IRBY ROAD	VIA IRBY ROAD
FOOTBALL MATCH	VIA KINGS LANE	Blank
FRANKBY	VIA KINGS ROAD	VIA KINGS LANE
GREASBY	VIA LISCARD	VIA KINGS ROAD
GORSEY HEY	VIA LOWER BEBINGTON	VIA LISCARD
HGR BEBINGTON		
HAYMARKET	Blank	VIA LOWER BEBINGTON
HGR TRANMERE	VIA NEW CHESTER ROAD	VIA NEW CHESTER ROAD
HESWALL	VIA OLD CHESTER ROAD	VIA OLD CHESTER ROAD
HEYGARTH ROAD	VIA OXTON ROAD	VIA OXTON ROAD
HURRELL ROAD	VIA PARK ROAD WEST	VIA PARK ROAD WEST
IRBY	VIA PARK STATION	VIA PARK STATION
KINGS LANE	VIA POULTON BRIDGE	VIA POULTON BRIDGE
LAIRD STREET	VIA PRENTON ROAD WEST	VIA PRENTON ROAD WEST
LISCARD VILLAGE	VIA SEACOMBE	VIA RAEBURN AVENUE
MANOR ROAD	VIA SINGLETON AVENUE	VIA SEACOMBE FERRY
MORETON.BERMUDA RD.	VIA ST. JAMES CHURCH	VIA SINGLETON AVENUE
MORETON SHORE	VIA THURSTASTON	VIA ST. JAMES CHURCH
MORETON CROSS	VIA TOWN LANE	Blank
Blank	VIA UPTON	VIA THURSTASTON
WOODSIDE	VIA WHETSTONE LANE	VIA TOWN LANE
NEW BRIGHTON	VIA WOODCHURCH ROAD	VIA UPTON
NEW FERRY	VIA WOODCHURCH ESTATE	VIA WHETSTONE LANE
NORTH CIRCLE	BEBINGTON ROAD	ENGAGED
OSMASTON ROAD	BEDFORD ROAD	FOOTBALL MATCH
OXTON CIRCLE	BOLTON ROAD	LIMITED STOP
PARK STATION	BRIDGE STREET	{ PASSENGERS FOR BEYOND
PORT SUNLIGHT	Blank	{ FOREST ROAD
PRENTON	BROMBOROUGH POWER STATION	{ PASSENGERS FOR BEYOND
PRENTON DELL ROAD	CENTRAL STATION	{ LAIRD STREET DEPOT
SINGLETON AVENUE	DUPLICATE	{ PASSENGERS FOR AND
ST.JAMES CHURCH	ENGAGED	{ BEYOND LANDICAN LANE
WOODSIDE	GREEN LANE	{ PASSENGERS FOR BEYOND
ST. PAULS ROAD	GERALD ROAD	{ NEW FERRY DEPOT
SAUGHALL MASSIE	HEYGARTH ROAD	{ PASSENGERS FOR AND
SEACOMBE FERRY	KINGSMEAD ROAD	{ BEYOND NOCTORUM LANE
SPITAL CROSS ROADS	LANDICAN LANE	{ PASSENGERS FOR BEYOND
STATION ROAD	LIMITED STOP	{ PRENTON ROAD EAST
STORETON ROAD	PORT CAUSEWAY	{ PASSENGERS FOR BEYOND
STORK MARGARINE WORKS	PRENTON ROAD EAST	{ SINGLETON AVENUE
THORNTON ROAD	ROCK FERRY STATION	{ PASSENGERS FOR BEYOND
THURSTASTON	TUNNEL ENTRANCE	{ TOLLEMACHE ROAD
THURSTASTON SHORE		
TOWN LANE		
UPTON		
WOODCHURCH ESTATE		
VILLAGE ROAD		
Blank		

REVISED BLINDS 1950
Fitted to buses 206-225

TOP BLIND	BOTTOM BLIND	SIDE BLIND
ALLPORT ROAD	VIA ALLPORT LANE	VIA ALLPORT LANE
ARROWEBROOK ROAD	VIA ARROWE PARK	VIA ARROWE PARK
ARROWE PARK	VIA BARNSTON	VIA BARNSTON
BEBINGTON STATION	VIA BIDSTON	VIA BIDSTON
BEDFORD DRIVE	VIA BEDFORD AVENUE	VIA BEDFORD ROAD
BEBINGTON ROAD	VIA BOROUGH ROAD	VIA BOROUGH ROAD
BEDFORD ROAD	VIA CONWAY STREET	VIA CONWAY STREET
BOLTON ROAD	VIA CLAUGHTON ROAD	VIA CLAUGHTON ROAD
BOUNDARY ROAD	VIA CLEVELAND STREET	VIA CLEVELAND STREET
BRIDGE STREET	VIA CENTRAL STATION	VIA CENTRAL STATION
BROMBOROUGH	VIA CHARING CROSS	VIA CHARING CROSS
BROMBOROUGH CROSS	VIA CLAUGHTON VILLAGE	VIA CLAUGHTON VILLAGE
BROMBOROUGH DOCK	VIA DERBY ROAD	VIA DERBY ROAD
BROMBOROUGH POOL VILLAGE	VIA FOUR BRIDGES	VIA FOUR BRIDGES
BROMBOROUGH POWER STATION	VIA HEYGARTH ROAD	VIA HEYGARTH ROAD
CENTRAL STATION	VIA HIGHER TRANMERE	VIA HIGHER TRANMERE
CHARING CROSS	VIA IRBY ROAD	VIA IRBY ROAD
CIRCULAR TOUR	VIA KINGS LANE	VIA KINGS LANE
CLATTERBRIDGE	VIA KINGS ROAD	VIA KINGS ROAD
CLAUGHTON VILLAGE	VIA LISCARD	VIA LISCARD
CROSS LANE	VIA LOWER BEBINGTON	VIA LOWER BEBINGTON
EASTHAM FERRY	VIA NEW CHESTER ROAD	VIA NEW CHESTER ROAD
EASTHAM VILLAGE	VIA NEW FERRY	VIA NEW FERRY
WOODSIDE	White Blank	White Blank
PARK STATION	VIA OLD CHESTER ROAD	VIA OLD CHESTER ROAD
FOOTBALL MATCH	VIA OXTON ROAD	VIA OXTON ROAD
FRANKBY	VIA PARK ROAD WEST	VIA PARK ROAD WEST
GERALD ROAD	VIA PARK STATION	VIA PARK STATION
GREASBY	VIA PORT CAUSEWAY	VIA PORT CAUSEWAY
GREEN LANE	VIA POULTON BRIDGE	VIA POULTON BRIDGE
GORSEY HEY	VIA PRENTON ROAD WEST	VIA PRENTON ROAD WEST
HIGHER BEBINGTON	VIA SEACOMBE	VIA SEACOMBE
HAYMARKET	VIA SINGLETON AVENUE	VIA SINGLETON AVENUE
HIGHER TRANMERE	VIA ST. JAMES CHURCH	VIA ST. JAMES CHURCH
HESWALL	VIA THURSTASTON	VIA THURSTASTON
HEYGARTH ROAD	VIA TOWN LANE	VIA TOWN LANE
HURRELL ROAD	VIA UPTON	VIA UPTON
IRBY	VIA WHETSTONE LANE	VIA WHETSTONE LANE
IVY STREET	VIA WOODCHURCH ROAD	VIA WOODCHURCH ROAD
KINGS LANE	VIA WOODCHURCH ESTATE	VIA WOODCHURCH ESTATE
KINGSMEAD ROAD	White Blank	White Blank
KINGS SQUARE	BYRNE AVENUE BATHS	ENGAGED
LAIRD STREET	CIRCULAR TOUR	FOOTBALL MATCH
LANDICAN LANE	DUPLICATE	LIMITED STOP
LISCARD VILLAGE	TO THE SHOW	{ PASSENGERS FOR AND BEYOND FOREST ROAD
LOWER BEBINGTON VILLAGE		{ PASSENGERS FOR BEYOND LAIRD STREET DEPOT
BROMBOROUGH		
MANOR ROAD		{ PASSENGERS FOR AND BEYOND LANDICAN LANE
MARKET PLACE SOUTH		
MORETON,BERMUDA ROAD		{ PASSENGERS FOR BEYOND NEW FERRY DEPOT
MORETON SHORE		
MORETON CROSS		{ PASSENGERS FOR AND BEYOND NOCTORUM LANE
White Blank		
WOODSIDE		{ PASSENGERS FOR BEYOND PRENTON ROAD EAST
CENTRAL STATION		
CHARING CROSS		{ PASSENGERS FOR BEYOND SINGLETON AVENUE
NEW BRIGHTON		
NEW FERRY		{ PASSENGERS FOR AND BEYOND TOLLEMACHE ROAD
NEW FERRY TOLL BAR		
NORTH CIRCLE		CIRCULAR TOUR
OSMASTON ROAD		TO THE SHOW
OXTON CIRCLE		
PARK STATION		
PARK ENTRANCE		
PORT CAUSEWAY		
PORT SUNLIGHT		
(continued on next page)		

REVISED BLINDS 1950

TOP BLIND (continued)

PRENTON
PRENTON ROAD EAST
PRENTON DELL ROAD
QUARRY ROAD EAST
ROCK FERRY STATION
SINGLETON AVENUE
SOUTH CIRCLE
ST. JAMES CHURCH
WOODSIDE
CENTRAL STATION
CHARING CROSS
ST. PAULS ROAD
SAUGHALL MASSIE
SEACOMBE FERRY
SPITAL CROSS ROADS
ST. CATHERINES HOSPITAL

(continued in second column)

(continuation from previous column)
STATION ROAD
STORETON ROAD
STORK MARGARINE WORKS
THINGWALL CORNER
THORNTON ROAD
THURSTASTON
THURSTASTON SHORE
TOWN LANE
TUNNEL ENTRANCE
TO THE SHOW
UPTON
VILLAGE ROAD
WARWICK ROAD
WOODCHURCH ESTATE

REVISED BLINDS 1969
From Bus 168

TOP BLIND	BOTTOM BLIND	SIDE BLIND
White Blank	White Blank	White Blank
ACKERS ROAD	VIA ALLPORT LANE	VIA ALLPORT LANE
ALLPORT ROAD	VIA ARROWE PARK	VIA ARROWE PARK
ARROWEBROOK ROAD	VIA BIDSTON	VIA BIDSTON
ARROWE PARK	VIA BEDFORD AVENUE	VIA BEDFORD AVENUE
BEBINGTON STATION	VIA BOROUGH ROAD	VIA BOROUGH ROAD
BEBINGTON ROAD	VIA BROMBOROUGH PORT ESTATE	VIA BROMBOROUGH PORT ESTATE
BEDFORD ROAD	VIA CONWAY STREET	VIA CONWAY STREET
BOLTON ROAD	VIA CLAUGHTON ROAD	VIA CLAUGHTON ROAD
White Blank	VIA CLEVELAND STREET	VIA CLEVELAND STREET
BRIDGE STREET	VIA CENTRAL STATION	VIA CENTRAL STATION
BROMBOROUGH (ACRE LANE)	VIA CHARING CROSS	VIA CHARING CROSS
BROMBOROUGH (CROFT AVENUE)	VIA CLAUGHTON VILLAGE	VIA CLAUGHTON VILLAGE
BROMBOROUGH CROSS	VIA DERBY ROAD	VIA DERBY ROAD
BROMBOROUGH DOCK	VIA FOUR BRIDGES	VIA FOUR BRIDGES
BROMBOROUGH POWER STATION	VIA HEYGARTH ROAD	VIA HEYGARTH ROAD
BROMBOROUGH (BROOKHURST ESTATE)	VIA HIGHER TRANMERE	VIA HIGHER TRANMERE
CENTRAL STATION	VIA IRBY ROAD	VIA IRBY ROAD
CHARING CROSS	VIA KINGS LANE	VIA KINGS LANE
CIRCULAR TOUR	VIA KINGS ROAD	VIA KINGS ROAD
CLATTERBRIDGE	VIA LISCARD	VIA LISCARD
CLAUGHTON VILLAGE	VIA LOWER BEBINGTON	VIA LOWER BEBINGTON
DURLEY DRIVE	VIA NEW CHESTER ROAD	VIA NEW CHESTER ROAD
CROSS LANE	VIA NEW FERRY	VIA NEW FERRY
EASTHAM FERRY	White Blank	White Blank
EASTHAM VILLAGE	VIA NEW HEY ROAD	VIA NEW HEY ROAD
WOODSIDE	VIA OLD CHESTER ROAD	VIA OLD CHESTER ROAD
PARK STATION	VIA OXTON ROAD	VIA OXTON ROAD
FOOTBALL MATCH	VIA PARK STATION	VIA PARK STATION
FORD ESTATE	White Blank	VIA PEMBERTON ROAD
FRANKBY	VIA PEMBERTON ROAD	VIA PORT CAUSEWAY
White Blank	VIA PORT CAUSEWAY	VIA POULTON BRIDGE
GREASBY	VIA POULTON BRIDGE	VIA PRENTON ROAD WEST
GREEN LANE	VIA PRENTON ROAD WEST	VIA SEACOMBE
HESWALL	VIA SEACOMBE	VIA SINGLETON AVENUE
HEYGARTH ROAD	VIA SINGLETON AVENUE	VIA ST.JAMES CHURCH
HURRELL ROAD	VIA ST.JAMES CHURCH	VIA THURSTASTON
IRBY	VIA THURSTASTON	VIA TOWN LANE
IVY STREET	VIA TOWN LANE	VIA UPTON
KINGS LANE	VIA UPTON	VIA WHETSTONE LANE
LAIRD STREET	VIA WHEATLAND LANE	VIA WHEATLAND LANE
LANDICAN CEMETERY	VIA WHETSTONE LANE	VIA WOODCHURCH ROAD
LISCARD VILLAGE	VIA WOODCHURCH ROAD	VIA WOODCHURCH ESTATE
White Blank	VIA WOODCHURCH ESTATE	White Blank
LOWER BEBINGTON	White Blank	ENGAGED

174

TOP BLIND (continued)
MANOR ROAD
MANOR DRIVE
MILL PARK ESTATE
MORETON, BERMUDA ROAD
MORETON SHORE
MORETON CROSS
MOUNT ROAD/BEBINGTON ROAD
White Blank
WOODSIDE
CENTRAL STATION
CHARING CROSS
NEW BRIGHTON
NEW FERRY
NEW FERRY TOLL BAR
NORTH CIRCLE
NOCTORUM ESTATE
ORRETTS MEADOW ROAD
OSMASTON ROAD
OVERCHURCH ESTATE
OXTON CIRCLE
PARK STATION
PORT CAUSEWAY
PORT SUNLIGHT
PRENTON (WAR MEMORIAL)
PRENTON CIRCLE
PRENTON DELL
QUARRY ROAD EAST
ROCK FERRY STATION
SOUTH CIRCLE
ST. JAMES CHURCH
WOODSIDE
CENTRAL STATION
CHARING CROSS
White Blank
SAUGHALL MASSIE
SCHOOL BUS
SEACOMBE FERRY
SOMERSET ROAD
SPITAL CROSS ROADS
STATION ROAD
STORETON ROAD
STORK MARGARINE WORKS
THINGWALL CORNER
THORNTON ROAD
THURSTASTON
THURSTASTON SHORE
TOWN LANE
TRAFALGAR ROAD
TUNNEL ENTRANCE
UPTON
VILLAGE ROAD
WOODCHURCH ESTATE
White Blank

BOTTOM BLIND (continued)
CIRCULAR TOUR
ENGAGED
LIMITED STOP
TO THE SHOW
White Blank

SIDE BLIND (continued)
FOOTBALL MATCH
LIMITED STOP
{ PASSENGERS FOR AND BEYOND
{ BEDFORD ROAD/GROVE ROAD
{ PASSENGERS FOR BEYOND
{ LAIRD ST. DEPOT
{ PASSENGERS FOR AND BEYOND
{ LANDICAN LANE
{ PASSENGERS FOR BEYOND
{ NEW FERRY DEPOT
{ PASSENGERS FOR BEYOND
{ PRENTON ROAD EAST
{ PASSENGERS FOR BEYOND
{ SINGLETON AVENUE
{ PASSENGERS FOR AND BEYOND
{ TOLLEMACHE ROAD
{ PASSENGERS FOR AND BEYOND
{ UPTON ROAD/TOLLEMACHE ROAD
{ PASSENGERS FOR BEYOND
{ ARROWE PARK
CIRCULAR TOUR
TO THE SHOW
White Blank

A further pre-delivery view of No. 201 shows that the rear number plate was on the lower panel instead of on the waistband.

Massey Bros.

APPENDIX 5
PRODUCER GAS VEHICLES

Instruction sheet, apparently produced by Birkenhead Corporation, and probably based on a national document prepared for the guidance of bus operators generally.

Producer gas is regarded by the Ministry of War Transport as the most suitable alternative fuel to petrol. In the present emergency the Government have issued instructions that operators must convert a certain proportion of their fleet in order to conserve shipping and so save liquid fuel, every gallon of which has to be imported.

When it is considered that a bus converted to operate on Producer Gas will save 25 gallons for every 100 miles run, and that when our quota of vehicles are all converted and in full use, there will be a saving of 200,000 gallons of petrol per year, it will be appreciated how important this matter is.

The saving can only be achieved by intelligent driving and servicing and the wholehearted co-operation of all drivers is required in order that we can make a success of the services operated by Producer Gas Vehicles.

There is nothing mysterious about a Producer Gas Plant. The Gas is made in the appliance which is towed behind the bus and is produced as a result of passing a current of air through incandescent fuel. The fuel we are using at present is known as anthracite.

After the gas is produced. it is necessary to pass it through various filters and coolers in order to reduce the bulk and to eliminate certain undesirable elements which cause unnecessary wear and tear in the engine.

The following notes are designed to assist drivers in understanding exactly how the apparatus works in order that they can obtain the best results from the vehicle they are driving.

POWER

Producer Gas has a lower heat value than Petrol and, in consequence, when a Petrol engine has been converted, there is some loss of power. This is met to a large extent by a higher compression ratio and advancing the ignition timing.

The Gas is generated by combustion which is induced by suction from the engine and has to be made in quantities sufficient to meet the demands of the engine at any given moment, therefore the intelligent use of engine speeds and gear changing is essential in order to maintain an adequate supply of gas at the time it is required.

Engines run very smoothly on Gas and there is no pinking or knocking as with Petrol and it is necessary not to labour too long in a higher gear before changing down.

CONTROLS

The controls have been modified in the conversion as follows:-

Foot. The accelerator pedal controls the main gas and air valves (which are linked together) on the Zenith Gas Mixer.

Hand. The Hand Throttle control under the steering wheel on the right-hand side controls the idling speed of the engine (to close, push forward).

Ignition. The ignition control under the steering wheel on the left-hand side controls the ignition timing and is fully advanced in the forward position.

Extra Air. The extra air control is on the engine casing on the left of the Driver. This is closed by a forward movement and vice versa.

Petrol Carburettor. A small Zenith Carburettor is seen under the Gas mixer and is solely for the purpose of starting the engine and thus creating the suction on the Fire. It can only be operated by hand from the nearside of the engine. The air choke and throttle act directly on the carburettor and for convenience an extra starter button is placed within easy reach so that the engine can be started on Petrol without entering the cab.

Jets. Should the jets require attention it will be found the dismantling screw on the Float Chamber also forms a jet key; the jets are situated at the bottom of the Float Chamber.

Lubrocharger. Upper cylinder lubrication is provided by a Redex Lubrocharger fitted on the dash panel and needs no attention beyond noting a trickle of 'Redex' through the U-tube.

Taking over. When a driver takes over at the depot, he will find the preliminary starting on Petrol has been done and the engine is running on Gas ready to drive away on service. He will be interested mainly in learning how to manipulate the controls and drive on gas to the best advantage to get results and save Solid Fuel.

Driving on Gas. To obtain a good supply of Gas for starting off, the engine revs should be kept at 400-500 per minute whilst the bus is stationary by opening the hand throttle slightly. To facilitate gear changing, it can be closed whilst the bus is in motion.

In starting under load or on inclines, always engage First Gear; when changing up, take the engine revs to the maximum, to ensure maximum gas output and engine power for the greater load.

Hill Climbing. Change gear early and keep the engine revs high; losing speed in too high a gear will diminish the suction through the fire and the gas supply will fail or weaken accordingly.

Extra Air Setting. This control is very sensitive in action and its correct setting has a marked effect on engine performance. With very little practice, the Driver can soon feel this correct setting relative to the maximum power to be obtained from the engine. When starting on a fresh charge of fuel, it may be found necessary to vary the adjustment during the first 20 minutes or so. When climbing, it will be found advantageous to close it slightly to increase the suction on the fire.

Do not alter the control whilst running down hill and do not coast down hill in neutral or with the clutch held out and finally do not run down hill with the accelerator completely shut off..

Standing Time. If not exceeding 10 to 15 minutes, keep the engine running; set at 400-500 revs per minute.

To stop the engine. Close the extra air control and switch off the ignition.

Starting up on Gas. After standing, an idea as to whether the engine will start up on Gas can be obtained by opening the Tuyere flap to see if the fire is bright. In opening this flap, stand clear in case there is a flash back of flame. This, of course, only applies when the engine is not running.

If the fire is bright close the flap again and the engine may start on Gas. Close the extra air control, retard the ignition, switch on, press the starter button and flick the accelerator. When the engine starts, re-adjust the air control and advance the ignition.

Starting up on Petrol. When the engine has been stopped longer than 15 minutes, it will be necessary to start up on Petrol. Open the Tuyere flap and gently poke the fire to remove any clinker that may have formed around the Tuyere nose in the fire box, then reclose the flap. In the cab, close the air control, retard the ignition well and switch on. Then, on the nearside of the engine, turn on the petrol, close the air choke and open the carburettor throttle, operate the side starter button. When the engine starts, do not advance the ignition, always bearing in mind that compression ratio is now so high that heavy knocking will result whilst running on petrol. When the engine is running on petrol, open the Gas mixer throttle slightly. If the engine does not speed up, wait and repeat. When the revs do increase, maintain them and open the extra air control slowly. Finally, turn off the petrol, advance the ignition and set the extra air and hand throttle. When the engine revs up freely on Gas, it is ready for service.

Air Leaks. Air leaks are one of the chief causes of trouble in the operation of Gas Producers and all precautions should be taken to avoid them. An air leak adjacent to the fire zone causes the fire in the hopper to spread, with consequent overheating, whilst air leaks between the hopper and the engine will reduce suction through the fire and cause loss of power and bad pulling. Overheating at the hopper may also be caused by shortage of Fuel or shortage of water in the Tuyere cooling tank.

Overheating at the hopper or fire zone must have immediate attention.

Trailers. It will be necessary to check the Trailer couplings occasionally, making sure that the pin and safety chain are secure. Examine the tyres and wheels.

The conductor can keep it under observation and inform the Driver if anything seems to require attention.

Number plates are detachable and care must be taken to see they correspond with the registration of the vehicle.

For the purpose of recording Fuel consumptions, the number of the Trailer must be entered on the Driver's card and any change of trailer also entered showing time and place.

Reversing. It is not, at this stage, proposed to use Gas vehicles on routes where reversing is necessary and no attempt should be made in this respect but if, on any occasion, it is essential, the Trailer must be watched closely and the bus steering lock be used to counteract any undue tendency of the Trailer to get square to the vehicle with possible damage to the couplings and flexible gas pipe.

Lights. Always see that the light lead is coupled to show Trailer side and rear lights when in use in the dark.

APPENDIX 6
THE ANNALS OF BIRKENHEAD TRANSPORT

22 9.1840	Omnibuses commenced running between Grange Lane and Monks Ferry for railway passengers.
23 10.1844	Railway extended to Monks Ferry - omnibuses withdrawn.
1848	Woodside - Oxton omnibuses commenced
1851	Henry Gough, George Stacey and Bretherton running omnibuses in the town
1854	Thomas Evans omnibus service between Woodside and Talbot Hotel, Oxton commenced.
30 8.1860	Birkenhead Street Railway opened between Woodside and Park Entrance
8.1861	Street Railway extended to top of Palm Grove
1862	Thos.Evans' omnibus service commenced between Egerton Park and Woodside
8 2.1864	Theobald's Line of Docks omnibus service commenced.
9.1864	Street Railway diverted outward via Price Street and Vittoria Street
1 10.1866	David Edwards commenced omnibus service between New Ferry (Farmer's Arms) and Castle Hotel, Chester Street.
6 9.1873	Hoylake Railway's tramway opened between Docks Station and Woodside
9 11.1875	Omnibus service commenced between New Ferry and Castle Hotel, Chester Street.
22 3.1877	Wirral Tramway Co's line opened between New Ferry and Ivy Street
24 7.1877	Wirral Tramway extended to Woodside
2 8.1877	Street Railway Co. dissolved and Birkenhead Tramways Co. formed.
11 7.1878	Official opening of Borough Road tramway to North Road
1 8.1878	Woodside - North Road tramway service commenced
5.1879	Price Street tramway replaced by omnibus to Vittoria Street
12 10.1879	Birkenhead Tramways Co. acquired Line of Docks tramway from Hoylake Railway
1 6.1881	Prenton tramway extended from North Road to Prenton Road East
29 10.1883	Birkenhead & District Omnibus & Carriage Co.Ltd. formed.
31 3.1884	Thomas Evans & Sons omnibus business acquired by District company.
2. 1.1888	Docks tramway curtailed at Ilchester Road (Borough boundary)
4 8.1889	Birkenhead United Tramway, Omnibus & Carriage Co.Ltd formed.
11 3.1891	Upton Bus Co.licensed to run between Upton and Birkenhead
21 12.1891	Tramway opened along new part of Argyle Street between Grange Lane and Borough Road and line along Wilbraham Street abandoned.
1898	Wirral Tramway Co. commenced omnibus service between New Ferry & Bromborough
8 5.1900	Wirral Tramway Co. ceased trading - Bromborough service taken over by United Co.
4 2.1901	Electric tramway opened between New Ferry & Brandon Street
6 6.1901	New Ferry tramway extended to Woodside
14 8.1901	Electric tramways opened to Higher Tranmere (Bebington Road), Laird Street & Claughton Road (Park Road East) Horse car service curtailed to Park Road East-top of Palm Grove
12 9.1901	Line of Docks horse tramway closed
27 9.1901	Electric tramways opened to Prenton and Shrewsbury Road via Borough Road
8 11.1901	Horse car service Park Road East-Palm Grove withdrawn
16.11.1901	Claughton Road tramway extended to Egerton Road.
24 12.1901	Woodside-Graving Docks Hotel Line of Docks electric tramway opened
2 3.1902	Laird Street and Shrewsbury Road tramways linked as a circular.
8.1903	Oxton Carriage Co. - Rock Ferry Pier-Dacre Hill omnibus service commenced (did not run for very long)
9.1903	Peters' horse bus service commenced between Charing Cross & Seacombe
10.1903	Birkenhead Carriage Co.Ltd. (former United Co.) in liquidation. New Ferry-Bromborough service taken over by Oxton Carriage Co.
9 12.1905	Mersey Railway buses first ran between Park Station and Football Ground
11 12.1905	Mersey Railway commenced running between Central Station and Slatey Road
26 12.1905	Mersey Railway Sunday and holiday service commenced between Central Station & Gayton
1.1906	Mersey Railway buses extended from Gayton to Heswall
29 1.1906	Mersey Railway buses extended from Slatey Road to Kingsmead Road South
26 2.1906	Kingsmead Road South route reorganised as a circular route
8 3.1906	Mersey Railway buses withdrawn following legal action by Birkenhead Corporation
16 5.1907	Mersey Railway buses started running between Port Sunlight & Rock Ferry Station via Bolton Road & New Chester Road.
29 5.1907	Port Sunlight-Rock Ferry Station via Old Chester Road commenced on weekdays only.
8 7.1907	Mersey Railway buses finally withdrawn
25 1.1913	Crosville buses started running between Chester & New Ferry and local service commenced on Saturdays between New Ferry & Bromborough later in the year. Oxton Carriage Co's service probably ceased about this time.
31 7.1914	Birkenhead Corporation Act 1914 authorising running of motor buses
5.1919	Crosville New Ferry-Bromborough-Eastham daily local service commenced
1919	Charing Cross-Seacombe horse bus service motorised by Birkenhead Motor Works
12 7.1919	First Birkenhead Corporation bus service started between Rock Ferry & Park Station
30 8.1919	Rock Ferry-Park Station service extended to Moreton Cross
14 7.1920	Charing Cross-Park Station-Upton bus service commenced
16 8.1920	Upton service extended to Central Station
4 10.1920	Rock Ferry Pier-Woodhey (Town Lane) bus service commenced
12 3.1921	Rock Ferry-Woodhey service extended to Port Sunlight
19 3.1921	Charing Cross-Seacombe via Duke Street Bridge service started. Company buses withdrawn
14 5.1921	Woodside-Moreton Cross Sunday morning service commenced

1921	Laird Street-Woodside via Shrewsbury Road Sunday morning service commenced
26 6.1921	Charing Cross-Harrison Drive summer service commenced
10.1921	Sunday morning bus services withdrawn
24 10.1921	Charing Cross-Liscard Village service commenced
11 8.1923	Charing Cross-Harrison Drive service withdrawn
16 9.1923	Woodside-Moreton Cross daily service commenced
23 3.1925	Charing Cross-Port Sunlight via Derby Road service commenced
8 6.1925	New Ferry-Charing Cross via Old Chester Road service commenced
12 6.1925	Market Place South-Balls Road 'shopping bus' commenced
10 8.1925	Shopping bus extended to Half Way House, Storeton Road
30 8.1925	Woodside-St.James' Church via Claughton Road service replaced Claughton Road trams
30 11.1925	New Ferry-Charing Cross-Upton through service commenced
9 8.1926	Woodside-Kings Road (Cavendish Drive) via Church Road service commenced (weekdays only)
10.1926	First series of route numbers introduced
1 2.1927	Woodside and Rock Ferry-Moreton Cross services extended to Bermuda Road
c28.3.1927	Post boxes introduced on trams
1 6.1927	Port Sunlight-Charing Cross service extended to Park Station via Park Road East
5 6.1927	Sunday morning service commenced between Charing Cross & Seacombe/Liscard
6 6.1927	Moreton Cross-Moreton Shore service commenced
28 8.1927	Sunday morning cross docks services withdrawn
1 9.1927	Woodside-Moreton Shore through service commenced
1 1.1928	Upton-Moreton Shore service commenced
1 4.1928	Bus and ferry through return tickets introduced universally
14 7.1928	Woodside-Osmaston Road via Singleton Avenue service commenced
29 9.1928	Woodside-Arrowe Park Saturday afternoon service commenced
7 10.1928	Tranmere tram service curtailed at Whitfield Sreet Sunday bus service to Kings Road commenced
25 10.1928	Upton-Moreton Shore service withdrawn for winter
3 3.1929	Woodside-Lower Bebington (Spital Cross Roads) service commenced
21 10.1929	New Ferry-New Brighton via Charing Cross joint service commenced
1.12 1929	Port Sunlight-Park Station extended to Claughton Village pm
14 1.1930	New Brighton service rerouted via Argyle Street & Cleveland Street
4 2.1930	Tranmere tram service reopened to Allerton Road
3 3.1930	Kings Road service extended from Cavendish Drive to Kings Lane
1 6.1930	Woodside-Upton via Arrowe Park service commenced
14 7.1930	Woodside-Upton service extended to Woodside via Park Station (circular)
23 7.1930	Shopping bus extended from Half Way House to Birch Road
1 8.1930	All principal Crosville services terminating at New Ferry extended to Woodside
	Woodside-Eastham (Village and Ferry) service commenced by Corporation
	New Ferry-Bromborough Pool Village service (Fridays & Saturdays pm) commenced
	Upton-New Ferry service extended to Bromborough Cross
1 10.1930	Woodside-Eastham Ferry service replaced by St.Paul's Road-Eastham Ferry service
	Heswall-Singleton Avenue via Thurstaston & Irby transferred from Crosville to Corporation and extended to Woodside
	Woodside-Osmaston Road service extended to Prenton Dell Road
	Crosville Heswall and West Kirby services extended from Singleton Avenue and Parkgate service from Prenton tram terminus to Woodside
26 10.1930	Woodside-Upton Circular and Upton-Moreton Shore services combined as Woodside-Moreton Shore via Arrowe Park & Upton
3 11.1930	New Ferry Hotel-Bromborough (Allport Road) via Trafalgar commenced
1 1.1931	New route numbers officially introduced.
	46 New Ferry-Bromborough via Trafalgar curtailed to run between Toll Bar & The Cross
1 7.1931	41 Woodside-Eastham Ferry seasonal daily service reintroduced
5 7.1931	16 Park Station-Arrowe Park seasonal Sunday service commenced
31 8.1931	41 Woodside-Eastham Ferry service discontinued on weekdays
13 9.1931	41 Woodside-Eastham Ferry service withdrawn on Sundays and never reintroduced.
28 12.1931	49 Woodside-New Ferry service replaced trams
1 4.1932	85 Woodside-Thurstaston via Park Station, Greasby & Frankby commenced
5 6.1932	26 Moreton-Rock Ferry diverted to Bromborough Cross after 11.30am
21 8.1932	64 Woodside-New Ferry (Great Eastern) via Church Road & Kings Road commenced
c. 6.1933	49 Woodside-New Ferry peak hour service extended to Pool Lane (38)
Btwn12.33 & 1.4.34	49 Woodside-New Ferry off-peak service extended to Bolton Road (39)
31 7.1933	44 St.Paul's Road-Eastham Ferry diverted via Raeburn Avenue
3 9.1933	26 Moreton-Bromborough diverted via Borough Road instead of Derby Road
	20-23, rerouted out via Hamilton Street in via Argyle Street in lieu of Chester Street both ways
16 7.1934	44 diverted via Trafalgar absorbing route 46, New Ferry-Bromborough
1 10.1934	64 Woodside-New Ferry via Kings Road diverted via Borough Road instead of Church Road
	60 Woodside-Kings Road diverted as 64 and extended to Village Road
	61 Woodside-Thornton Road via Pearson Road peak hour service commenced
	65 Woodside-Bedford Drive via Pearson Road service commenced replacing trams
	80 Woodside-Storeton Road service commenced replacing trams
12 11.1934	65 replaced by all day service on 61
1.1935	42 Route number allocated to New Ferry-Bromborough Pool Village service

180

3	2.1935	60 Woodside-Village Road reverted to Church Road route; 61 operated at peak hours only
1	4.1935	90/94 North Circle commenced, replacing Line of Docks trams
		10 New Ferry-New Brighton diverted via Chester Street & Bridge Street
5	8.1935	60 extended from Village Road to Gorsey Hey
19	4.1936	Revised Children's and Workmen's fares introduced.
29	6.1936	16 Park Station-Arrowe Park extended to New Ferry and operated daily in summer
13	7.1936	00 Hurrell Road-Stork Margarine Works workers' service commenced
?13	7.1936	21/22 Moreton-Woodside early journeys diverted inward via Chester Street
c	7.1936	61 Pearson Road service replaced by journeys via Whetstone Lane (66)
		11/12 diverted via Cole Street & Grange Road West on journeys to Charing Cross
		70-3, 75, 77, 85 diverted out via Hamilton Street in lieu of Chester Street
Between 7.36 & 7.37		39 Woodside-Bolton Road off peak service extended to Pool Lane (38)
c28.8.1936		Post boxes on buses discontinued
5	4.1937	60 extended from Gorsey Hey to Pulford Road (Heath Road)
by	6.1937	40/44 Eastham services diverted inward via Eastham By-pass
18	7.1937	2/6 Oxton Circle bus service commenced replacing last trams
	7.1937	16 diverted via Laird Street and Tollemache Road instead of Claughton Village
31	10.1937	80 Woodside-Storeton Road extended to Prenton War Memorial
12	3.1938	Laird Street-Plaza (Evenings)/Football Ground (Sat) experimental service commenced
16.	7.1938	Laird St-Plaza evening journeys operated Saturdays only
	7.1938	38 Woodside-Bromborough (Manor Road) commenced
?	12.1938	26, 43 Bromborough Cross terminus moved to Gratrix Road
10	1.1939	71,72,73 all inward buses rerouted via Woodchurch Road, Oxton Road and Whetstone Lane before 9.0am weekdays.
14	2.1939	54 Rock Ferry-Port Sunlight service diverted via Bedford Avenue & Bebington Road
1	5.1939	57 Port Sunlight-Bidston Road afternoon peak hour service commenced
?	1939	15, 43 Upton terminus moved to by-pass, (Arrowe Park Road) out via Rake Lane, in via by-pass (Arrowe Park Road).
		16, 77 diverted via Upton by-pass (Arrowe Park Road) in lieu of Rake Lane, The Village
30	6.1939	Rock Ferry closed
2	7.1939	78 Woodside-Greasby via Arrowe Park commenced
		85 Woodside-Thurstaston diverted via Claughton Road instead of Park Station
9	7.1939	84 Woodside-Lever Causeway via Prenton Road West commenced
31	7.1939	26 morning service diverted from Rock Ferry Pier to New Ferry
by	8.1939	99 Hurrell Road-Green Lane workmen's service commenced
24	9.1939	Reduced wartime services commenced; 16 (except Sundays), 38/40 (off-peak), 42, 44, 54, 71, 79, 85 withdrawn
29	10.1939	37 Woodside-Allport Road loop off peak service commenced
9	12.1939	79 Haymarket-Birch Road service reintroduced
10	1.1940	71 Woodside-Heswall via Irby service recommenced at peak hours
13	11.1942	Revision of loading arrangements at Woodside and Hamilton Square Station
27	5.1943	10 Virginia Road, New Brighton adopted as permanent terminus all year round
?	3.1944	50 workmen's journeys to Clatterbridge commenced
2	1.1945	Forces night service from Liverpool (Lime Street) commenced
7	8.1945	60 diverted from Pulford Road to Stanton Road
7	1.1946	43 Bromborough-Upton extended to Overchurch Road and renumbered 46
		58 Woodside-Clatterbridge public service commenced (extension of journeys on 50)
1	5.1946	85/86 South Circle commenced
		All suspended services except 54 reinstated
		42 New Ferry-Bromborough Pool Village renumbered 32 with journeys to Woodside as 34
		85 Woodside-Thurstaston via Greasby renumbered 96
?31	1.1947	Forces night service from Liverpool (Lime Street) withdrawn
1	6.1947	11 Liscard-Charing Cross extended at both ends to run between New Brighton & Thornton Road (The Wiend)
		18 New Brighton-Arrowe Park via Poulton Bridge service commenced
2	6.1947	79/97 Woodside-Storeton Road-Park Station-Woodside service commenced (absorbing 79)
3	11.1947	79/97 rerouted via Park Road East & Conway Street in lieu of Ashville Road & Price Street; rerouted clockwise via Borough Road & Whetstone Lane instead of Grange Road from 5.10pm to finish
12	1.1948	26 Moreton (Bermuda Road)-Bromborough Cross extended to Acre Lane and renumbered 28
		46 Overchurch Road-Bromborough Cross extended to Eastham Village and renumbered 42
18	1.1948	41 Arrowe Park-Eastham Village via Upton Sunday service commenced
3	5.1948	79/97 circular withdrawn. 79 Woodside-Storeton Road (Birch Road) commenced
31	1.1949	84 Woodside-Thornton Road (Lever Causeway) via Mount Road peak hour service commenced
29	5.1949	74 Woodside-Thurstaston Shore summer service commenced
30	5.1949	10 New Brighton-New Ferry extended to Bromborough
		11 New Brighton-The Wiend extended to Gorsey Hey and through journeys diverted in Wallasey via Poulton Road & Mill Lane in lieu of Oxton Road, Woodstock Road. Charing Cross-Liscard journeys continued to use latter route.
		12 Seacombe-Charing Cross extended at both ends as New Brighton-Bebington Station
16	1.1950	41/42 diverted to Heygarth Road (Raeburn Avenue) instead of Eastham Village
23	1.1950	10,11,12 extended journeys withdrawn at certain times
24	9.1950	12 extended journeys withdrawn for winter
4	6.1951	9 Liscard-Charing Cross via Poulton Bridge service commenced and through journeys on service 11 reverted to route via Oxton Road & Woodstock Road, Wallasey
		71 diverted inwards via Hamilton Street in lieu of Argyle Street
		71A Woodside-Heswall via Irby Road and Quarry Road commenced

1 10.1951	18 New Brighton-Arrowe Park withdrawn in winter
27 1.1952	41 Arrowe Park-Heygarth Road (Sundays) withdrawn
9 2.1952	16 Park Station-Arrowe Park extended to Landican Cemetery
11 4.1952	18 New Brighton-Arrowe Park extended to Ackers Road
28 4.1952	44 Eastham Ferry-St.Pauls Road service curtailed at New Ferry depot
	42 Overchurch Rd-Heygarth Road service curtailed at Bromborough Cross (as 46) except at peak hours and Saturdays pm
21 8.1952	Town Tours commenced
15 12.1952	70 Woodside-Prenton Dell Road extended to Woodchurch Estate (Grasswood Road)
25 5.1953	70 extended from Grasswood Road to Orrets Meadow Road
31 10.1953	57 Port Sunlight-Boundary Road peak hour journeys withdrawn
2 11.1953	51 Port Sunlight-Claughton Village diverted via Laird Street & Mallaby Street
	79 Curtailed at Haymarket off peak
	96 Woodside-Thurstaston curtailed at Frankby Green off peak & Sundays
18 4.1954	96 Sunday afternoon service reinstated to Thurstaston in summer if fine
24 5.1954	28A Moreton (Bermuda Road)-Bromborough (Croft Avenue) service commenced
	42,43,46 Upton-Bromborough services diverted via Mallaby Street & Laird Street
31 7.1954	18 New Brighton-Ackers Road extended to Orrets Meadow Road via Home Farm Road
9.1954	41 Woodside-Eastham (Mill Park) service commenced for building workers
17 1.1955	13 Central Station-Egremont (Trafalgar Road) peak hour service commenced Mondays to Fridays
1 4.1955	Transport and Ferries Committees combined and title of undertaking changed to Birkenhead Municipal Transport
23 5.1955	70A Woodside-Woodchurch Estate (Ferny Brow Road) via Pemberton Road service commenced
	70A Prenton Dell Road journeys renumbered 75; 75 Arrowe Park renumbered 76
11 5.1956	11 withdrawn between The Wiend and Gorsey Hey
13/14 5.1956	Mersey Tunnel bus service commenced replacing Woodside night ferry service. Birkenhead ran first three-month period. Joint with Liverpool Corporation.
17 12.1956	Emergency reduced services - Suez crisis
10 3.1958	70A extended to Hoole Road via Pemberton Road & Houghton Road
	75 Woodside-Prenton Dell Road - some journeys extended to Prenton Village Road
14 9.1959	70 extended to Leeswood Road (Houghton Road) via New Hey Road
5 6.1960	87 New Ferry-Moreton Shore via Bedford Drive, Mount Road & Arrowe Park summer service commenced
17 10.1960	38 Woodside-Bromborough extended to Eastham Village via Heygarth Road as 39
	40 Woodside-Eastham Village extended to Mill Park (all day service) as 41
	39 works buses to Bromborough Dock via Borough Road renumbered 37
28 8.1961	Extensive revision of routes and stops in Town Centre in preparation for traffic management scheme commencing 1st September
	10 rerouted north via Argyle Street, Hamilton Square Station, Canning Street, Taylor Street; south via Canning Street, Hamilton Street; 10A Liscard-Kings Square peak hour service commenced
	13 Egremont-Central Station rerouted via Canning Street & curtailed at Kings Square
	71-74 rerouted IN via Argyle Street in lieu of Hamilton Street
	94/95 rerouted OUT via Bridge Street, Argyle Street.
	24 terminus IN at Argyle Street; OUT at Hamilton Street (Bernards Corner)
4 6.1962	79 Woodside-Prenton Dell Estate service commenced
	79 Woodside-Birch Road renumbered 97
9 9.1962	87 New Ferry-Moreton Shore withdrawn after operation
29 6.1963	12 summer service curtailed to run between Bebington Road (Mount Road) and New Brighton Saturdays and Sundays only
early 1964	44 diverted from Depot to Great Eastern Hotel, New Ferry
22 6.1964	51 Port Sunlight-Claughton Village extended to Upton & Saughall Massie at certain times; 51A Upton, 51B Claughton Village; 56 daytime service Bebington Station-Park Station introduced
	14,15 most journeys withdrawn
?13.9.1964	12 summer extension withdrawn after operation this day.
26 10.1964	71-73 morning peak journeys routed IN via Grange Road (traffic congestion)
23 11.1964	42 diverted to Brookhurst Estate at peak hours and Saturday afternoons
	38 some Manor Road journeys extended to Heygarth Road to replace 42.
29 3.1965	44 New Ferry-Eastham Ferry diverted via Spital and curtailed at Mayfield Drive except some early journeys
12 4.1965	97 Woodside-Birch Road rerouted inwards via Rose Mount, Fairclough Lane, Village Road, Claughton Firs & Bennetts Hill & converted to single deck one man operation
4 10.1965	79/80 linked to form Prenton Circle; 79A to Prenton Village Road; 80A to Glenavon Road
26. 6.1967	85/86 South Circle - reduced to peak hours & Sundays
c. 7.1967	10A, 13 curtailed from St. Mary's Gate to Bridge Street (after 26th June; before August)
13 3.1967	12 converted to one-man operation to run Seacombe-Charing Cross only.
2 10.1967	11 - some journeys diverted via Mount Road instead of Woodchurch Lane as 11A
1. 5.1968	All buses outward from Woodside via Hamilton Street diverted via Hinson Street & Argyle Street instead of Haymarket, etc.
1 7.1968	15A Park Station-Ford Estate service commenced
?9.68or 69	18 New Brighton-Woodchurch withdrawn for season but never restarted
	74 Woodside-Thurstaston Shore withdrawn for season but never restarted
20 1.1969	85/86 South Circle converted to one man operation on Sundays
3 11.1969	2, 6 Oxton Circle converted to double-deck one man operation
1 12.1969	Merseyside Passenger Transport Executive acquired Birkenhead transport undertaking

182

APPENDIX 7
LIVERY

Birkenhead trams were finished in a livery of maroon and cream. Buses from 1 to 17 were finished in the tram livery but from No. 18 the buses were painted a much darker chocolate brown (almost black in a poor light), apparently described officially as 'scotch purple'. The difference between tram and bus was perhaps comparable to that of milk and plain chocolate. This depressing livery was relieved only by elaborate gilt lining-out and 'BIRKENHEAD CORPORATION MOTORS' in shaded gilt lettering.

When the LG1 Leviathan double-deckers arrived, the upper decks were finished in cream with dark-coloured beading. The PLSP2 Leviathans, however, at first had cream window surrounds on both decks. The Titans introduced a scheme with three cream bands, the lower one containing the title in rather compressed letters and this arrangement was extended to the Leviathans and Lions on repaint. Fleet numbers were usually applied on each side of the front; they became much smaller with the new paint scheme and from the TD3c's there was only one, on the cab front as there was nowhere for a number on the special header tank used for the torque converter. The municipal arms were carried centrally on the lower deck panels. This general layout remained standard for many years though, in accordance with the general trend, lining-out was simplified.

The AEC 'Q' No. 185 introduced a new blue livery which was used on all subsequent deliveries. It was also unusual in having a fleet number at the rear as well as on the front. Earlier buses were repainted gradually over about five years. In 1934, the title of the undertaking was changed from 'MOTORS' to 'TRANSPORT'. All new buses carried the new title and the older vehicles were progressively changed on repaint.

The war brought a few changes, not the least of which was the change from white to blue roofs following the strafing of a Liverpool Corporation bus at Speke by an enemy aircraft. In 1940 the remaining petrol-engined double-deckers had their cream bands painted black; three diesel buses, 179, 199 and 224 were also so treated. The petrol buses were parked in the yard at Laird Street and the black paint made them less conspicuous to enemy aircraft. From 1943, a start was made on repainting back to normal livery, the last to be done being 145 in June 1945. Nos. 161 and 166 were withdrawn in 1944 and remained in blue and black until sold in 1947 and 1946 respectively.

When the buses with replacement bodies re-entered service in 1942, they carried rear fleet numbers in addition to those on the cab front and this practice was continued on the utility Guys. From 1944, the municipal arms were additionally applied to the upper deck panels, No. 316 being the first in February but this practice ceased in 1946 when exterior advertising commenced, No. 249 being the first bus to carry an advertisement - for Genasprin - on the offside in July 1946.

May 1944 saw an experimental change to the fleet name when BIRKENHEAD CORPORATION TRANSPORT was not applied to buses on repaint but 'Birkenhead Corporation Passenger Transport' was applied above the general manager's name on the lower nearside panel. Eleven buses were so treated - 148, 187, 189, 287, 322-3, 333, 339-42. The idea was then abandoned and there was a reversion to the original style, the 11 receiving the former title, though the additional legend remained until the next repaint.

A variation in livery was made in 1950 on new Daimlers 176-90 on which the area between the centre and lower cream bands was also painted cream. The fleet numbers were applied in Gill Sans letters and the title was soon similarly changed. Following the merger of the Bus and Ferries undertakings in 1953, 'CORPORATION' was omitted from the title. There were no further changes until 1964 when the first rear-engined buses were delivered in a simplified livery - all blue with cream lower deck window surrounds. However, this was not viewed with favour and they were soon repainted with a cream band below the upper deck windows which improved their appearance considerably. The central band was restored on the second batch of Atlanteans which also had cream upper deck window surrounds.

APPENDIX 8
BIRKENHEAD CORPORATION BUS STATISTICS 1919-69

Year Ended 31 March	Revenue £	Passengers Carried	Miles Run	Net Surplus or (Deficit) £	Average Pasengers per Mile d	Average Fare per Passenger d
1920	8,032	556,684	103,348	2,140	5.38	3.47
1921	21,624	1,443,315	219,975	1,251	6.57	3.60
1922	33,908	2,256,863	308,597	8,351	7.32	3.61
1923	38,617	2,585,750	374,581	13,028	6.91	3.59
1924	44,998	3,401,777	527,643	11,797	6.45	3.18
1925	55,051	4,459,325	697,006	12,272	6.40	2.97
1926	75,803	6,996,226	1,060,750	14,972	6.60	2.60
1927	98,589	10,096,012	1,422,326	16,024	7.10	2.35
1928	124,773	13,408,093	1,770,867	28,343	7.58	2.24
1929	150,446	18,298,839	2,220,633	26,705	8.24	1.99
1930	183,017	22,218,135	2,649,645	25,000	8.39	1.98
1931	196,888	23,963,713	3,217,203	31,000	7.45	1.98
1932	216,395	26,090,850	3,683,866	27,814	7.09	1.99
1933	224,911	28,017,895	4,098,851	22,127	6.84	1.93
1934	234,168	29,162,450	4,198,688	24,973	6.95	1.93
1935	243,712	31,693,632	4,431,758	34,716	7.16	1.85
1936	264,727	36,353,339	5,041,216	40,018	7.22	1.75
1937	272,947	39,339,820	5,251,416	43,092	7.49	1.67
1938	318,649	46,863,083	5,989,830	43,744	7.83	1.64
1939	341,160	50,920,138	6,357,526	47,608	8.01	1.61
1940	338,192	49,442,170	5,583,642	51,456	8.86	1.65
1941	325,143	50,025,608	4,641,477	36,379	10.78	1.56
1942	351,866	51,220,904	4,750,205	18,320	10.79	1.65
1943	382,595	53,215,417	4,682,368	23,974	11.37	1.73
1944	405,501	55,143,225	4,719,596	36,630	11.69	1.77
1945	413,533	56,237,861	4,779,357	37,144	11.77	1.77
1946	429,240	57,749,211	5,051,460	40,144	11.44	1.79
1947	496,426	66,889,342	6,322,442	41,389	10.58	1.79
1948	559,038	72,734,022	6,860,132	42,101	10.61	1.85
1949	574,798	75,578,515	7,163,381	9,451	10.55	1.83
1950	597,912	78,129,842	7,646,863	8,256	10.22	1.84
1951	602,936	77,356,704	7,451,195	(19294)	10.39	1.87
1952	701,929	74,659,968	7,358,656	(27786)	10.15	2.26
1953	754,686	72,102,044	7,049,287	18,277	10.23	2.52
1954	819,676	68,980,482	7,166,647	71,350	9.63	2.86
1955	826,044	67,859,110	7,252,940	52,600	9.36	2.93
1956	848,285	68,745,087	7,364,344	21,773	9.34	2.97
1957	885,512	67,811,619	7,184,079	26,125	9.44	3.14
1958	883,294	65,632,817	7,191,872	(14037)	9.13	3.23
1959	979,528	63,635,462	7,234,627	60,619	8.80	3.70
1960	994,246	64,431,000	7,331,143	67,144	8.79	3.71
1961	992,989	64,361,000	7,384,678	27,999	8.72	3.71
1962	1,010,652	65,030,000	7,589,288	(29005)	8.57	3.73
1963	1,087,278	63,103,000	7,591,225	4,319	8.32	4.14
1964	1,191,254	61,732,000	7,504,833	54,612	8.23	4.64
1965	1,228,770	59,532,000	7,470,098	9,756	7.97	4.92
1966	1,305,134	54,702,000	7,278,710	50,858	7.55	5.71
1967	1,392,776	51,466,000	6,867,110	86,411	7.50	6.50
1968	1,180,754	41,351,000	5,859,263	(23064)	7.06	6.86
1969	1,224,181	41,308,706	5,889,152	(74399)	7.02	7.12

Woodside bus station in 1966. The red funnelled ferry, also part of the Corporation Transport Dept., has just left the landing stage for Liverpool.

Courtesy A.Allison

THE OMNIBUS
SOCIETY

* Caters for all those interested in buses, coaches, trams and trolleybuses

* Branches across Great Britain

* Regular meetings

* Visits to bus operators' depots

* Publishes *The Omnibus Magazine*

* Historical research groups

* Library of books, timetables and related material

For details visit our website: www.omnibussoc.org
or see current advertisements

**Other books published by the
Provincial Historical Research Group**

Primrose of Leominster £6.95
Trams & Buses of the Great Cities
in the 1880s £9.95
Tocia - Buses of the Llyn Peninsula
in North Wales £9.95